Workshop on Computational Linguistics and Clinical Psychology 2014

Held at ACL 2014

Baltimore, Maryland, USA
27 June 2014

ISBN: 978-1-63439-212-9

Printed from e-media with permission by:

Curran Associates, Inc.
57 Morehouse Lane
Red Hook, NY 12571

Some format issues inherent in the e-media version may also appear in this print version.

Printed by Curran Associates, Inc. (2014)

For permission requests, please contact the Association for Computational Linguistics
at the address below.

Association for Computational Linguistics
209 N. Eighth Street
Stroudsburg, Pennsylvania 18360

Phone: 1-570-476-8006
Fax: 1-570-476-0860

acl@aclweb.org

Additional copies of this publication are available from:

Curran Associates, Inc.
57 Morehouse Lane
Red Hook, NY 12571 USA
Phone: 845-758-0400
Fax: 845-758-2634
Email: curran@proceedings.com
Web: www.proceedings.com

Introduction

Mental health problems are among the costliest challenges we face, in every possible sense of cost. The numbers are staggering: to cite just a few, in the United States mental health spending accounted for $33 billion in 1986, $100 billion in 2003, and is projected to increase to $203 billion for 2014; some 25 million American adults will have an episode of major depression this year; and suicide is the third leading cause of death for people between 10 and 24 years old. The importance of clinical psychology as a problem space cannot be overstated.

For clinical psychologists, language plays a central role in diagnosis. Indeed, many clinical instruments fundamentally rely on what is, in effect, manual annotation of patient language. Applying language technology in this domain, e.g. in language-based assessment, could potentially have an enormous impact, because many individuals are motivated to underreport psychiatric symptoms (consider active duty soldiers, for example) or lack the self-awareness to report accurately (consider individuals involved in substance abuse who do not recognize their own addiction), and because many people — e.g. those without adequate insurance or in rural areas — cannot even obtain access to a clinician who is *qualified* to perform a psychological evaluation. Bringing language technology to bear on these problems could potentially lead to inexpensive screening measures that could be administered by a wider array of healthcare professionals, which is particularly important since the majority of individuals who present with symptoms of mental health problems do so in a primary care physician's office. Given the burden on primary care physicians to diagnose mental health disorders in very little time, the American Academy of Family Physicians has recognized the need for diagnostic tools for physicians that are "suited to the realities of their practice".

Although automated language analysis connected with mental health conditions goes back at least as far as the 1990s, it has not been a major focus for computational linguistics compared with other application domains. However, recently there has been noticable uptick in research activity on this topic. One recent shared task brings together research on the Big-5 personality traits, and another involved research on identification of emotion in suicide notes. Research has been done on language analysis in the context of, for example, autistic spectrum disorders, dementia, depression, post-partum depression, general life satisfaction , and suicide risk. This increase in attention is consistent with, and gains power from, the recent rise in computational linguistics activity connected with computational social science more broadly.

With computational linguistics research on this topic moving toward critical mass, one key goal of this workshop was to bring together researchers to discuss the current state of the art, share methods, and set directions for the future. The workshop had a second goal also, though: to directly engage clinical *practitioners* in mental health. By including clinicians on our program committee and as discussants, the workshop was designed to increase NLP practitioners' understanding of what mental health clinicians do and what their real needs are, and to increase clinical practitioners' understanding of what is possible in NLP and what it might have to offer.

We received a total of 17 submissions. Of these, 7 (41%) were accepted for oral presentation and discussion, and an additional 7 were selected for inclusion in the workshop's poster session.

We wish to thank everyone who showed interest and submitted a paper, all of the authors for their contributions, the members of the Program Committee for their thoughtful reviews, our clinical practitioner discussants, and all the attendees of the workshop. We also wish to extend sincere thanks to the Association for Computational Linguistics for making this workshop possible, and to CHIB, the Center for Health-related Informatics and Bioimaging at the University of Maryland, for its generous sponsorship.

Workshop co-chairs:

Philip Resnik, PhD, University of Maryland

Rebecca Resnik, PsyD, Mindwell Psychology Bethesda

Margaret Mitchell, PhD, Microsoft Research

Organizers:

Philip Resnik, PhD, University of Maryland
Rebecca Resnik, PsyD, Mindwell Psychology Bethesda
Margaret Mitchell, PhD, Microsoft Research

Program Committee:

Steven Bedrick, Oregon Health and Science University
Craig Bryan, University of Utah
Jesus Caban, Walter Reed National Military Medical Center
Munmun De Choudhury, Microsoft Research
Michael Gamon, Microsoft Research
Kristy Hollingshead, Department of Defense
Arthur Horton, Psych Associates of Maryland
Loring Ingraham, George Washington University
Molly Ireland, Texas Tech
Michal Kosinski, Cambridge University
Antolin Llorente, University of Maryland Medical School
Elmar Nöth, University of Erlangen-Nuremberg
Serguei Pakhomov, University of Minnesota
Emily Prud'hommeaux, University of Rochester
Nan Bernstein Ratner, University of Maryland
Ehud Reiter, University of Aberdeen
Brian Roark, Google Research
Andy Schwartz, University of Pennsylvania
Kathy Seifert, Eastern Shore Psychological Services
Thamar Solorio, Univ of Alabama at Birmingham
David Stillwell, Cambridge University
Paul Thompson, Dartmouth College
Lyle Ungar, University of Pennsylvania
Marilyn Walker, UC Santa Cruz
Karin Scheetz Walsh, Children's National Medical Center

Table of Contents

Workshop Program

Friday, June 27, 2014

9:00 Introduction

9:10 Presentations and discussion 1

Predicting military and veteran suicide risk: Cultural aspects
Paul Thompson, Craig Bryan and Chris Poulin

Linguistic Indicators of Severity and Progress in Online Text-based Therapy for Depression
Christine Howes, Matthew Purver and Rose McCabe

10:30 Morning break

11:00 Presentations and discussion 2

Comparison of different feature sets for identification of variants in progressive aphasia
Kathleen C. Fraser, Graeme Hirst, Naida L. Graham, Jed A. Meltzer, Sandra E. Black and Elizabeth Rochon

Aided diagnosis of dementia type through computer-based analysis of spontaneous speech
William Jarrold, Bart Peintner, David Wilkins, Dimitra Vergryi, Colleen Richey, Maria Luisa Gorno-Tempini and Jennifer Ogar

12:20 Poster teasers

12:30 Lunch (provided) and poster session

Friday, June 27, 2014 (continued)

2:00 Presentations and discussion 3

3:30 Afternoon break

4:00 Presentations and discussion 4

4:45 General discussion

5:30 Workshop ends

+

Posters

Friday, June 27, 2014 (continued)

Predicting military and veteran suicide risk: Cultural aspects

Paul Thompson
Dartmouth College

Paul.Thompson@dartmouth.edu

Chris Poulin
Durkheim Project

chris@durkheimproject.org

Craig J. Bryan
National Center for Veterans Studies

craig.bryan@utah.edu

Abstract

This paper describes the three phases of the Durkheim Project. For this project we developed a clinician's dashboard that displays output of models predicting suicide risk of veterans and active duty military personnel. During phase one, we built the clinician's dashboard and completed a Veterans Affairs (VA) predictive risk medical records study, based on an analysis of the narrative, or free text, portions of VA medical records, In phase two, we will predict suicide risk based on opt-in social media postings by patients using social media websites, e.g., Facebook. We describe the software infrastructure that we have completed for this phase two system. During phase three we will provide a three layer intervention strategy. We discuss our methodology for the three phases, including IRB-approved protocols for the first two phases and a soon-to-be approved IRB protocol for phase three.

1 Introduction

Diagnosis of psychological health and the prediction of negative events, such as suicide, or suicide ideation, is limited by: a) a lack of understanding of the true differentiating risks of suicidality (Health Promotion, 2010; Treating Soldiers, 2010) and b) a lack of near real-time reaction capability to large volumes of data. There is a need for broader coverage suicide risk detection and a better understanding of the expression of suicide ideation through data mining of text and images. The Durkheim Project's proposed solution is to provide continuous monitoring of text based information, such as found in social network user behavioral intent enabling intervention; facilitated by social / online data sources, powered by a medically-validated suicide risk classifier.

2 Suicide risk and military culture

The suicide rate among members of the United States Armed Forces has continued to rise for the past decade, beginning soon after the onset of military operations in Iraq and Afghanistan. Suicide is now the second-leading cause of death among military personnel, with more service members dying by suicide in 2012 than by combat-related causes (Zoroya, 2012). In response to steadily rising suicide rates among military personnel and veterans, researchers, clinicians, policy-makers, and military leaders have responded with an overwhelming and concerted effort to reverse these trends. Despite these considerable efforts, however, no evidence of effectiveness has been observed to date, resulting in considerable frustration for all involved. Although specific reasons explaining the lack of success to date are not yet known, it has been noted that most suicide prevention efforts used with military and veteran populations lack cultural relevance and do not incorporate several critical characteristics of the military culture that can create unique challenges from a suicide prevention perspective (Bryan et al., 2012). For instance, mental toughness and suppressive coping, fearlessness of death, and self-sacrifice are qualities that are valued in the military, but can serve as barriers to traditional prevention efforts.

The military culture values strength, resilience, courage, and personal sacrifice when faced with adversity. Weakness is not tolerated, and service members are expected to "shake it off" or "suck it up" when experiencing problems or illness.

Workshop on Computational Linguistics and Clinical Psychology: From Linguistic Signal to Clinical Reality, pages 1–6, Baltimore, Maryland USA, June 27, 2014.

Suppression and avoidance have long been linked to mental health problems and emotional distress (Hayes et al., 1996), including suicidal ideation and suicide attempts (Najmi et al., 2007). Yet despite this "common sense" piece of knowledge, suppression and avoidance are nonetheless taught and reinforced within the military culture as a coping strategy because, in the short term after a stressful or traumatic event, suppression can actually reduce emotional distress and foster adaptation to extreme adversity (Beck et al., 2006; Bonanno 2004). This is especially relevant in combat situations, when natural grief responses may need to be suppressed to sustain adequate performance and achieve mission objectives. For example, crying in the midst of a fire fight is not adaptive or conducive to survival, and therefore must be stifled. Suppression and avoidance therefore presents the first paradox for understanding military and veteran suicide: a skill that is adaptive and useful in the short-term following a traumatic event can be detrimental and impair adaptive functioning in the long-term.

Military personnel are also explicitly trained to overcome their fear of injury and death, typically through repeated exposure to scenarios and environments that increasingly mimic actual combat situations, which habituates them to fear and eventually replaces this fear with exhilaration and/or other positive emotions (i.e., the opponent-process). Indeed, greater exposure to combat, especially combat marked by higher levels of violence and injury, are associated with less fear of death among military personnel (Bryan and Cukrowicz, 2011; Bryan et al. 2011). Fearlessness is an essential quality of a service member; retreating from danger and life-threatening situations are generally not conducive to an effective fighting force. Yet at the same time, fear of death is a well-known protective factor for suicide, given that individuals who are afraid to die are unlikely to attempt suicide, and fearlessness is associated with more severe levels of suicide risk among military personnel relative to civilian samples, and is associated with increased severity of suicide risk among military personnel (Bryan et al., 2010). Consequently, fearlessness about death paradoxically serves both as a necessary strength and asset for military personnel, yet also serves as a risk factor for suicide.

The military culture also places a premium on selflessness in the service of a higher good, and does not necessarily view life as the highest good in every situation. In the military, one's life might actually be viewed as subordinate to other, higher "goods" such as the well-being of others or ideals and principles such as freedom and justice. Laying down one's life for a greater good is widely considered to be one of the highest honors a service member can achieve. A considerable amount of research has converged on a very suicide-specific and dangerous thought process for suicidal behavior: perceived burdensomeness. Perceived burdensomeness entails the mistaken perception that "others would be better off without me" or that one's death is of greater value than one's life. Perceived burdensomeness and self-sacrifice are in many ways opposite sides of the same coin, and it is not yet clear how or when perceived burdensomeness ("taking" one's life) becomes mistaken for self-sacrifice ("giving" one's life) among military personnel and veterans.

These characteristics simultaneously function as an asset (in terms of military performance) and as a liability (in terms of suicide prevention) for military personnel and veterans, thereby creating a paradox for suicide prevention in military and veteran populations, and contributing directly to mental health stigma. Furthermore, the values of the military culture are generally at odds with the values and ideals of mental health systems, which value emotional vulnerability and help-seeking, and focus on deficiencies and clinical disorders, thereby reinforcing stigma even more. In essence, traditional prevention approaches have conceptualized suicide in a way that conflicts with the core identity and values of military personnel and veterans. To be effective, suicide prevention efforts must be culturally-relevant and integrate these values and ideals of military personnel and veterans.

3 Related work

In addition to the work related to military culture issues discussed in section 2, there are many linguistic approaches to analyzing suicide risk (Barak and Miron, 2005; Jones and Bennell, 2007; Lester, 2008a; Lester, 2008b; Lester, 2010a; Lester, 2010b; Lester et al., 2010; Lester and McSwain, 2010; Stirman and Pennebaker, 2001). In 2011, one of the Informatics for Integrating Biology & the Bedside (i2b2) shared tasks was a sentiment analysis task to identify emotion in suicide notes (Combined Objective, 2011). Of this literature only Barak and Miron

(2005) considers online text. Most other text analysis suicide research concerns analysis of suicide notes. There are studies of the writings of suicidal poets (Lester and McSwain, 2010; Stirman and Pennebaker, 2001) and studies involving distinguishing genuine and simulated suicide notes (Jones and Bennell, 2007; Lester, 2010a).

4 The Durkheim Project

4.1 Overview

The Durkheim Project consists of three phases. During the first phase, described in section 4.2, a clinician's dashboard was built and a Veterans Affairs (VA) predictive risk medical records study was completed, based on an analysis of the narrative, or free text, portions of VA medical records. Also during the first phase, the initial software infrastructure to collect and analyze the social media data for phase two, was designed and implemented. During the second phase, section 4.3, now underway, opt-in social media postings are being collected and will be analyzed. During the third phase, section 4.4, a pilot program will isolate serious suicide risk for individuals in real-time, and develop a prediction triage model for improved suicide intervention

4.2 Phase 1: Veteran Affairs medical records study

During phase 1 linguistics-driven prediction models were developed to estimate the risk of suicide. These models were generated from unstructured clinical notes taken from a national sample of United States VA medical records. The protocol for this study was approved by the Institutional Review Board (IRB) of the VA Medical Center, where the study was conducted. We created three matched cohorts: veterans who completed suicide, veterans who used mental health services and did not complete suicide, and veterans who did not use mental health services and did not complete suicide during the observation period (n = 70 in each group). From the clinical notes, we generated datasets of single keywords and multi-word phrases, and constructed prediction models using a supervised machine-learning algorithm based on a genetic programming framework, MOSES (Looks, 2006, 2007; Goertzel et al., 2013). MOSES can be described as a variant of a decision-tree forest, with certain genetic and maximum entropy techniques mixed in: maximum entropy to apply pressure to minimize tree size and genetic to ensure tree species diversity. In our prior research we have found that MOSES consistently outperforms standard text classification approaches, such as Support Vector Machines (SVMs). The primary hyper-parameter that we used was the dynamic feature size. The resulting inference accuracy was at first 65% and then consistently 67% or more. This was the prediction accuracy for assigning a patient to the correct cohort. These data suggest that computerized text analytics can be applied to unstructured sections of medical records to estimate the risk of suicide (Poulin et al. 2014). The resulting system could potentially allow clinicians to screen seemingly healthy patients at the primary care level, and to continuously evaluate suicide risk among psychiatric patients.

4.3 Phase 2: Predicting risk with opt-in social media postings

Although data collection and analysis for phase 2 is just beginning, the software development required for this data collection and analysis was completed during phase 1. A phase 2 protocol for collecting and analyzing opt-in social media postings and presenting predictions to clinicians via the Durkheim Project's Clinicians' dashboard has also been approved by our IRB. When the system is fully operational, a clinician will see predictive models of suicide risk for a patient constructed from the patient's medical records and the patient's opt-in social media postings. Subjects are being recruited via targeted efforts. Subjects will be recruited through our collaboration with Facebook (PR Newswire 2013). A Facebook pop-up window will be used to recruit people that Facebook has identified as being military personnel or veterans.

4.4 Phase 3: Intervention

For phase 3, a protocol has been completed, which will soon be submitted to a final IRB. This protocol includes an unblinded, 3-cohort design, for a pilot program, which proposes to isolate serious suicide risks for individuals in real-time and to develop a prediction triage model for improved suicide intervention. Plans are to use and improve upon the linguistically-based prediction capabilities of the model developed during phase 1. The phase 1 retrospective study was able to predict with limited accuracy before suicides occurred. The theoretic assumption is that wording chosen by those at risk will vary at different stages of risk. By building from ongoing observations from the phase 2 study and feedback obtained during the conduct of the phase 3 study, the aim is to adjust the linguistics-driven model to predict suicide risk within the critical period for interventions of various levels of severity.

In this protocol, ongoing monitoring of the network will allow continuous updating and change in value of risk alert levels among the green-to-red color coding. When the predictive system detects postings that indicate a certain threshold level of potential suicide risk, risk alerts are triggered in real-time and sent to either a monitoring clinician or a pre-identified buddy monitor, or to an automated system, which will generate supportive messages that are sent to the at-risk individual.

To better characterize the risk for the population of active-duty military and veterans, the analysis for this study will be limited to the primary participants. These primary participants may be newly recruited via the dedicated Facebook and mobile applications or, through that same dedicated application, from among those already participating in the phase 2 study. In either case, all primary participants must provide informed consent for this specific study. That is, those already involved in the phase 2 study must provide separate consent to participate in the phase 3 study. However, outside of the context of this study, the computerized intervention will be open to members of the general public who might wish to take advantage of the program's intervention potential. Primary participants are active duty U.S. military or veterans with English as a primary or secondary language, who agree to post to social media using English. The age limit for primary participants in the phase 3 study, as with phase 2 study, targets the age group most likely to actively use social media, i.e., those between the ages of 18 and 45.

5 Results

So far results are only available for the phase 1 study. For single-word models, the predictive accuracy was approximately 59% (the average for 100 models), and scores for individual candidate models ranged from 46-67%. Because our training sets are balanced, we have used accuracy as a surrogate for precision and recall. Accuracy was computed using five-way cross-validation. Models that used certain word pairs had significantly better scores than single-word models, though they are far less human readable. The phrases "negative assessment for PTSD" and "positive assessment for PTSD" carry different meanings. This phrase-based approach was more accurate than a single-word approach. For pre-selected word pairs, the individual model scores ranged from 52-69%, with an average of 64% (for 100 models). In the final experiments, the combined Cohorts '1v2v3 classifier' had a peak performance of 70%, and an average performance of 67%.

6 Discussion

Our analyses were successful at determining useful text-based signals of suicide risk. We obtained accuracies of greater than 60% for ensemble averages of 100 models, and our individual model accuracies reached 67-69%. Given the small size of the dataset and the fragmentary nature of the clinical notes, this performance level represents a significant achievement. For a classifier, these results represent a statistically significant 'signal'. Meanwhile, we showed that, methodologically, word pairs are more useful than single words for model construction on electronic medical record (EMR) data. Furthermore, the predictive feature words that distinguished each group were highly revealing, especially for the suicidal cohort, and were consistent with the existing medical literature on suicide. Many medical conditions have been associated with an increased risk for suicide, but these conditions have generally not been included in suicide risk assessment tools. These conditions include gastrointestinal conditions, cardiopulmonary conditions, oncologic conditions, and pain conditions. Also, some research has emerged that links care processes to suicide risk. The word "integrated" emerged as a key term in our study and is also reflected in the integrated care literature (Bauer et al., 2013).

Although the text on which our predictive model was based for the phase 1 medical records study was text written by a physician or other healthcare provider, our hypothesis is that some of the highly predictive features learned during phase 1 will carry over to the predictive modeling of opt-in social media postings during phase 2. This text is written by the patient. However, we expect that some of the features, or concepts, will be the same due to the ability to do software based synonym matches Additionally, a physician or other healthcare worker may sometimes quote or paraphrase what a patient said when adding a note to the clinical record. A key predictive feature, such as the word "anxiety," may be used either by a clinician or a patient. We believe that the use of specialized text-analytic resources such as linguistic inquiry and word count (LIWC) would also help improve our results. Some preliminary results have been obtained using LIWC on our dataset.

In future research we plan to scale up the phase 1 medical records study from our current study where each cohort had 70 subjects to a study, using the same protocol, with at least 1000 subjects in each cohort. We also plan to transfer the predictive model built from the phase 1 study to the analysis of phase 2 opt-in social media postings. Once our phase 3 protocol has IRB approval, we plan to begin the phase 3 of the Durkheim Project, informed by the results, and ongoing follow-on research, of our phase 1 and 2 studies. In our future research we plan to use additional features from the structured portions of the medical record, as well as to use LIWC. In both our medical records and social media research we plan to use temporal analysis.

7 Conclusion

Although the phase 1 study was successful in distinguishing the cohort of completed suicides both from the control group cohort and the psychiatric cohort, it was difficult to distinguish text based noise from signal with high accuracy in our initial results. We expect that our planned follow-on study with 1000 subjects in each cohort will have much less problem in distinguishing signal from noise. Suicide risk prediction is a very difficult problem. We believe that studies such as our phases 1 and 2 studies, which use supervised machine learning techniques, can uncover predictive risk factors that are not clearly understood by the medical community. At the same time, we also believe that more effective suicide risk prediction systems can be built based on the integration of machine learning methods and the expertise of suicidologists. In particular, building an understanding of military culture into our methods will be important.

References

Amy M. Bauer, Ya-Fen Chan, Hsiang Huang, Steven Vannoy, Jurgen Unützer. 2013. Characteristics, Management, and Depression Outcomes of Primary Care Patients Who Endorse Thoughts of Death or Suicide on the PHQ-9. *J Gen Intern Med.* Mar; 28(3):363-9. doi: 10.1007/s11606-012-2194-2. Epub 2012 Aug 31.

Azy Barak, Ofra Miron. 2005. Writing Characteristics of Suicidal People on the Internet: A Psychological Investigation of Emerging Social Environments. *Suicide and Life-Threatening Behavior* 35(5) October.

Ben Goertzel, Nil Geisweiller, Pennachin, Cassio. 2013. Integrating Feature Selection into Program Learning. *Proceedings of AGI-13*, Springer. http://goertzel.org/agi-13/FS-MOSES_v1.pdf.

Chris Poulin, Brian Shiner, Paul Thompson, Linas Vepstas,Yinong Young-Xu, Benjamin Goertzel, Bradley Watts, Laura Flashman, Thomas McAllister. 2014. Predicting the Risk of Suicide by Analyzing the Text of Clinical Notes. *PLoS ONE* 9(1): e85733. doi:10.1371/journal.pone.0085733.

Combined Objective & Subjective Shared Task Announcement: Call for Participation. 2011. https://www.i2b2.org/NLP/Coreference/Call.php.

Craig J. Bryan, Kelly C. Cukrowicz. 2011. Associations between types of combat violence and the acquired capability for suicide. *Suicide and Life-Threatening Behavior, 41,*126-136.

Craig J. Bryan, Kelly C. Cukrowicz, Christopher L. West, Chad E. Morrow. 2010. Combat experience and the acquired capability for suicide. *Journal of Clinical Psychology*, 66, 1044-1056.

Craig J. Bryan, Keith W. Jennings, David A. Jobes, John C. Bradley. 2012. Understanding and preventing military suicide. *Archives of Suicide Research, 16,* 95-110.

Craig J. Bryan, Chad E. Morrow, Michael D. Anestis, Thomas E. Joiner. 2010. A preliminary test of the interpersonal-psychological theory of suicidal behavior in a military sample. *Personality and Individual Differences*, 48, 347-350.

David Lester. 2008a. Computer Analysis of the Content of Suicide Notes from Men and Women. *Psychological Reports*, 102, 575-576.

David Lester. 2008b. Differences Between Genuine and Simulated Suicide Notes. *Psychological Reports*, 103, 527-528.

David Lester. 2010a. Linguistic Analysis of a Blog from a Murder-Suicide. *Psychological Reports*, 106(2): 342.

David Lester. 2010b. The Final Hours: A Linguistic Analysis of the Final Words of a Suicide. *Psychological Reports*, 106(3): 791-797.

David Lester, Janet Haines, Christopher Williams. 2010. Content Differences in Suicide Notes by Sex, Age, and Method: A Study of Australian Suicide Notes. *Psychological Reports*, 106(2): 475-476.

David Lester, Stephanie McSwain. 2010. Poems by a Suicide: Sara Teasdale. *Psychological Reports*, 106(3): 811-812.

George Bonanno. 2004. Loss, trauma, and human resilience: Have we underestimated the human capacity to thrive after extremely aversive events? *American Psychologist, 59*, 20-28.

Gregg Zoroya. Army, Navy suicides at record high. 2012. *USA Today.* http://www.usatoday.com/story/news/nation/2012/11/18/navy-suicides-army/1702403/, November 18.

Health Promotion Risk Reduction Suicide Prevention. 2010. U.S. ARMY HP/RR/SP REPORT: http://usarmy.vo.llnwd.net/e1/HPRRSP/HP-RR-SPReport2010_v00.pdf.

J. Gayle Beck, Berglind Gudmundsdottir, Sarah Palyo, Luana M. Miller, DeMond Grant. 2006. Rebound effects following deliberate thought suppression: does PTSD make a difference? *Behavior Therapy, 37*, 170-180.

LIWC. 2014. Linguistic Inquery and Word Count. http://www.liwc.net/ Accessed 28 April 2014.

Moshe Looks. 2006. Competent Program Evolution. PhD thesis, Washington University.

Moshe Looks. 2007. Meta-optimizing semantic evolutionary search. In: Lipson, H. (ed.), *Genetic and Evolutionary Computation Conference, GECCO 2007, Proceedings*, London, England, UK, July 7-11, p. 626.

Natalie J. Jones, Craig Bennell. 2007. The Development and Validation of Statistical Prediction Rules for Discriminating Between Genuine and Simulated Suicide Notes. *Archives of Suicide Research*, 11:21-233.

PR Newswire. 2013 http://www.prnewswire.com/news-releases/the-durkheim-project-will-analyze-opt-in-data-from-veterans-social-media-and-mobile-content----seeking-real-time-predictive-analytics-for-suicide-risk-213922041.html Accessed 28 April 2014.

Sadia Najmi, Daniel M. Wegner, and Matthew K. Nock. 2007. Thought suppression and self-injurious thoughts and behaviors. *Behaviour Research and Therapy, 45*, 1957-1965.

Shannon W. Stirman, James W. Pennebaker. 2001. Word Use in the Poetry of Suicidal and Nonsuicidal Poets. *Psychosomatic Medicine* 63:517-522.

Steven Hayes, Kelly G. Wilson, Elizabeth V. Gifford, Victoria M. Follette, and Kirk Strosahl. 1996. Experiential avoidance and behavioral disorders: A functional dimensional approach to diagnosis and treatment. *Journal of Consulting and Clinical Psychology, 64*, 1152-1168.

Treating Soldiers with Brain Injuries. 2010. *Diane Rehm*, NPR: June 24.

Linguistic Indicators of Severity and Progress in Online Text-based Therapy for Depression*

Christine Howes, Matthew Purver
Cognitive Science Research Group
School of Electronic Engineering and Computer Science
Queen Mary University of London
London, UK
{c.howes,m.purver}@qmul.ac.uk

Rose McCabe
University of Exeter Medical School
Exeter, UK
r.mccabe@exeter.ac.uk

Abstract

Mental illnesses such as depression and anxiety are highly prevalent, and therapy is increasingly being offered online. This new setting is a departure from face-to-face therapy, and offers both a challenge and an opportunity – it is not yet known what features or approaches are likely to lead to successful outcomes in such a different medium, but online text-based therapy provides large amounts of data for linguistic analysis. We present an initial investigation into the application of computational linguistic techniques, such as topic and sentiment modelling, to online therapy for depression and anxiety. We find that important measures such as symptom severity can be predicted with comparable accuracy to face-to-face data, using general features such as discussion topic and sentiment; however, measures of patient progress are captured only by finer-grained lexical features, suggesting that aspects of style or dialogue structure may also be important.

1 Introduction

Mental illnesses such as depression and anxiety have been called "the biggest causes of misery in Britain today" (Layard, 2012). The main avenue of treatment for such conditions is talking therapies, such as Cognitive Behavioural Therapy (CBT); however, there is far greater demand than can currently be met, and currently only 25% of sufferers in the UK receive treatment. Therapy is therefore increasingly being delivered online: this helps to improve access and reduce waiting times, and is just as effective as standard therapy (Kessler et al., 2009). However, this new online setting provides a challenge of evaluation and optimisation (Hanley and Reynolds, 2009; Beattie et al., 2009). Online therapy is a significant departure from face-to-face therapy, and it is not yet known exactly what features or approaches are likely to lead to successful outcomes, or help identify negative outcomes such as risk to the patient or others. Current methods (e.g. controlled studies) are expensive and time-consuming; we need fast, accurate methods to ensure treatment can be made effective and efficient in this new context.

Professional communication varies widely (McCabe et al., 2013b) and aspects of doctor-patient interaction and language are known to influence outcomes such as patient satisfaction, treatment adherence and health status (Ong et al., 1995; McCabe et al., 2013a). For therapists, automated methods to analyse therapist-client communication are of interest as there is little known about *how* the quality of communication influences patient outcome. Identifying patterns of effective communication – both in terms of what is spoken about and how it is spoken about – would help guide training of therapists. Moreover, it may assist in identifying successful therapy and perhaps, more importantly, where communication is not therapeutic and patients are failing to improve. This may warrant a different or more intensive therapeutic intervention. Applying computational linguistic techniques to therapy data could therefore offer potential to produce tools which can aid clinicians in predicting outcomes, diagnosing severity of symptoms and/or evaluating progress. Recent work on spoken therapy dialogue has shown promising results in a range of mental health tasks, including diagnosis of post-traumatic stress disorder (PTSD) and depression (DeVault et al., 2013; Yu et al., 2013),

*This work was partly supported by the ConCreTe project. The project ConCreTe acknowledges the financial support of the Future and Emerging Technologies (FET) programme within the Seventh Framework Programme for Research of the European Commission, under FET grant number 611733.

Workshop on Computational Linguistics and Clinical Psychology: From Linguistic Signal to Clinical Reality, pages 7–16,
Baltimore, Maryland USA, June 27, 2014.

and prediction of outcomes in schizophrenia treatment (Howes et al., 2013).

Online therapy data provides a new challenge – language and interaction styles differ to face-to-face – but also an opportunity in the availability of large amounts of text data without the need for automatic speech recognition or manual transcription. Here, we present an initial investigation into the application of computational linguistic techniques to online therapy for depression and anxiety. We find that important measures such as symptom severity can be predicted with comparable accuracy to face-to-face data, and that general aspects such as discussion topic and sentiment are useful predictors; and suggest some ways in which techniques can be adapted for improved performance in future.

2 Background

2.1 Computational analysis & mental health

Research into computer-based diagnosis in mental health goes back at least to the 1960s – see (Overall and Hollister, 1964; Hirschfeld et al., 1974) amongst others – but most systems rely on doctor- or patient-reported data rather than naturally occurring language. Much recent work similarly uses self-reported clinical and socio-demographic data, e.g. to predict treatment resistance in depression (Perlis, 2013). Some recent natural language processing (NLP) research examines features of the language used by patients when discussing conditions or treatment, e.g. discovering topics and opinions from online doctor ratings (Paul et al., 2013) or social media (Paul and Drezde, 2011).

However, aspects of the communication *during treatment itself* are also associated with patient outcomes (Ong et al., 1995). In the mental health domain, recent work suggests that, for patients with schizophrenia both conversation structure (*how* communication proceeds in therapy), and content (*what* is talked about), can affect outcomes (McCabe et al., 2013a; John et al., under review). NLP research has now begun to examine both. Wallace et al. (2013) model speech acts to characterise doctor-patient consultations on medication adherence; Angus et al. (2012) use unsupervised topic models to visualise shared content in clinical dialogue; Cretchley et al. (2010) use a similar approach for a qualititative analysis of topic and communication style between patients with schizophrenia and carers. DeVault et al. (2013) use features of speech, and Yu et al. (2013) multimodal features, from video-mediated dialogue to detect depression and PTSD with promising accuracies (0.66 to 0.74 depending on condition and task). In face-to-face therapy for schizophrenia, Howes et al. (2012; 2013) use a combination of supervised and unsupervised approaches to predict a range of diagnostic and outcome measures, including future adherence to treatment (accuracy 0.70); fine-grained lexical features gave reasonable accuracy, with more general topic features giving weaker prediction of some outcomes.

2.2 Topic modelling

One focus of research for mental health is therefore on methods for analysing content (*what* is talked about). Traditional methods, while effective, involve time-consuming hand-coding of data (Beattie et al., 2009; John et al., under review); NLP techniques can reduce this requirement. Unsupervised probabilistic models (e.g. Latent Dirichlet Allocation (LDA) Blei et al. (2003) and variants) have been widely applied to learn topics (word distributions) from the data itself, connecting words with similar meanings and even distinguishing between uses of words with multiple meanings (Steyvers and Griffiths, 2007). Such techniques have been applied successfully to structured dialogue e.g. meetings and tutorials (Purver et al., 2006; Eisenstein and Barzilay, 2008), and more recently to dialogues in the clinical domain (Cretchley et al., 2010; Howes et al., 2013), with topics found to identify important themes within therapy conversation such as medication, symptoms, family and social issues, and to correlate with outcomes.

2.3 Sentiment and emotion analysis

One aspect of conversation process and style is the affect or emotion present. NLP research has generally approached this via the task of *sentiment* detection, distinguishing positive from negative (and sometimes neutral) stance (Pang and Lee, 2008). Methods generally take either a knowledge-rich approach (relying on e.g. dictionaries of sentiment-carrying words (Pennebaker et al., 2007)), or a data-rich approach via (usually supervised) machine learning over datasets of sentiment-carrying text (e.g. Socher et al. (2013)). The former can provide deeper insights, but are less robust in the face of unexpected vocabulary, unusual or errorful spelling; the latter are more robust but require training from large datasets. Recent research has attempted finer-grained distinctions, e.g. detecting specific emotions such as anger, surprise, fear etc; again, approaches can be characterised as dictionary-based or machine-learning-based (Chuang and Wu, 2004; Seol et al., 2008; Purver and Battersby, 2012; De Choudhury et al., 2012). The resulting sentiment or emotion ratings have been widely used to determine aspects of personality and mental state in various domains. In social media text, Quercia et al. (2011; 2012) found correlations between sentiment and levels of popularity, influence and general well-being; O'Connor et al. (2010) with measures of public opinion. Closer to our application, Liakata et al. (2012) show that these methods can be applied to analyse emotion in suicide notes.

2.4 Research questions

Here, similar to (DeVault et al., 2013; Howes et al., 2013), our primary question is whether these approaches can be usefully applied to diagnose conditions and predict outcomes, but in a new modality – online text-based therapy – which may require different and/or more robust methods. In addition, we would like to gain some insight into which features of language and interaction might be predictive, in order to help clinicians improve therapeutic methods, and to assess how general and transferable any model might be. Our main questions here are therefore:

- What features of text-based online therapy dialogue might help predict symptoms and/or outcomes? Specifically, how predictive are conversation topic and emotional content?
- Can we detect them accurately and reliably, using approaches generalisable to large datasets, across different subjects and conditions?
- Can the features provide any insights into the treatment process and/or the online modality?

3 Method

3.1 Data

The data used in this study consisted of the transcripts from 882 Cognitive Behavioural Therapy (CBT) treatment dialogues between patients with depression and/or anxiety and their therapists using an online text-based chat system. The transcripts are from online CBT provided by Psychology Online, who deliver 'live' therapy from a qualified psychologist accessed via the internet (`http://www.psychologyonline.co.uk`). Of the 882 transcripts, 837 are between therapists and patients who were in an ongoing treatment program or had completed their treatment by the time our sample was collected. There are 167 patients in this sample (125 females and 42 males), with 35 different therapists (for 2 patients the identity of the therapist is unknown). The number of transcripts per patient ranges from 1 to 14, with a mean of 5.011 (s.d. 2.73). For all of the measures based on the transcripts, as outlined below, we included all text typed by both the therapist and the patient. In addition to the transcripts themselves, each patient normally filled out two questionnaires prior to each session with their therapist. These are described below.

3.2 Outcomes

Patient Health Questionnaire (PHQ-9) This is a self-administered diagnostic instrument for common mental disorders (Kroenke and Spitzer, 2002). The PHQ-9 is the depression module, which scores each of the 9 DSM-IV criteria as '0' (not at all) to '3' (nearly every day). A higher score indicates higher levels of depression, with scores ranging from 0-27. It has been validated for use (Martin et al., 2006).

Generalised Anxiety Disorder scale (GAD-7) Similarly, the GAD-7 (Spitzer et al., 2006) is a brief self-report scale of generalised anxiety disorder. This is a 7-item scale which scores each of the items as '0' (not at all) to '3' (nearly every day). A higher score indicates higher levels of anxiety.

Outcome measures For the data in our sample, PHQ-9 and GAD-7 were highly correlated ($r = 0.811$, $p < 0.001$) so for the results reported below we focus on PHQ-9. As each patient filled in the PHQ-9 before each consultation, we used two different outcome measures: *PHQ now* – the PHQ-9 score of the patient for the questionnaire completed immediately prior to the consultation; and *PHQ start-now* – the difference between the PHQ-9 score prior to any treatment and *PHQ now*, i.e. a measure of progress (how much better or worse the patient is since the start of their treatment). Although these two measures are numerical, one of the general aims of our research is to identify patients at risk. We therefore binarised the outcome measures and treated our task as a categorisation problem to identify the group of interest. For *PHQ now*, these were patients with moderate to severe symptoms; for *PHQ start-now*, patients whose PHQ score had not improved.

3.3 Topics

The transcripts from the 882 treatment consultations were analysed using an unsupervised probabilistic topic model, using MALLET (McCallum, 2002) to apply standard Latent Dirichlet Allocation (Blei et al., 2003), with the notion of *document* corresponding to a single consultation session, represented as the sequence of words typed by any speaker. Stop words (common words which do not contribute to the content, e.g. 'the', 'to') were removed as usual (Salton and McGill, 1986), but the word list had to be augmented for text chat conventions and spellings (e.g. unpunctuated "ive"). Additionally, common mispellings were mapped to their correctly spelled equivalents using Microsoft Excel's in-built spellchecker. This was due to the nature of text chat, in contrast to transcribed speech or formal text – the word 'questionnaire', for example, was found to have been typed in 21 different ways. Following (Howes et al., 2013) we set the number of topics to 20,[1] used the default setting of 1000 Gibbs sampling iterations, and enabled automatic hyperparameter optimisation to allow an uneven distribution of topics via an asymmetric prior over the document-topic distributions (Wallach et al., 2009).

As Howes et al. (2013) did in face-to-face therapy, we found most topics were composed of coherent word lists, with many corresponding to common themes in therapy e.g. family (Topic 12), symptoms (16), treatment process (2, 14), and issues in work and social life (19, 5) – see Table 5.

3.4 Sentiment and emotion analysis

Each turn in the transcripts was then annotated for strength of positive and negative sentiment, and level of anger. We compared three approaches: the dictionary-based LIWC (Pennebaker et al., 2007) and two machine learning approaches, the Stanford classifier based on deep neural nets and parse structure trained on standard text (Socher et al., 2013), and one based on distant supervision over social media text, Sentimental (Purver and Battersby, 2012).[2] None are specifically designed for therapy dialogue data; however, given the unorthodox spelling and vocabulary used in text chat, we expect machine-learning based approaches, and training on "noisy" social media text, to provide more robustness.

We used each to provide a positive/negative/neutral sentiment value; for LIWC, we took this from the relative magnitudes of the `posemo` and `negemo` categories. Two human judges then rated the 85 utterances in one transcript independently. Inter-annotator agreement was good, with Cohen's kappa = 0.66. Agreement with LIWC was poor (0.43-0.45); with Stanford better (0.51-0.54); but best with Sentimental (0.63-0.80). For anger, LIWC gave only one utterance a non-zero rating, while Sentimental provided a range of values. We therefore used Sentimental in our experiments. Raw values per turn were scaled to [-1,+1] for sentiment (-1 representing strong negative sentiment, +1 strong positive), and [0,1] for anger; we then derived minimum, maximum, mean and standard deviation values per transcript.

3.5 Classification experiments

We performed a series of experiments, to investigate whether various features of the transcripts could enable automatic detection of patient responses to the PHQ-9. The full range of possible features were calculated for each transcript – see Table 1. As well as topic, sentiment and emotion features as detailed above, we include raw lexical features to characterise details of content, and some high-level features (amount of talk; patient demographics; and therapist identity, known to affect outcomes).

In each case, we used the Weka machine learning toolkit (Hall et al., 2009) to pre-process data, and a decision tree classifier (J48), a logistic regression model and the support vector machine implementation LibLINEAR (Chang and Lin, 2001) as classifiers. *PHQ now* was binarised based on the classification in Kroenke and Spitzer (2002), whereby scores of 10 or over are moderate to severe and scores of less than 10 are mild. *PHQ start-now* was binarised according to whether there was an improvement (reduction) in the PHQ score or not. Positive scores indicate

[1]An arbitrary decision, but Howes et al. (2013) chose it to match the number defined by manual coders in a therapy domain.

[2]Available from `liwc.net`, `nlp.stanford.edu` and `sentimental.co` respectively.

Feature set	Description
AgentID	Identity of the therapist
High level	Client gender; client age group; session number; client/agent number of words and turns used; proportion of all words per participant
Topic	Probability distribution of topics per transcript (one value per topic per transcript)
Sentiment	Overall sentiment mean, standard deviation, minimum and maximum; overall anger mean, standard deviation, minimum and maximum
Word	Unigrams, for all words that appeared in at least 20 of the transcripts, regardless of speaker; the features were the normalised counts of each word
N-gram	As word, but including unigrams, bigrams and trigrams

Table 1: Feature sets for classification experiments

an improvement; scores of 0 or lower indicate no change or a worsening of PHQ score. Each outcome indicator was tested with different feature sets using 10-fold cross-validation.[3]

4 Results

4.1 Correlations

First, we examined statistical associations between our four outcome measures and our available features (see Section 3). R-values are shown for all significant correlations (at the $p < 0.05$ level) in Tables 2-4. For the *PHQ now* measure, a positive correlation means a greater value of the feature is associated with a greater value of the PHQ score (i.e. a higher level of symptoms). For the *PHQ start-now* measures, a positive correlation means that a greater value of the feature is associated with a greater improvement in the PHQ score since the start of treatment. Correlations greater than ± 0.2 are shown in bold.

High-level With patients with a worse (higher) PHQ score (*PHQ now*), more words and turns are typed by both participants. Better overall progress scores are also weakly associated with the amount of talk, with fewer turns typed by both participants if patients' PHQ score has improved by a greater amount since the start of their treatment program (see Table 2).

Sentiment As shown in Table 3, more negative sentiment expressed in the transcripts (mean and minimum), a higher variability of sentiment between negative and positive (s.d.), and greater levels of anger (mean and maximum) are associated with worse PHQ scores. More positive sentiments (mean and maximum) are also associated with better progress.

Topic Topics 2, 6, 9, 10, 16 and 17 are negatively correlated with PHQ scores, i.e. higher levels of these topics are associated with better PHQ (see Table 4). Some of these topics involve words related to assessing the patient's progress and feedback, e.g. topic 2 includes *session*, *goals* and *questionnaires*, and topic 17 includes *good*, *work* and *positive*. Others relate to specific concerns of the patient, e.g. topic 6 (*worry*, *worrying* and *problem*) and topic 16 (*anxiety*, *fear* and *sick*). The top twenty words assigned to each topic by LDA, and the direction of significant correlations are shown in Table 5.

Conversely, topics 4, 5, 7, 8, 11 and 18 are positively correlated with PHQ scores, meaning more talk assigned to these topics is associated with worse PHQ. Several of these topics relate to specific issues, such as topic 5 (*sleep*, *bed*, *night*) and topic 18 (*eating*, *food*, *weight*). Some of these topics display overlap with the previous group (e.g. topics 2 and 4 both contain words reviewing progress such as *session*, *week*, *next* and *last*); this suggests that some topics (e.g. progress or particular issues) are discussed in importantly (and recognisably) different ways or contexts (possibly different emotional valences – see below), and these differences are being identified by the automatic topic modelling.

Similarly, greater amounts of talk in topics 2, 15 and 17 are weakly associated with better progress. These are the topics identified above as involving words related to assessing progress, and feedback. Greater amounts of talk in topic 8 (*checking*, *OCD*, *anxiety*, *rituals*) is associated with worse progress.

Cross-correlations between topic and sentiment features Previous work has hypothesised that automatically derived topics may differ from hand-coded topics in picking up additional factors of the communication such as valence (Howes et al., 2013). To explore this on a global level (i.e.

[3] We partition the data into 10 equal subsamples, and use each subsample as the test data for a model trained on the remaining 90%. This is repeated for each subsample (the 10 folds), and the test predictions collated to give the overall results. This partitioning is done by transcript: different transcripts from the same patient may therefore appear in training and test data within the same fold; our use of low-dimensional topic/sentiment features should minimise over-fitting, but future work will investigate the extent of this effect.

Measure	PHQ now	PHQ start-now
Agent number of words	**0.231**	
Client number of words	0.195	
Agent number of turns	0.149	-0.080
Client number of turns	0.193	-0.071

Table 2: Significant correlations of high-level features and outcomes

Measure	PHQ now	PHQ start-now
Sentiment mean	**-0.237**	0.119
Sentiment s.d.	0.161	
Sentiment minimum	-0.167	
Sentiment maximum		0.074
Anger mean	0.185	
Anger s.d.	0.074	
Anger minimum		
Anger maximum	0.192	

Table 3: Significant correlations of sentiment features and outcomes

at the level of the transcript, rather than at the finer-grained level of the turn) we examined cross-correlations between sentiment and topic. This initial exploration offers support for this hypothesis, as can be seen in Table 6. For example, topics 3 and 4 both contain words relating to feelings and thoughts, but topic 3 is positively correlated with sentiment, while topic 4 is negatively correlated. These correlations indicate a complex relationship between topic and sentiment which should be explored further in future research; a joint topic-sentiment model might be appropriate e.g. (Paul et al., 2013). Although some topics pattern consistently with sentiment (e.g. topic 12, with words about relatives and relationships, is associated with negative sentiments and higher levels of anger) some do not (e.g. topic 19 is associated with more positive sentiment, but greater anger). Examination suggests that this topic involves discussions *about* feelings of anger, but not necessarily *expressing* anger, and also may include talk on how to deal with such feelings (with words like *assertive*). These observations may indicate that in this domain, in which people explicitly talk about their feelings, fully accurate sentiment and emotion analysis may require a different approach than in domains such as social media analysis.

4.2 Classification experiments

Results of classification experiments on different feature sets are shown in Tables 7-9. For each experiment, the weighted average f-score is shown, with the f-score for the class of interest shown in brackets. For *PHQ now* the class of interest is patients with high (moderate to severe) PHQ-9 scores; for *PHQ start-now* we are concerned with patients who are *not* getting better. As a baseline, the proportion of the data in the class of interest in each case is shown in the first column in Table 7 – note that these are not exactly 50%, but reflect the actual proportions in the data (see Section 3.5).

High-level As can be seen in Table 7, if we use a feature set consisting of high-level features and AgentID, we are able to predict *PHQ now* and *PHQ start-now* reasonably well (> 0.7). However, given the nature of the data, it is uncommon for a therapist to have many clients of the same age group and gender; these features can therefore act as a reasonable proxy for identifying individual patients, meaning that this result is somewhat spurious. Also, although identity of therapist is an important factor in therapeutic outcomes (McCabe et al., 2013a; McCabe et al., 2013b), we would like to identify aspects of the communication that explain *why* particular therapists are more successful than others, and generalise our findings to new therapists. AgentID was therefore removed in all subsequent experiments.

Sentiment and topic As shown in Table 8, using the proportions of derived topics by transcript as features does allow us to predict whether a patient has a high *PHQ now* score reasonably well; but sentiment alone performs poorly. Combining sentiment and topic features, however, allows us to predict *PHQ now* with scores of around 0.7 (i.e. approaching the accuracy achieved using high-level and AgentID features above). Prediction of the progress measure is less effective.

Words and n-grams For the symptom measure, using words and n-grams gives f-scores in

Measure	PHQ now	PHQ start-now
Topic 2	-0.157	0.112
Topic 4	0.124	
Topic 5	0.176	
Topic 6	-0.117	
Topic 7	**0.217**	
Topic 8	0.093	-0.126
Topic 9	-0.077	
Topic 10	-0.149	
Topic 11	0.140	
Topic 12	0.080	
Topic 15		0.072
Topic 16	-0.112	
Topic 17	**-0.211**	0.079
Topic 18	0.121	

Table 4: Significant correlations of topic features and outcomes

Topic	PHQ +/-	Sentiment +/-	Anger +/-	keywords
Topic 0		-	+	good thought re well also mindfulness hw thoughts now vc maybe prob message neg just wk one self bit
Topic 1				people good others self evidence thought enough wrong negative esteem thinking say confidence beliefs person true someone belief situation
Topic 2	-	+	-	session send goals next week last sent read great think questionnaires also homework goal appointment set time cbt able
Topic 3		+		thoughts thinking unhelpful helpful look thought behaviours go feelings may think anxiety negative try aware behaviour agenda start self
Topic 4	+	-		feel think like just good really week now know last session next say felt people thoughts going feeling bit
Topic 5	+	-	+	sleep bed day week work get night mood time diary see better much sleeping activity house routine done activities
Topic 6	-			worry worrying worries bit stop train worried problem go example idea control hierarchy driving exposure home happen worst car
Topic 7	+	-		help feel gp depression thank understand therapy now feeling life today think problems able little message medication sorry make
Topic 8	+			check checking ocd thoughts anxiety try something difficult danger brain week sense threat helpful away rituals anxious elephant images
Topic 9	-		-	think time like much way sure see though know look lot sounds well also right thing sorry sense different
Topic 10	-	+		thought thoughts anxiety really situation situations one week next example social experience record great emotions thanks notice see make
Topic 11	+		+	things get time go need like want now just something feel know one work good day going give next
Topic 12	+	-	+	mum relationship husband life family dad parents never love feelings children said years mother much hard way told sister
Topic 13				really week think appointment homework however lets teeth questions great just ready start may dentist set end sure therapy
Topic 14		+	-	great right sure appointment just thank well tonight loo lol good say really cool get going sorry transcript absolutely
Topic 15		+	-	things like get bit good sounds feeling also something really great today think idea send week useful anything make
Topic 16	-		-	anxiety panic breathing get anxious feeling going go attack fear physical control try happen sick symptoms times cope distraction
Topic 17	-	+	-	good work well positive back help really time still last much weeks use thanks session better keep done things
Topic 18	+			eating eat food weight day week meal lunch dinner pie energy good mum put table public walk believe ate
Topic 19		+	+	work job anger angry school stress thanks wife team stuff issues also boss year assertiveness assertive meeting kids times

Table 5: Top 20 words per topic

line with those using only the reduced dimensionality of sentiment and topic. This is surprising; one might expect finer-grained lexical features (which provide more information via a much higher-dimensional feature space) to increase predictivity, as per Howes et al. (2013); on the other hand, it is also promising as it suggests that meaningful generalisations can be drawn out of this data using NLP techniques.

For the progress measure, on the other hand, n-gram features perform better than topic/sentiment (though not as well as on the symptom measures); this suggests that there are aspects of the communication that can assist in predicting patient progress, but that they are not captured by the topic and sentiment information as currently defined. This suggests that dialogue structure or style may play a role; one possibility for exploration is to look at topic and/or sentiment at a finer-grained level and examine their dynamics (e.g. are positive sentiments expressed near the start or end of a consultation linked to better progress)?

5 Discussion

Standard topic, sentiment and emotion modelling can be usefully applied to online text therapy dialogue, although care is needed choosing and applying a technique suitable for the idiosyncratic language and spelling. The resulting information allows us to predict aspects of symptom severity and patient progress with reasonable degrees of accuracy (similar to those achieved with face-to-face data (DeVault et al., 2013; Howes et al., 2012)), without requiring knowledge of therapist identity. However, some measures of patient progress are predicted better with fine-grained, high-dimensional lexical features, suggesting that insight into style and/or dialogue structure is required, beyond simple topic or sentiment analysis.

	Sentiment				Anger			
Measure	mean	s.d.	min	max	mean	s.d.	min	max
Topic 0	-0.083	0.189	**-0.234**	**0.206**	**0.329**	**0.343**	-0.144	**0.267**
Topic 1				0.087		0.083		
Topic 2	**0.245**	-0.180	**0.202**	-0.135	-0.175	-0.109	0.076	-0.176
Topic 3	0.113	**-0.213**	0.159	-0.135		-0.123	0.110	0.095
Topic 4	**-0.350**	**0.324**	**-0.201**	0.099		0.074		
Topic 5	-0.079				0.119			
Topic 6				0.068				
Topic 7	-0.083			-0.167		-0.109	0.110	
Topic 8		0.078		0.123			-0.104	
Topic 9		-0.072			-0.071		-0.075	
Topic 10	0.100	-0.167	0.133	-0.073				
Topic 11		0.086			0.161	0.132		0.121
Topic 12	**-0.338**	0.182	-0.156		**0.233**	0.092	-0.087	0.146
Topic 13		-0.111		-0.112		**-0.243**	0.077	-0.089
Topic 14	0.112	0.156	-0.183	0.186	-0.087	0.225	-0.116	0.204
Topic 15	0.140	-0.179	0.072	-0.064	-0.161	-0.156		-0.070
Topic 16					-0.090	-0.089	0.073	-0.115
Topic 17	**0.385**	-0.156	**0.267**	-0.116	**-0.408**	-0.139	0.078	**-0.288**
Topic 18						-0.071		
Topic 19	0.177				**0.209**			

Table 6: Significant correlations between topic and sentiment features

	Baseline	Agent		High-level (H/L)			
Measure	Proportion	OneR	(Worse)	inc Agent J48		exc Agent J48	
PHQ Now	*40.5%*	0.584	(0.360)	**0.738**	(0.637)	0.640	(0.561)
PHQ Start-now	*38.1%*	0.639	(0.446)	**0.707**	(0.611)	0.545	(0.299)

Table 7: Weighted average f-scores of outcomes using different high-level feature groups (figures in brackets are the f-scores for the class of interest; i.e. *PHQ Now* – patients with higher/more symptomatic PHQ; *PHQ Start-now* – patients showing no change or a worsening in PHQ)

		Sentiment		Topic		Sentiment + Topic	
		inc H/L	exc H/L	inc H/L	exc H/L	inc H/L	exc H/L
J48	PHQ Now	0.625 (0.528)	0.610 (0.437)	0.642 (0.548)	0.650 (0.512)	0.641 (0.544)	0.638 (0.522)
	PHQ Start-now	0.630 (0.412)	0.508 (0.094)	0.628 (0.479)	0.477 (0.024)	0.619 (0.474)	0.526 (0.147)
Logistic Regr.	PHQ Now	0.626 (0.497)	0.610 (0.432)	**0.689** (0.585)	0.658 (0.537)	**0.707** (0.613)	**0.674** (0.559)
	PHQ Start-now	0.532 (0.218)	0.605 (0.025)	0.593 (0.369)	0.569 (0.283)	0.591 (0.377)	0.557 (0.295)

Table 8: Weighted average f-scores using sentiment/topic features (figures in brackets are the f-scores for the class of interest)

	Words		N-grams	
Measure	inc H/L	exc H/L	inc H/L	exc H/L
PHQ NOW	0.655 (0.575)	0.676 (0.614)	**0.696** (0.615)	**0.686** (0.616)
PHQ Start-now	0.616 (0.528)	0.623 (0.506)	0.626 (0.459)	**0.645** (0.532)

Table 9: Weighted average f-scores using raw lexical features (words/ngrams) using LibLINEAR (figures in brackets are the f-scores for the class of interest)

References

D. Angus, B. Watson, A. Smith, C. Gallois, and J. Wiles. 2012. Visualising conversation structure across time: Insights into effective doctor-patient consultations. *PLoS ONE*, 7(6):1–12.

A. Beattie, A. Shaw, S. Kaur, and D. Kessler. 2009. Primary-care patients' expectations and experiences of online cognitive behavioural therapy for depression: a qualitative study. *Health Expectations*, 12(1):45–59.

D. Blei, A. Ng, and M. Jordan. 2003. Latent Dirichlet allocation. *Journal of Machine Learning Research*, 3:993–1022.

C.-C. Chang and C.-J. Lin, 2001. *LIBSVM: a library for Support Vector Machines*. Software available at `http://www.csie.ntu.edu.tw/~cjlin/libsvm`.

Z.-J. Chuang and C.-H. Wu. 2004. Multi-modal emotion recognition from speech and text. *Computational Linguistics and Chinese Language Processing*, 9(2):45–62, August.

J. Cretchley, C. Gallois, H. Chenery, and A. Smith. 2010. Conversations between carers and people with schizophrenia: a qualitative analysis using Leximancer. *Qualitative Health Research*, 20(12):1611–1628.

M. De Choudhury, M. Gamon, and S. Counts. 2012. Happy, nervous or surprised? Classification of human affective states in social media. In *Proceedings of the Sixth International Conference on Weblogs and Social Media (ICWSM)*.

D. DeVault, K. Georgila, R. Artstein, F. Morbini, D. Traum, S. Scherer, A. S. Rizzo, and L.-P. Morency. 2013. Verbal indicators of psychological distress in interactive dialogue with a virtual human. In *Proceedings of the SIGDIAL 2013 Conference*, pages 193–202.

J. Eisenstein and R. Barzilay. 2008. Bayesian unsupervised topic segmentation. In *Proceedings of the 2008 Conference on Empirical Methods in Natural Language Processing*, pages 334–343.

M. Hall, E. Frank, G. Holmes, B. Pfahringer, P. Reutemann, and I. H. Witten. 2009. The WEKA data mining software: An update. *SIGDKDD Explorations*, 11(1):10–18.

T. Hanley and D. Reynolds. 2009. Counselling psychology and the internet: A review of the quantitative research into online outcomes and alliances within text-based therapy. *Counselling Psychology Review*, 24(2):4–13.

R. Hirschfeld, R. L. Spitzer, and M. R.G. 1974. Computer diagnosis in psychiatry: A Bayes approach. *Journal of Nervous and Mental Disease*, 158:399–407.

C. Howes, M. Purver, R. McCabe, P. G. T. Healey, and M. Lavelle. 2012. Helping the medicine go down: Repair and adherence in patient-clinician dialogues. In *Proceedings of the 16th Workshop on the Semantics and Pragmatics of Dialogue (SemDial 2012)*.

C. Howes, M. Purver, and R. McCabe. 2013. Using conversation topics for predicting therapy outcomes in schizophrenia. *Biomedical Informatics Insights*, 6(Suppl. 1):39–50, July.

P. John, M. Lavelle, S. Mehnaz, and R. McCabe. under review. What do psychiatrists and patients with schizophrenia talk about and does it matter? *Psychiatric Bulletin*.

D. Kessler, G. Lewis, S. Kaur, N. Wiles, M. King, S. Weich, D. Sharp, R. Araya, S. Hollinghurst, and T. Peters. 2009. Therapist-delivered internet psychotherapy for depression: a randomised controlled trial in primary care. *Lancet*, 374:628–634.

K. Kroenke and R. L. Spitzer. 2002. The PHQ-9: a new depression diagnostic and severity measure. *Psychiatr Ann*, 32(9):1–7.

R. e. a. Layard. 2012. How mental illness loses out in the NHS. Technical report, Mental Health Policy Group, Centre for Economic Performance, London School of Economics, June.

M. Liakata, J.-H. Kim, S. Saha, J. Hastings, and D. Rebholz-Schuhmann. 2012. Three hybrid classifiers for the detection of emotions in suicide notes. *Biomedical Informatics Insights*, 5(1):175–184.

A. Martin, W. Rief, A. Klaiberg, and E. Braehler. 2006. Validity of the brief patient health questionnaire mood scale (PHQ-9) in the general population. *General hospital psychiatry*, 28(1):71–77.

R. McCabe, P. G. T. Healey, S. Priebe, M. Lavelle, D. Dodwell, R. Laugharne, A. Snell, and S. Bremner. 2013a. Shared understanding in psychiatrist-patient communication: Association with treatment adherence in schizophrenia. *Patient Education and Counselling*.

R. McCabe, H. Khanom, P. Bailey, and S. Priebe. 2013b. Shared decision-making in ongoing outpatient psychiatric treatment. *Patient education and counseling*, 91(3):326–328.

A. K. McCallum. 2002. MALLET: A machine learning for language toolkit. http://mallet.cs.umass.edu.

B. O'Connor, R. Balasubramanyan, B. R. Routledge, and N. A. Smith. 2010. From tweets to polls: Linking text sentiment to public opinion time series. In *Proceedings of the 4th AAAI International Conference on Weblogs and Social Media*, pages 122–129.

L. Ong, J. De Haes, A. Hoos, and F. Lammes. 1995. Doctor-patient communication: a review of the literature. *Social science & medicine*, 40(7):903–918.

J. Overall and L. Hollister. 1964. Computer procedures for psychiatric classification. *Journal of the American Medical Association*, 187:583–585.

B. Pang and L. Lee. 2008. Opinion mining and sentiment analysis. *Foundations and Trends in Information Retrieval*, 2(1–2):1–135.

M. Paul and M. Drezde. 2011. You are what you tweet: Analyzing twitter for public health. In *Proceedings of the 5th International AAAI Conference on Weblogs and Social Media (ICWSM)*.

M. Paul, B. Wallace, and M. Dredze. 2013. What affects patient (dis)satisfaction? Analyzing online doctor ratings with a joint topic-sentiment model. In *Proceedings of the AAAI Workshop on Expanding the Boundaries of Health Informatics Using AI (HIAI)*.

J. W. Pennebaker, R. J. Booth, and M. E. Francis. 2007. Linguistic inquiry and word count (LIWC): A computerized text analysis program. Austin, TX: LIWC.net.

R. H. Perlis. 2013. A clinical risk stratification tool for predicting treatment resistance in major depressive disorder. *Biological Psychiatry*, 74(1):7–14. Sources of Treatment Resistance in Depression: Inflammation and Functional Connectivity.

M. Purver and S. Battersby. 2012. Experimenting with distant supervision for emotion classification. In *Proceedings of the 13th Conference of the European Chapter of the Association for Computational Linguistics (EACL)*, pages 482–491.

M. Purver, K. Körding, T. Griffiths, and J. Tenenbaum. 2006. Unsupervised topic modelling for multi-party spoken discourse. In *Proceedings of the 21st International Conference on Computational Linguistics and 44th Annual Meeting of the Association for Computational Linguistics (COLING-ACL)*, pages 17–24.

D. Quercia, J. Ellis, L. Capra, and J. Crowcroft. 2011. In the Mood for Being Influential on Twitter. In *Proceedings of the* 3rd *IEEE Conference on Social Computing (SocialCom)*.

D. Quercia, J. Crowcroft, J. Ellis, and L. Capra. 2012. Tracking "gross community happiness" from tweets. In *Proceedings of the ACM Conference on Computer Supported Cooperative Work (CSCW)*, pages 965–968.

G. Salton and M. McGill. 1986. *Introduction to modern information retrieval*. McGraw-Hill, Inc.

Y.-S. Seol, D.-J. Kim, and H.-W. Kim. 2008. Emotion recognition from text using knowledge based ANN. In *Proceedings of ITC-CSCC*.

R. Socher, A. Perelygin, J. Wu, J. Chuang, C. D. Manning, A. Ng, and C. Potts. 2013. Recursive deep models for semantic compositionality over a sentiment treebank. In *Proceedings of the 2013 Conference on Empirical Methods in Natural Language Processing*, pages 1631–1642.

R. L. Spitzer, K. Kroenke, J. B. Williams, and B. Löwe. 2006. A brief measure for assessing generalized anxiety disorder: the GAD-7. *Archives of internal medicine*, 166(10):1092–1097.

M. Steyvers and T. Griffiths. 2007. Probabilistic topic models. *Handbook of latent semantic analysis*, 427(7):424–440.

B. C. Wallace, T. A. Trikalinos, M. B. Laws, I. B. Wilson, and E. Charniak. 2013. A generative joint, additive, sequential model of topics and speech acts in patient-doctor communication. In *Proceedings of the 2013 Conference on Empirical Methods in Natural Language Processing*, pages 1765–1775.

H. M. Wallach, D. M. Mimno, and A. McCallum. 2009. Rethinking LDA: Why priors matter. In *NIPS*, volume 22, pages 1973–1981.

Z. Yu, S. Scherer, D. Devault, J. Gratch, G. Stratou, L.-P. Morency, and J. Cassell. 2013. Multimodal prediction of psychological disorder: Learning nonverbal commonality in adjacency pairs. In *Proceedings of the SemDial 2013 Workshop*, pages 193–202.

Comparison of different feature sets for identification of variants in progressive aphasia

Kathleen C. Fraser[1], Graeme Hirst[1], Naida L. Graham[2], Jed A. Meltzer[3], Sandra E. Black[4], and Elizabeth Rochon[2]
[1]Dept. of Computer Science, University of Toronto
[2]Dept. of Speech-Language Pathology, University of Toronto, & Toronto Rehabilitation Institute
[3]Rotman Research Institute, Baycrest Centre, Toronto
[4]LC Campbell Cognitive Neurology Research Unit, Sunnybrook Health Sciences Centre, Toronto
{kfraser,gh}@cs.toronto.edu, {naida.graham,elizabeth.rochon}@utoronto.ca
jmeltzer@research.baycrest.org, sandra.black@sunnybrook.ca

Abstract

We use computational techniques to extract a large number of different features from the narrative speech of individuals with primary progressive aphasia (PPA). We examine several different types of features, including part-of-speech, complexity, context-free grammar, fluency, psycholinguistic, vocabulary richness, and acoustic, and discuss the circumstances under which they can be extracted. We consider the task of training a machine learning classifier to determine whether a participant is a control, or has the fluent or nonfluent variant of PPA. We first evaluate the individual feature sets on their classification accuracy, then perform an ablation study to determine the optimal combination of feature sets. Finally, we rank the features in four practical scenarios: given audio data only, given unsegmented transcripts only, given segmented transcripts only, and given both audio and segmented transcripts. We find that psycholinguistic features are highly discriminative in most cases, and that acoustic, context-free grammar, and part-of-speech features can also be important in some circumstances.

1 Introduction

In some types of dementia, such as primary progressive aphasia, language deficit is a core symptom, and the analysis of narrative or conversational speech is important for assessing the extent of an individual's language impairment. Analysis of connected speech has been limited in the past because it is time-consuming and requires expert annotation. However, studies have shown that it is possible for machine learning classifiers to achieve high accuracy on some diagnostic tasks when trained on features which were automatically extracted from speech transcripts.

In this paper, we summarize previous research on the automatic analysis of speech samples from individuals with dementia, focusing in particular on primary progressive aphasia. We discuss in detail different types of features and compare their effectiveness in the classification task. We suggest some benefits and drawbacks of these different features. We also examine the interactions between different feature sets, and discuss the relative importance of individual features across feature sets. Because we examine a large number of features on a relatively small data set, we emphasize that this work is exploratory in nature; nonetheless, our results are consistent with, and extend, previous work in the field.

2 Background

In recent years, there has been growing interest in using computer techniques to automatically detect dementia from speech and language features derived from a sample of narrative speech. Some researchers have explored ways to use methods such as part-of-speech tagging, statistical parsing, and speech signal analysis to detect disorders such as dementia of the Alzheimer's type (DAT) (Bucks et al., 2000; Singh et al., 2001; Thomas et al., 2005; Jarrold et al., 2010) and mild cognitive impairment (MCI) (Roark et al., 2011).

Here, we focus on a type of dementia called primary progressive aphasia (PPA). PPA is a subtype of frontotemporal dementia (FTD) which is characterized by progressive language impairment without other notable cognitive impairment. There are three subtypes of PPA: semantic dementia (SD), progressive nonfluent aphasia (PNFA), and logopenic progressive aphasia (LPA). SD, sometimes called "fluent" progressive aphasia, is typically marked by fluent but empty speech, anomia,

Workshop on Computational Linguistics and Clinical Psychology: From Linguistic Signal to Clinical Reality, pages 17–26,
Baltimore, Maryland USA, June 27, 2014.

deficits in comprehension, and spared grammar and syntax (Gorno-Tempini et al., 2011). In contrast, PNFA is characterized by halting and sometimes agrammatic speech, reduced syntactic complexity, word-finding difficulties, and relatively spared single-word comprehension (Gorno-Tempini et al., 2011). The third subtype, LPA, is characterized by slow speech and frequent word finding difficulties; this subtype is not included in the current analysis.

Although clear diagnostic criteria for PPA have been established (Gorno-Tempini et al., 2011), there is no one test which can provide a diagnosis. Classification of PPA into subtypes requires evaluation of spoken output, as well as neuropsychological assessment and brain imaging. Qualitative evaluation of speech often can be done accurately by clinicians or researchers, but the ability to do this evaluation can require years of training and experience. Some researchers have performed detailed quantitative characterization of speech in PPA, but the precise characteristics of speech are not yet fully understood and this process is too time-consuming for most clinicians.

Peintner et al. (2008) conducted one of the earliest automatic analyses of speech from individuals with FTD, including SD and PNFA as well as a behavioural variant. They considered psycholinguistic features as well as phoneme duration features extracted from the audio samples. Although they were fairly successful in classifying participants according to their subtype, they did not report many details regarding the specific features which were useful or how those features might reflect the underlying impairment of the speakers.

Pakhomov et al. (2010a) examined FTD speech from an information-theoretic approach. They constructed a language model of healthy control speech, and then calculated the perplexity and out-of-vocabulary rate for each of the patient groups relative to that model. In another study, Pakhomov et al. (2010b) extracted speech and language features from samples of FTD speech. In a principal components analysis, they discovered four components which accounted for most of the variance in their data: speech length, hesitancy, empty content, and grammaticality. However, they did not perform any classification experiments.

Fraser et al. (2013a) attempted to classify participants as either SD patients, PNFA patients, or healthy controls using a large number of language

	SD ($N = 11$)	PNFA ($N = 13$)	Control ($N = 16$)
Male/Female	8/3	7/6	9/7
Age (yrs)	65.9 (7.1)	64.5 (10.4)	67.8 (8.2)
Education (yrs)	17.5 (5.8)	14.0 (3.5)	16.8 (4.3)

Table 1: Demographic information. Numbers are given in the form: mean (standard deviation).

features extracted from manually-transcribed transcripts. They distinguished between SD and control participants with very high accuracy, and were also successful at distinguishing between PNFA and control participants. However, their method did not perform as well on the task of classifying SD vs. PNFA speakers. In subsequent work (Fraser et al., 2013b), they expanded their feature set to include acoustic features extracted directly from the audio file.

3 Methods

3.1 Data

Twenty-four patients with PPA were recruited through three Toronto memory clinics, and 16 age- and education-matched healthy controls were recruited through a volunteer pool. All participants were native speakers of English, or had completed some of their education in English. Exclusion criteria included a known history of drug or alcohol abuse and a history of neurological or major psychiatric illness. Each patient was diagnosed by a behavioural neurologist and all met current criteria for PPA (Gorno-Tempini et al., 2011). Table 1 shows demographic information for each group.

To elicit a sample of narrative speech, participants were asked to tell the well-known story of *Cinderella*. They were given a wordless picture book to remind them of the story; then the book was removed and they were asked to tell the story in their own words. This procedure, described in full by Saffran et al. (1989), is commonly used in studies of connected speech in aphasia.

The narrative samples were transcribed by trained research assistants. The transcriptions include filled pauses, repetitions, and false starts, and were annotated with the total speech time. Sentence boundaries were marked according to semantic, syntactic, and prosodic cues.

3.2 Classification framework

Given the audio files and transcripts, we can then calculate our features (described in detail below) and use them to train a support vector machine (SVM) classifier. We use a leave-one-out cross-validation framework and report the average accuracy (i.e. proportion of correctly classified instances) across folds. We optimize the complexity parameter and the kernel type in a nested cross-validation loop over the training set. For comparison, we also tested a naïve Bayes classifier; however we found that the results were consistently poorer and we do not report them here.

3.3 Features

In the following sections we will describe each of the feature sets that we use and explain how the features are computed, and we will discuss some of the potential advantages and disadvantages associated with each set. In particular, we discuss what types of data are necessary for the extraction of these features. The data types are: unsegmented transcripts, segmented transcripts, and audio.

3.3.1 Part-of-speech features

Different categories of words may be selectively impaired in different types of dementia. In PPA, individuals with SD tend to be more impaired with respect to nouns than verbs, and may replace nouns with pronouns or circumlocutory phrases. In contrast, individuals with PNFA may have more difficulty with verbs and may even demonstrate agrammatism, which can result in the omission of grammatical morphemes and function words. Thus, it is often useful to compare the relative frequencies with which words representing the different parts-of-speech (POS) are produced in a sample, as in Table 2. Similar features have been reported in computational studies of MCI (Roark et al., 2011), FTD (Pakhomov et al., 2010b), and DAT (Bucks et al., 2000). Numerous POS taggers exist, although we use the Stanford tagger here (Toutanova et al., 2003).

3.3.2 Complexity features

Changes in linguistic complexity may accompany the onset of dementia, although some studies have found a decrease in complexity (e.g. Kemper et al. (2001)) while others have found an increase (e.g. Le et al. (2011)).

The features in Table 3 vary in their ease of computation. Mean word length can be calculated from an unsegmented transcript, while mean sentence length requires only sentence boundary segmentation. Other measures, such as Yngve depth (Yngve, 1960), require full parses of the sentences (we use the Stanford parser (Klein and Manning, 2003) and Lu's Syntactic Complexity Analyzer (Lu, 2010)).

Nouns	# nouns / # words
Verbs	# verbs / # words
Noun-verb ratio	# nouns / # verbs
Noun ratio	# nouns / (# nouns + # verbs)
Inflected verbs	# inflected verbs / # verbs
Determiners	# determiners / # words
Demonstratives	# demonstratives / # words
Prepositions	# prepositions / # words
Adjectives	# adjectives / # words
Adverbs	# adverbs / # words
Pronoun ratio	# pronouns / (# nouns + # pronouns)
Function words	# function words / # words
Interjections	# interjections / # words

Table 2: Part-of-speech features.

Max depth	maximum Yngve depth of each parse tree, averaged over all sentences
Mean depth	mean Yngve depth of each node in the parse tree, averaged over all sentences
Total depth	total sum of the Yngve depths of each node in the parse tree, averaged over all sentences
Tree height	height of each parse tree, averaged over all sentences
MLS	mean length of sentence
MLC	mean length of clause
MLT	mean length of T-unit
Subordinate conjunctions	number of subordinate conjunctions
Coordinate conjunctions	number of coordinate conjunctions
Subordinate:coordinate ratio	ratio of number of subordinate conjunctions to number of coordinate conjunctions
Mean word length	mean length, in letters, of each word in the sample

Table 3: Complexity features.

3.3.3 CFG features

Although many of the complexity features above are derived from parse trees, in this section we present a set of features that take into account the context-free grammar (CFG) labels on each of the nodes. CFG features have been previously used to assess the grammaticality of sentences in an artificial error corpus (Wong and Dras, 2010) and to distinguish human from machine translations (Chae and Nenkova, 2009). However, this is the first time such features have been applied to speech from participants with dementia.

In Table 4 we list a few examples of our 134 CFG features, as well as the three phrase-level features (calculated for noun phrases, verb phrases, and prepositional phrases).

NP → NNS	Noun phrases consisting of only a plural noun
VP → VBN PP	Verb phrases consisting of a past-participle verb and a prepositional phrase
ROOT → INTJ	Trees consisting of only an interjection
Phrase type proportion	Length of each phrase type (noun phrase, verb phrase, or prepositional phrase), divided by total narrative length
Average phrase type length	Total number of words in a phrase type, divided by the number of phrases of that type
Phrase type rate	Number of phrases of a given type, divided by total narrative length

Table 4: CFG features.

Um	Frequency of filled pause *um*
Uh	Frequency of filled pause *uh*
NID	Frequency of words Not In Dictionary (e.g. paraphasias, neologisms)
Verbal rate	Number of words per minute
Total words	Total number of words produced

Table 5: Fluency features.

3.3.4 Fluency features

Park et al. (2011) found that listeners' judgements of fluency were affected by a number of different variables, and the three most discriminative features were "speech rate, speech productivity, and audible struggle." For our list of fluency features (Table 5), we include only those features which could be extracted from the transcripts alone (assuming the total speech time is given). We count pauses filled by *um* and *uh* separately, as research has suggested that they may indicate different cognitive processes (Clark and Fox Tree, 2002).

The number of words in a sample could be easily generated using the word count feature in most text-editing software (although we first exclude filled pauses and NID tokens), and the verbal rate can subsequently be calculated directly. The other three features are easily calculated using string matching and an electronic dictionary.

3.3.5 Psycholinguistic features

Some types of dementia are characterized by impairments in semantic access. Such impairments may be sensitive to psycholinguistic features such as lexical frequency, familiarity, imageability, and age of acquisition (Table 6). We use the SUBTL frequency norms (Brysbaert and New, 2009) and the combined Bristol and Gilhooly-Logie norms (Stadthagen-Gonzalez and Davis, 2006; Gilhooly and Logie, 1980) for familiarity, imageability, and age of acquisition (see Table 6). We compute the average of each of these measures for all content words, as well as for nouns and verbs separately.

Frequency	Frequency with which a word occurs in some corpus of natural language
Familiarity	Subjective rating of how familiar a word seems
Imageability	Subjective rating of how easily a word generates an image in the mind
Age of acquisition	Subjective rating of how old a person is when they first learn that word
Light verbs	Number of occurrences of *be, have, come, go, give, take, make, do, get, move,* and *put*, normalized by total number of verbs

Table 6: Psycholinguistic features.

Another measure that fits into this category is the frequency of occurrence of light verbs, which an impaired speaker may use to replace a more specific verb. We use the same list of light verbs as Breedin et al. (1998), given in Table 6.

One challenge associated with psycholinguistic features is finding norms which provide adequate coverage for the given data. Fraser et al. (2013a) reported that the SUBTL frequency norms had a coverage of above 90% on their data, but the Bristol-Gilhooly-Logie norms had a coverage of only around 30%.

3.3.6 Vocabulary richness features

Individuals experiencing semantic difficulty may use a limited range of vocabulary. We can measure the vocabulary richness or lexical diversity of a narrative sample using a number of different metrics (see Table 7). Type-token ratio has been a popular choice, perhaps due to its simplicity; however it is sensitive to the length of the sample. Bucks et al. (2000) were the first to apply Honoré's statistic and Brunét's index to the study of dementia, and found significant differences between individuals with DAT and healthy controls. Covington and McFall (2010) proposed a new measure called the moving-average type-token ratio (MATTR), which is independent of text length. This feature was later applied to aphasic speech in a study by Fergadiotis and Wright (2011), and was found to be one of the most unbiased indicators of lexical diversity in impaired speakers.

The measures given in Table 7 are easily computed from their respective formulae. In this work, we lemmatize each word using NLTK (Bird et al., 2009) before calculating the features. For MATTR, we consider $w = 10, 20, 30, 40, 50$.

Honoré's statistic	$N^{V^{-0.165}}$ / where V is the number of word types and N is the number of word tokens.
Brunét's index	$100 \log N/(1-V_1/V)$ where V_1 is the number of words used only once, V is the total number of word types, and N is the number of word tokens.
Type-token ratio (TTR)	V/N where V is the number of word types and N is the number of word tokens.
Moving-average type-token ratio (MATTR$_w$)	TTR calculated over a moving window of size w, and averaged over all windows.

Table 7: Vocabulary richness features.

3.3.7 Acoustic features

What we call *acoustic* features are extracted directly from the audio file. We consider the features given in Table 8. Acoustic features have been shown to be useful when automatically detecting conditions such as Parkinson's disease, in which changes in speech are common (Little et al., 2009; Tsanas et al., 2012). Acoustic features have also been examined in studies of DAT (Meilán et al., 2014), FTD (Pakhomov et al., 2010b), and PPA (Fraser et al., 2013b, whose software we use here).

An obvious benefit to acoustic features is that they do not require a transcription, and can be calculated immediately given an audio sample. The corresponding drawback is that they tell us nothing about the linguistic content of the narrative.

Total duration of speech	Total length of all non-silent segments
Phonation rate	Total duration of speech / total duration of the sample (including pauses)
Mean pause duration	Mean length of pauses > 0.15 ms
Short pause count	# Pauses > 0.15 ms and < 0.4 ms
Long pause count	# Pauses > 0.4 ms
Pause:word ratio	Ratio of silent segments longer than 150 ms to non-silent segments
$F_{0:3}$ mean	Mean of the fundamental frequency and the first three formant frequencies
$F_{0:3}$ variance	Variance of the fundamental frequency and the first three formant frequencies
Mean instantaneous power	Measure related to the loudness of the signal
Mean 1st ACF	Mean first autocorrelation function
Max 1st ACF	Maximum first autocorrelation function
Skewness	Measure of lack of symmetry, associated with tense or creaky voice
Kurtosis	Measure of the peakedness of the signal
ZCR	Zero-crossing rate, can be used to distinguish between voiced and unvoiced regions
MRPDE	Mean recurrence period density entropy, a measure of periodicity
Jitter	Measure of the short-term variation in the pitch (frequency) of a voice
Shimmer	Measure of the short-term variation in the loudness (amplitude) of a voice

Table 8: Acoustic features.

4 Experiments

We report the results of three experiments exploring the discriminative power of the different features. We first compare the classification accuracies using each individual feature set. We then perform an ablation study to determine which combination of feature sets leads to the highest classification accuracy. We also look at individual features across sets and discuss which ones are the most discriminative, particularly in situations where data might be limited.

4.1 Individual comparison of accuracy by set

The accuracies which result from using each feature set individually are given in Table 9. The highest accuracy across the three tasks is achieved in distinguishing SD participants from controls. An accuracy of .963 can be achieved using all the features together, or using the psycholinguistic or POS features alone. This is consistent with the semantic impairments that are observed in SD. The measures of vocabulary richness do not distinguish between the SD and control groups, suggesting it is the words themselves, and not the number of different words being used, that is important.

In the case of PNFA participants vs. controls, we find that the highest accuracy is achieved using all the features, and the second highest by using only acoustic features. This is not surprising, considering that the acoustic features include measures of pausing and phonation rate, which can detect the characteristic halting speech of PNFA. The third best accuracy is achieved using the fluency features, which also fits with this explanation. However, we might have expected that the complexity and CFG features would be more sensitive to the grammatical impairments of PNFA.

Finally, the best accuracy for SD vs. PNFA is lower than in the previous two cases, and is achieved using only CFG features. This suggests that there are some grammatical constructions which occur with different frequencies in the two groups. These differences do not appear to be captured by the complexity features, which could explain why Fraser et al. (2013a) did not find syntactic differences between the SD and PNFA groups. Interestingly, the results using CFG fea-

Feature set	SD vs. controls	PNFA vs. controls	SD vs. PNFA
All	**.963**	**.931**	.708
Acoustic	.778	.862	.167
Psycholinguistic	**.963**	.724	.708
POS	**.963**	.690	.375
Complexity	.852	.621	.667
Fluency	.667	.828	.500
Vocab. richness	.481	.586	.583
CFG	.630	.690	**.792**

Table 9: Classification accuracies for each feature set individually using a SVM classifier. Bold indicates the highest accuracy for each task.

tures are actually higher than the results using all features. This demonstrates that classifier performance can be adversely affected by the presence of irrelevant features, especially in small data sets.

4.2 Combining feature sets

In the previous section we examined the feature sets individually; however, one type of feature may complement the information contained in another feature set, or it may contain redundant information. To examine the interactions between the feature sets, we perform an ablation study. Starting with all the features, we remove each feature set one at a time and measure the accuracy of the classifier. The feature set whose removal causes the smallest decrease in accuracy is then removed permanently from the experiment, the reasoning being that the most important feature sets will cause the greatest decrease in accuracy when removed. In some cases, we observe that the classification accuracy actually *increases* when a set is removed, which suggests that those features are not relevant to the classification (at least in combination with the other sets). In the case of a tie, we remove the feature set whose individual classification accuracy on that task is lowest. The procedure is then repeated on the remaining feature sets, continuing until only one set remains.

The results for SD vs. controls are given in Table 10a. The best result, 1.00, is achieved by combining the psycholinguistic and POS features. This is unsurprising, since each of those feature sets perform well individually. Curiously, the same result can also be achieved by also including the complexity, vocabulary richness, and CFG features, but not in the intermediate stages between those two optimal sets. We attribute this to the interactions between features and the small data set.

For PNFA vs. controls, shown in Table 10b, the

(a) SD vs. controls.

Removed	Remaining Features	Accuracy
	A+P+POS+C+F+VR+CFG	.963
F	A+P+POS+C+VR+CFG	.963
A	P+POS+C+VR+CFG	1.00
VR	P+POS+C+CFG	.926
CFG	P+POS+C	.926
C	**P+POS**	**1.00**
POS	P	.963

(b) PNFA vs. controls.

Removed	Remaining Features	Accuracy
	A+P+POS+C+F+VR+CFG	.931
VR	A+P+POS+C+F+CFG	.931
C	A+P+POS+F+CFG	.931
POS	A+P+F+CFG	.931
CFG	A+P+F	.966
F	**A+P**	**.966**
P	A	.862

(c) SD vs. PNFA.

Removed	Remaining Features	Accuracy
	A+P+POS+C+F+VR+CFG	.708
POS	A+P+C+F+VR+CFG	.750
VR	A+P+C+F+CFG	.833
F	A+P+C+CFG	.833
A	P+C+CFG	.792
C	**P+CFG**	**.917**
P	CFG	.792

Table 10: A=acoustic, P=psycholinguistic, POS=part-of-speech, C=complexity, F=fluency, VR=vocabulary richness, CFG=CFG production rule features. Bold indicates the highest accuracy with the fewest feature sets.

best result of .966 is achieved using a combination of acoustic and psycholinguistic features. In this case the removal of the fluency features, which gave the second highest individual accuracy, does not make a difference to the accuracy. This suggests that the fluency features contain similar information to one of the remaining sets, presumably the acoustic set.

In the case of SD vs. PNFA, we again see that the best accuracy can be achieved by combining two feature sets, as shown in Table 10c. Using psycholinguistic and CFG features, we can achieve an accuracy of .917, a substantial improvement over the best accuracy for this task in Table 9. In fact, in all three cases we see that using a carefully selected combination of feature sets can result in better accuracy than using all the feature sets together or using any one set individually.

4.3 Best features for incomplete data

Up to this point, we have examined complete feature sets. We now briefly explore which individual features are the most discriminative across feature sets. We approach this as a practical consideration: given the data that a researcher has, and limited resources, what are the best features to measure? We consider the following four scenarios:

1. Given audio files only. This scenario often arises because it is relatively easy to record speech, but difficult to have it transcribed. Only acoustic features can be extracted.
2. Given basic transcriptions only (no audio). We assume there is no sentence segmentation and the time is not marked (e.g. as in the output of automatic speech recognition). Thus, we can measure psycholinguistic, POS, and vocabulary measures. We can also measure the fluency features except for verbal rate, as well as mean word length and subordinate/coordinate conjunctions from the complexity set. Without sentence boundaries, we cannot parse the transcripts.
3. Given fully segmented transcripts (no audio). We can measure all features except for acoustic features.
4. Given audio and fully segmented transcripts. We can measure all features.

For each scenario, we rank the available features by their χ^2 value and choose the top 10 only as input to the SVM classifier (see Manning et al. (2008) for a complete explanation of χ^2 feature selection). We only include features if $\chi^2 > 0$, so in cases where there are very few relevant features, fewer than 10 features may be selected. Because we perform cross-validation, the selected features may vary across different folds. In the tables that follow, we present the features ranked by the number of folds in which they appear (i.e. a feature with the value 1.00 was selected in every fold). Due to space constraints, only the top 10 ranked features are shown.

The results for Scenario 1 are given in Table 11a. For the SD vs. controls and PNFA vs. controls, the most highly ranked features tend to be related to fluency and rate of speech, as well as voice quality (skewness and MRPDE). However, when distinguishing between the two patient groups, the acoustic features are essentially useless. In most cases, we see that *none* of the acoustic features had a non-zero χ^2 value, and thus the classifier could not be properly trained.

For Scenario 2 (Table 11b), the results for SD vs. controls show that within the psycholinguistic and POS feature sets, features relating to familiarity and frequency are very important, as well as nouns and demonstratives. In the PNFA vs. controls case, we see that a number of the vocabulary richness features are selected, which is in contrast to the previous two experiments. However, it appears that only the MATTR feature is important (with varying window lengths), so when we considered only full feature sets, that information was obscured by the other, irrelevant features in that set. The SD vs. PNFA case shows a mix of features from the previous two cases.

For Scenario 3 (Table 11c), we add the complexity and CFG features. These features do not have a large effect in the SD vs. controls case, but a few CFG features are selected in the PNFA vs. controls and SD vs. PNFA cases.

In Scenario 4 (Table 11d), we consider all features. In the SD vs. controls case this increases the accuracy. However, for PNFA vs. controls and SD vs. PNFA, the classification accuracy actually decreases, relative to Scenario 3. When the number of features increases, the potential to overfit to the training data fold also increases, and it seems likely that that is occurring here. Nonetheless, we expect that the features which are selected in every fold are still highly relevant. These features are unchanged between Scenarios 3 and 4 in the SD vs. controls and SD vs. PNFA case, however in the PNFA vs. controls case, the acoustic features are now ranked more highly than some of the vocabulary richness and CFG features from Scenario 3.

5 Discussion

While it may be tempting to calculate as many features as possible and use them all in a classifier, we have shown here that better results can be achieved by choosing a small, relevant subset of features. In particular, psycholinguistic features such as frequency and familiarity were useful in all three classification tasks. Acoustic features were useful in discriminating patients from controls, but not for discriminating between the two PPA subtypes. We also found that MATTR was relevant in some cases, although the other vocabulary richness features were not, and that the CFG features were more useful than traditional measures of syntactic complexity. POS features were useful only in distinguishing between SD and controls.

One of the biggest challenges in this type of work is the small amount of data available.

(a) Scenario 1: audio only.

SD vs. control, Acc: .852		PNFA vs. control, Acc: .793		SD vs. PNFA, Acc: .500	
1.00	skewness	1.00	long pause count	.083	max 1st ACF
1.00	phonation rate	1.00	phonation rate	.042	mean F3
1.00	MRPDE	1.00	short pause count		
1.00	mean duration of pauses	1.00	MRPDE		
.037	long pause count	1.00	mean duration of pauses		
.037	mean 1st ACF	.966	pause:word ratio		
.037	kurtosis	.793	skewness		
		.793	ZCR		
		.345	mean inst. power		
		.035	jitter		

(b) Scenario 2: unsegmented transcripts.

SD vs. control, Acc: .926		PNFA vs. control, Acc: .621		SD vs. PNFA, Acc: .792	
1.00	familiarity	1.00	MATTR 50	1.00	familiarity
1.00	noun frequency	1.00	MATTR 40	1.00	noun frequency
1.00	noun familiarity	1.00	MATTR 30	1.00	noun familiarity
1.00	frequency	1.00	frequency	1.00	MATTR 20
1.00	verb frequency	1.00	MATTR 20	.708	MATTR 10
1.00	nouns	.931	total words	.208	MATTR 30
1.00	demonstratives	.759	light verbs	.042	MATTR 50
.778	pronoun ratio	.690	adjectives	.042	MATTR 40
.667	noun imageability	.241	age of acquisition	.042	light verbs
.630	Honoré's statistic	.241	MATTR 10	.042	verbs

(c) Scenario 3: segmented transcripts.

SD vs. control, Acc: .926		PNFA vs. control, Acc: .897		SD vs. PNFA, Acc: .792	
1.00	word length	1.00	MATTR 50	1.00	WHADVP → WRB
1.00	familiarity	1.00	MATTR 40	1.00	familiarity
1.00	noun frequency	1.00	WHNP → WP	1.00	noun familiarity
1.00	noun familiarity	1.00	frequency	1.00	noun frequency
1.00	frequency	1.00	MATTR 20	1.00	MATTR 20
1.00	demonstratives	1.00	verbal rate	1.00	NP → NNS
.889	nouns	.966	MATTR 30	1.00	SBAR → WHADVP S
.852	verb frequency	.827	S1 → INTJ	.667	MATTR 10
.630	MLS	.483	total words	.500	NP → DT JJ NNS
.630	total Yngve depth	.414	word length	.458	SQ → AUX NP VP

(d) Scenario 4: segmented transcripts + audio.

SD vs. control, Acc: .963		PNFA vs. control, Acc: .793		SD vs. PNFA, Acc: .750	
1.00	word length	1.00	frequency	1.00	WHADVP → WRB
1.00	familiarity	1.00	phonation rate	1.00	familiarity
1.00	noun frequency	1.00	MRPDE	1.00	noun familiarity
1.00	noun familiarity	1.00	verbal rate	1.00	noun frequency
1.00	frequency	1.00	mean duration of pauses	1.00	MATTR 20
1.00	demonstratives	.897	MATTR 50	1.00	NP → NNS
.963	phonation rate	.897	WHNP → WP	1.00	SBAR → WHADVP S
.741	verb frequency	.897	MATTR 20	.625	MATTR 10
.593	nouns	.690	MATTR 40	.500	NP → DT JJ NNS
.333	MLS	.690	MATTR 30	.458	SQ → AUX NP VP

Table 11: Classification accuracies and top 10 features for four different data scenarios.

Psychological studies are typically on the order of only tens to possibly hundreds of participants, while machine learning researchers often tackle problems with thousands to millions of data points. We have chosen techniques appropriate for small data sets, but acknowledging the potential weaknesses of machine learning methods when training data are limited, these findings must be considered preliminary. However, we also believe that this is a promising approach for future applications, including automated screening for language impairment, support for clinical diagnosis, tracking severity of symptoms over time, and evaluating therapeutic interventions.

Acknowledgments

This research was supported by the Natural Sciences and Engineering Research Council of Canada and the Canadian Institutes of Health Research (grant #MOP-8277). Thanks to Frank Rudzicz for the acoustic features software.

References

Steven Bird, Ewan Klein, and Edward Loper. 2009. *Natural language processing with Python*. O'Reilly Media, Inc.

Sarah D. Breedin, Eleanor M. Saffran, and Myrna F. Schwartz. 1998. Semantic factors in verb retrieval: An effect of complexity. *Brain and Language*, 63:1–31.

Marc Brysbaert and Boris New. 2009. Moving beyond Kučera and Francis: A critical evaluation of current word frequency norms and the introduction of a new and improved word frequency measure for American English. *Behavior Research Methods*, 41(4):977–990.

R.S. Bucks, S. Singh, J.M. Cuerden, and G.K. Wilcock. 2000. Analysis of spontaneous, conversational speech in dementia of Alzheimer type: Evaluation of an objective technique for analysing lexical performance. *Aphasiology*, 14(1):71–91.

Jieun Chae and Ani Nenkova. 2009. Predicting the fluency of text with shallow structural features: case studies of machine translation and human-written text. In *Proceedings of the 12th Conference of the European Chapter of the Association for Computational Linguistics*, pages 139–147. Association for Computational Linguistics.

Herbert H. Clark and Jean E. Fox Tree. 2002. Using uh and um in spontaneous speaking. *Cognition*, 84(1):73–111.

Michael A. Covington and Joe D. McFall. 2010. Cutting the Gordian knot: The moving-average type–token ratio (MATTR). *Journal of Quantitative Linguistics*, 17(2):94–100.

Gerasimos Fergadiotis and Heather Harris Wright. 2011. Lexical diversity for adults with and without aphasia across discourse elicitation tasks. *Aphasiology*, 25(11):1414–1430.

Kathleen C. Fraser, Jed A. Meltzer, Naida L. Graham, Carol Leonard, Graeme Hirst, Sandra E. Black, and Elizabeth Rochon. 2013a. Automated classification of primary progressive aphasia subtypes from narrative speech transcripts. *Cortex*.

Kathleen C. Fraser, Frank Rudzicz, and Elizabeth Rochon. 2013b. Using text and acoustic features to diagnose progressive aphasia and its subtypes. In *Proceedings of Interspeech*.

K.J. Gilhooly and R.H. Logie. 1980. Age-of-acquisition, imagery, concreteness, familiarity, and ambiguity measures for 1,944 words. *Behavior Research Methods*, 12:395–427.

M.L. Gorno-Tempini, A.E. Hillis, S. Weintraub, A. Kertesz, M. Mendez, S.F. Cappa, J.M. Ogar, J.D. Rohrer, S. Black, B.F. Boeve, F. Manes, N.F. Dronkers, R. Vandenberghe, K. Rascovsky, K. Patterson, B.L. Miller, D.S. Knopman, J.R. Hodges, M.M. Mesulam, and M. Grossman. 2011. Classification of primary progressive aphasia and its variants. *Neurology*, 76:1006–1014.

William Jarrold, Bart Peintner, Eric Yeh, Ruth Krasnow, Harold Javitz, and Gary Swan. 2010. Language analytics for assessing brain health: Cognitive impairment, depression and pre-symptomatic Alzheimer's disease. In Yiyu Yao, Ron Sun, Tomaso Poggio, Jiming Liu, Ning Zhong, and Jimmy Huang, editors, *Brain Informatics*, volume 6334 of *Lecture Notes in Computer Science*, pages 299–307. Springer Berlin / Heidelberg.

Susan Kemper, Marilyn Thompson, and Janet Marquis. 2001. Longitudinal change in language production: Effects of aging and dementia on grammatical complexity and propositional content. *Psychology and Aging*, 16(4):600–614.

Dan Klein and Christopher D. Manning. 2003. Accurate unlexicalized parsing. In *Proceedings of the 41st Meeting of the Association for Computational Linguistics*, pages 423–430.

Xuan Le, Ian Lancashire, Graeme Hirst, and Regina Jokel. 2011. Longitudinal detection of dementia through lexical and syntactic changes in writing: a case study of three British novelists. *Literary and Linguistic Computing*, 26(4):435–461.

Max A. Little, Patrick E. McSharry, Eric J. Hunter, Jennifer Spielman, and Lorraine O. Ramig. 2009. Suitability of dysphonia measurements for telemonitoring of Parkinson's disease. *Biomedical Engineering, IEEE Transactions on*, 56(4):1015–1022.

Xiaofei Lu. 2010. Automatic analysis of syntactic complexity in second language writing. *International Journal of Corpus Linguistics*, 15(4):474–496.

Christopher D. Manning, Prabhakar Raghavan, and Hinrich Schütze. 2008. *Introduction to Information Retrieval*. Cambridge University Press.

Juan José G. Meilán, Francisco Martínez-Sánchez, Juan Carro, Dolores E. López, Lymarie Millian-Morell, and José M. Arana. 2014. Speech in Alzheimer's disease: Can temporal and acoustic parameters discriminate dementia? *Dementia and Geriatric Cognitive Disorders*, 37(5-6):327–334.

Serguei V.S. Pakhomov, Glen E. Smith, Susan Marino, Angela Birnbaum, Neill Graff-Radford, Richard Caselli, Bradley Boeve, and David D. Knopman. 2010a. A computerized technique to asses language use patterns in patients with frontotemporal dementia. *Journal of Neurolinguistics*, 23:127–144.

S.V. Pakhomov, G.E. Smith, D. Chacon, Y. Feliciano, N. Graff-Radford, R. Caselli, and D. S. Knopman. 2010b. Computerized analysis of speech and language to identify psycholinguistic correlates of frontotemporal lobar degeneration. *Cognitive and Behavioral Neurology*, 23:165–177.

Hyejin Park, Yvonne Rogalski, Amy D. Rodriguez, Zvinka Zlatar, Michelle Benjamin, Stacy Harnish, Jeffrey Bennett, John C. Rosenbek, Bruce Crosson, and Jamie Reilly. 2011. Perceptual cues used by listeners to discriminate fluent from nonfluent narrative discourse. *Aphasiology*, 25(9):998–1015.

Bart Peintner, William Jarrold, Dimitra Vergyri, Colleen Richey, Maria Luisa Gorno Tempini, and Jennifer Ogar. 2008. Learning diagnostic models using speech and language measures. In *Engineering in Medicine and Biology Society, 2008. EMBS 2008. 30th Annual International Conference of the IEEE*, pages 4648–4651.

Brian Roark, Margaret Mitchell, John-Paul Hosom, Kristy Hollingshead, and Jeffery Kaye. 2011. Spoken language derived measures for detecting mild cognitive impairment. *IEEE Transactions on Audio, Speech, and Language Processing*, 19(7):2081–2090.

Eleanor M. Saffran, Rita Sloan Berndt, and Myrna F. Schwartz. 1989. The quantitative analysis of agrammatic production: procedure and data. *Brain and Language*, 37:440–479.

Sameer Singh, Romola S. Bucks, and Joanne M. Cuerden. 2001. Evaluation of an objective technique for analysing temporal variables in DAT spontaneous speech. *Aphasiology*, 15(6):571–583.

Hans Stadthagen-Gonzalez and Colin J. Davis. 2006. The Bristol norms for age of acquisition, imageability, and familiarity. *Behavior Research Methods*, 38(4):598–605.

Calvin Thomas, Vlado Keselj, Nick Cercone, Kenneth Rockwood, and Elissa Asp. 2005. Automatic detection and rating of dementia of Alzheimer type through lexical analysis of spontaneous speech. In *Proceedings of the IEEE International Conference on Mechatronics and Automation*, pages 1569–1574.

Kristina Toutanova, Dan Klein, Christopher Manning, and Yoram Singer. 2003. Feature-rich part-of-speech tagging with a cyclic dependency network. In *Proceedings of the 2003 Conference of the North American Chapter of the Association for Computational Linguistics: Human Language Technologies*, pages 252–259.

Athanasios Tsanas, Max A. Little, Patrick E. McSharry, Jennifer Spielman, and Lorraine O. Ramig. 2012. Novel speech signal processing algorithms for high-accuracy classification of Parkinson's disease. *IEEE Transactions on Biomedical Engineering*, 59(5):1264–1271.

Sze-Meng Jojo Wong and Mark Dras. 2010. Parser features for sentence grammaticality classification. In *Proceedings of the Australasian Language Technology Association Workshop*, pages 67–75.

Victor Yngve. 1960. A model and hypothesis for language structure. *Proceedings of the American Physical Society*, 104:444–466.

Aided Diagnosis of Dementia Type through Computer-Based Analysis of Spontaneous Speech

William Jarrold
Nuance Communications[1]
william.jarrold@gmail.com

Bart Peintner
Soshoma[1]
bpeintner@gmail.com

David Wilkins
Language & Linguistic Consulting
wilkinsdavidp@gmail.com

Dimitra Vergryi and **Colleen Richey**
SRI International
dverg@speech.sri.com,
colleen.richey@sri.com

Maria Luisa Gorno-Tempini and **Jennifer Ogar**
University of California, San Francisco
{marilu|jogar}@memory.ucsf.edu

Abstract

This pilot study evaluates the ability of machined learned algorithms to assist with the differential diagnosis of dementia subtypes based on brief (< 10 min) spontaneous speech samples. We analyzed recordings of a brief spontaneous speech sample from 48 participants from 5 different groups: 4 types of dementia plus healthy controls. Recordings were analyzed using a speech recognition system optimized for speaker-independent spontaneous speech. Lexical and acoustic features were automatically extracted. The resulting feature profiles were used as input to a machine learning system that was trained to identify the diagnosis assigned to each research participant. Between groups lexical and acoustic differences features were detected in accordance with expectations from prior research literature suggesting that classifications were based on features consistent with human-observed symptomatology. Machine learning algorithms were able to identify participants' diagnostic group with accuracy comparable to existing diagnostic methods in use today. Results suggest this clinical speech analytic approach offers promise as an additional, objective and easily obtained source of diagnostic information for clinicians.

1 Introduction

Accurately differentiating certain neurodegenerative disorders such as *Alzheimer's Disease* (AD) and variants of *Fronto-temporal Lobar Degeneration* (FTLD) is extremely difficult (Varma et al., 1999). Differential diagnosis is often left to tertiary care settings (e.g. Research I Universities with medical schools). While the most definitive diagnosis is made post-mortem using brain tissue samples, the treatment and prognostic implications of living patients are often determined in large part on the basis of language assessment.

Although language is clearly not the exclusive diagnostic factor for AD, existing literature suggests it is an important one. Studies show significant differences in the written language abilities of AD patients and healthy older adults (Pestell et al., 2008 and Platel et al., 1993). The speech of patients with AD is partly characterized by word-finding difficulties, smaller vocabularies, and problems with semantic processing (Forbes at el., 2002). These symptoms appear early in the disease's progression, however language assessment of AD patients can fail to identify early symptoms that family members report to be present in their conversations (Crockford and Lesser, 1994).

FTLD has a prevalence similar to AD in patients under the age of 65 years (Mendez at el., 1993). Misdiagnosis of FTLD is common Mendez at el., 1993). Three variants are defined by the widely adopted Neary criteria (Neary at el., 1998); one with altered social conduct, the behavioral variant of *frontotemporal dementia* (bvFTD); the second characterized by a deterioration of conceptual-semantic knowledge, *semantic dementia* (SD); and the third marked by a disorder of expressive language fluency, *progressive non-fluent aphasia* (PNFA).

Clinicians diagnose using a wide array of evidence including patient history, imaging and neuropsychological assessment in which speech and language diagnostics feature prominently. In AD, cognitive disturbance is a required diagnostic feature and language impairment one several sufficient signs of such impairment. In the case

[1] Research conducted while at SRI International

Workshop on Computational Linguistics and Clinical Psychology: From Linguistic Signal to Clinical Reality, pages 27–37,
Baltimore, Maryland USA, June 27, 2014.

of SD and PNFA, changes in speech and language are core diagnostic features, with changes in lexical content features being highly diagnostic of SD, and changes in the acoustic properties of speech being highly diagnostic of PNFA. Even in bvFTD, where changes in social behavior are the defining features, analysis of language-based differences is important, because language is an essential mediator of social behavior. To be sure, the clinician does not diagnose exclusively on language features -- patient history, imaging, memory functioning and more play a role. However, language does feature prominently in the differential diagnosis of AD, FTLD and its three subtypes. For this reason, computerized analysis of speech may offer an important aid to the clinical diagnosis of these syndromes.

Prior work in clinical speech analytics supports the possibility of computer-based diagnosis of dementia related syndromes. Singh (2001) describes a means of quantifying the degree of speech deficits derived from human transcriptions of the speech of patient with AD. Machine Learning has already been applied to distinguish AD from controls using human transcribed spontaneous speech (Thomas at el., 2005). Abel et al. (2009) applied a connectionist net that models patient speech errors (naming and repetition disorders) to the problem of diagnosis. Tur et al. (2010) have shown the ability to automatically score patient speech from a story recall and picture description task that is on par with human performance. Lehr et al. (2012) have developed a system that automatically transcribes and scores patient speech obtained during the story recall portion of the Wechsler Logical Memory test. The evaluation demonstrated it could distinguish mild cognition impairment from typical controls at performance level comparable to human scorers.

Our work builds upon these prior studies along a number of dimensions. First, we distinguish between a wider array of dementia subtypes, i.e. not only AD vs controls, but also the three subtypes of FTLD. Second, we use not just lexical features but also acoustic/prosodic related features. Third, in order to shed light on the opaque "black box" nature of many machine-learned classifiers, we identify relationships between model features and symptoms from the clinical literature. Fourth, our approach can claim to be more ecologically valid because it analyzes spontaneous speech as input rather than recall of a remembered passage. Fifth, we do not require human transcription - a labor-intensive step that hinders broader use in a clinical setting. Sixth we provide a comparison of our system performance against benchmarks obtained from practicing clinicians. Our paper is the first we know of to exhibit all of the above properties.

In sum we used computational techniques to analyze acoustic and lexical features of the speech of patients with AD and FTLD variants, and we investigated whether models derived from these features via machine learning could accurately identify a patient's diagnosis.

2 METHOD

2.1 Participant Recruitment and Diagnosis

We obtained spontaneous speech data from 9 controls, 9 AD patients and 30 FTLD patients—9 with frontotemporal dementia (bvFTD), 13 with semantic dementia (SD), and 8 with progressive nonfluent aphasia (PNFA). Table 1 shows demographic information.

Data were collected in an ongoing series of NIH-funded studies being performed at the UCSF Memory and Aging Center. Patients were diagnosed by expert clinicians at the center by applying current clinical criteria. Patients underwent detailed standard speech and language, cognitive, emotional, genetic, pathological, and neuroimaging evaluations. Age-matched healthy controls were community volunteers obtained by SRI In-

	bvFTD	PNFA	SD	AD	Controls
Male/Female	5/4	1/7	6/7	5/4	3/6
Age	63.00(8.25)	62.88(7.75)	65.23(6.61)	59.11(7.47)	61.7(6.0)
Education *	17.33(1.73)	16.13(2.30)	16.45(2.54)	15.44(2.30)	17.27(2.1)
MMSE	24.4(5.85)	22.0(9.34)	17.09(8.15)	18.67(7.53)	Not Administered

Table 1. Demographic information for participants

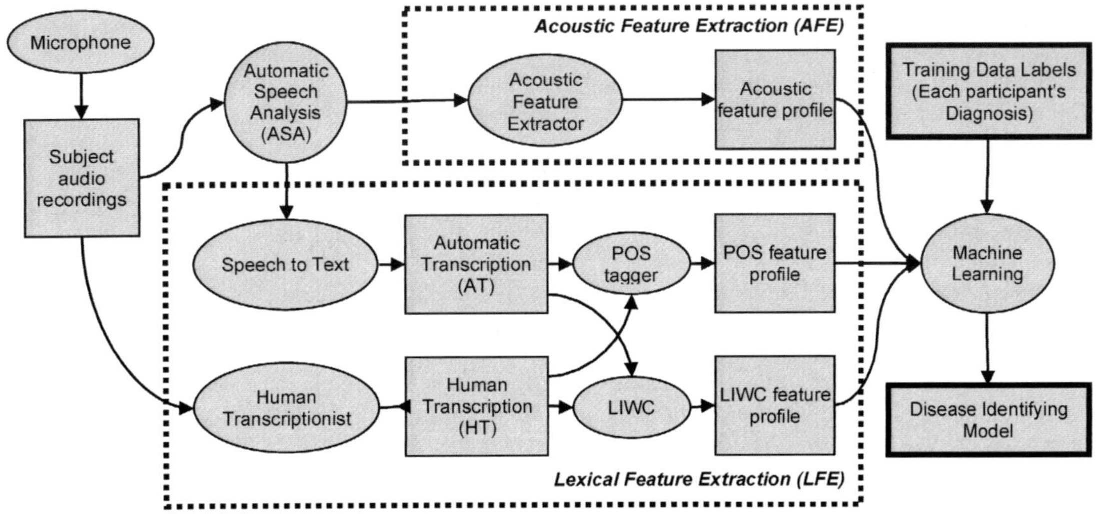

Figure 1. System Information Flow and Evaluation. Participant speech is subjected to automatic speech analysis of two kinds: Acoustic Feature Extraction (AFE) and Lexical Feature Extraction (LFE). Feature selection (not shown) is explained in Sects 2.3 and 2.6. Each machine learning algorithm produces a classification model based on labeled training data. All models used both acoustic and lexical features. Each such disease identifying model is evaluated against held-out training data (not shown). To measure sensitivity to ASR error, half of these models were based on lexical features derived from automatic transcription (AT), the other half from human transcription (HT).

ternational and were paid $10 for their participation.

2.2 Speech Samples

Speech samples were recordings of Part 1 of the Western Aphasia Battery (Kertesz, 1980). Participants are administered a semi-structured interview (e.g., questions such as "How are you?") and asked to describe a drawn picture of a picnic scene. The resulting 3 to 5 minutes of speech was recorded via wireless lapel microphones. Controls were recorded via digital audio recorder sampling at 48 kHz, 16 bit PCM, and later down-sampled to 16 kHz for use with the speech recognizer. Digital audio was down-sampled at 16 kHz, 16 bit PCM. Recordings were manually segmented in order to separate the interviewee's voice from the interviewer's. Only patient speech segments were subject to analysis

2.3 Procedure

To tackle speech-based diagnosis of AD, bvFTD, SD and PNFA, we employ several types of computer-based analyses (see Figure 1). Audio recordings were processed via the Meeting Understanding system (Stolcke at el., 2007), which was custom-tailored to recognize speaker-independent, multi-person speech. First, using this system we perform acoustic-level feature extraction (**AFE**), which obtains measures the duration of consonants, vowels, pauses, and other acoustic-phonetic categories. In parallel, we perform a lexical feature extraction (**LFE**) on transcripts of participant speech producing profiles of each speaker's language use. This profile characterizes frequencies of different types of words – e.g. frequency of nouns, verbs, function words, words about emotion, etc. – present in a language sample along ~100 dimensions.

Next, The AFE and LFE profiles are combined to form one large vector of features that collectively characterize the speaker. Feature selection is applied to select the most informative features. For feature selection, we performed a one-way ANOVA on each extracted feature to determine which features were significantly related to a diagnostic category using the Benjamini-Hochberg adjustment for multiple comparisons.

The vector of selected features for the speech samples in the *training set* is taken as input to machine learning. Based on these data machine learning automatically induces a diagnostic model that should predict any speaker's diagnosis based the AFE and LFE profiles of his or her speech sample.

The performance of a learned diagnostic model is measured in terms of ability to generalize to cases that it has not been trained on is measured by feeding *test set* cases – i.e. cases that have not been a part of the *training set*. We compared the accuracy of the machine learning induced algorithms with accuracy studies of traditional diagnostic methods in the literature.

In addition to the above, as part of a desire to achieve insight into the way these models were functioning, we sought verification that a differences in feature profiles as a function of diagnostic group correspond meaningfully to existing expectations derived from the literature. To do so, we formed and tested several predictions about specific feature differences based on the clinical literature (see Hypotheses below).

Finally, we wanted to determine how sensitive the feature differences and classification models were to speech recognition error. To do so we tested each hypothesis on both the human and automatic transcriptions. In addition, we learned a set of models based on automatic transcriptions and a second set of models based on human transcriptions and compared accuracies.

2.4 Acoustic Feature Extraction

We used the automatic speech recognition (**ASR**) system to extract a set of acoustic-level features corresponding to the overall rate, plus the mean and standard deviation of (a) pause lengths and (b) hypothesized phoneme durations. For each speech sample, the speech rate as well as the mean and standard deviation of the duration of pauses, vowels, and consonants were computed. The SRI speech processing system also further identified consonant classes based on manner features (e.g., fricative, stop, etc. ...) voicing features (voiced, voiceless) and measured the mean and standard deviation of the duration of these classes. Our Automatic Speech Analysis system produced 41 different duration-based measures extracted from the speech stream.

2.5 Lexical Feature Extraction (LFE)

For each transcript we performed two types of computer-based lexical analysis. The first determined frequencies of 14 different parts of speech (e.g. nouns, verbs, pronouns etc.) using an automatic part-of-speech (**POS**) tagger. The second involved Dr. Pennebaker's *Linguistic Inquiry and Word Count* (**LIWC**) software (Pennebaker, et al 2001), which determines word frequencies organized into 81 categories, such as psychological processes (e.g., emotional or cognitive) and linguistic dimensions (e.g. function words, verb tenses, negations).

To measure sensitivity to speech to text error, each ANOVA was performed twice, once for the "ground truth" human transcriptions (HT) and once for the automatic transcriptions (AT). During hypothesis testing, statistical significance of each pair of AT versus HT based LFEs (i.e., "ground truth") was compared. Additionally different models were learned, half using HT the other half using AT. To test for lexical-level differences between diagnostic categories, we performed a one-way ANOVA for each of the 95 LFE features (e.g. frequency of nouns) in which diagnosis was the independent variable and the given feature's frequency was the dependent variable.

2.6 Machine Learning

We assessed how well a variety of machine learning algorithms predicted a patient's diagnosis, using his or her combined AFE and LFE profile. Evaluation was conducted using five-fold cross-validation over the set of patients, with each "fold" consisting of two phases: a *training phase,* where the feature profiles and diagnoses from 4/5ths of the subjects are used to select features and then train the given learning algorithm, and a *test phase* where the trained learner is given just the feature profiles of the remaining patients, and attempts to predict their diagnoses. This procedure is executed five times, each time using different sets of subjects for the train and test phases, with overall accuracy being the average performance on the test subjects, across all five folds. We applied three learning methods, (1) logistic regression, a statistical learning technique for determining categorical outcomes, (2) Multi-Layered Perceptrons, an artificial intelligence (AI) learning method that roughly mimics biological neural networks, and (3) decision trees, another AI technique which induces sets of rules used to predict outcomes. All three are commonly used machine learning techniques, and for this study we used implementations available in Weka, an off-the-shelf machine learning toolkit (Witten and Frank, 2005).

2.7 Hypotheses

Machine learned classification models can be difficult to understand and often used merely as black boxes. To address this issue, we tried to draw a meaningful link between certain features and diagnosis. In particular, we formed and tested several hypotheses based on expectations derived from clinical literature. We used all the data (rather than one of the training folds) to test these hypotheses.

The hypotheses about the lexical features are as follows. First, based on (Forbes at el., 2002) we predicted that AD patients use more pronouns, verbs, and adjectives and fewer nouns than controls (**H1**).

In SD, one sees decreased lexical access to concrete concepts, so patients tend to use fewer nouns (**H2**). To compensate for such difficulties with word retrieval, they also use more pronouns (**H3**). This gives the impression of empty or circumlocutory speech. For example, rather than saying "The boy is flying a kite," a SD patient would be more prone to say "*He* is flying *that*." (Grossman and Ash, 2004).

In PNFA, one sees fewer verbs (**H4**) (Grossman and Ash, 2004). In addition, PNFA patients often exhibit *agrammatism*. Such speech is simplified and ungrammatical and involves fewer function words, for example "give cupcake" or "water now". Thus (**H5**) is that the speech of patients with PNFA will have fewer function words (**H5**) (Saffran at el., 1989). These hypotheses, along with whether each was supported by our analyses, are listed in Table 2 in Results.

The first acoustic hypothesis about acoustic features (**H6**) is related to the Neary criteria (Neary et al., 1998), which notes that PNFA is characterized by non-fluent spontaneous speech (among other required features). Additionally, patients in this group have significant *apraxia of speech* (Gorno-Tempini at el., 2004). Signs of this condition difficulty include articulatory groping – i.e. where the mouth searches for the correct configurations. Such trial and error speech often sounds "robotic" and can involve sounds that may be held out longer. Thus, given the duration features that are generally associated with apraxia of speech (Samuel at el., 1996; Edythe at el., 1996; Ballard and Robin, 2002), we hypothesize that PNFA patients would exhibit significantly longer vowel and consonant durations than controls (**H6**).

The second acoustic feature hypothesis (**H7**) is based on the fact that in the Neary criteria (Neary at el., 1998) *pressured speech* is a supportive (but not a core) diagnostic feature of both SD and bvFTD. In pressured speech one sees rapid

Hypothesis and source	**Supported in LFE of HT?**	**Supported in LFE or AFE of AT?**	**Figures (see Supplementary Materials)**
H1. AD patients use more pronouns, verbs, and adjectives and fewer nouns than controls (Forbes at el., 2002)	Yes, but only significant for nouns	Yes, significant for nouns, pronouns, and adjectives	Figure 3
H2. SD patients use fewer nouns (Grossman and Ash, 2004)	Yes	Yes, but not significant vs PNFA	Figure 3
H3. SD patients use more pronouns (Grossman and Ash, 2004)	Yes	Partial: SD sig. > CNTRL only	Figure 3
H4. Lower verb frequency in PNFA (Grossman and Ash, 2004)	Yes, but only significant vs. SD	No	Figure 3
H5. Fewer function words in PNFA (Saffran at el., 1989)	Yes	Yes, but only significant vs SD	Figure 3
H6. PNFA patients would exhibit longer vowel and consonant durations	N/A	Yes	Figure 2
H7. SD and bvFTD patients have shorter pauses than controls.	N/A	Yes	Figure 2

Table 2. Hypotheses extracted from literature and whether our measures—based on human transcripts (HT) and automatic transcripts (AT)—support them [Hypotheses 1-5 relate to Lexical Feature Extraction; Hypotheses 6-7 relate to Acoustic Level Analyses]

"flight of ideas" speech. We would thus expect *some* patients in these conditions to exhibit press of speech, and so hypothesize that the mean duration of pauses should be significantly less than controls (**H7**).

3 RESULTS

Results suggest that analyses at the lexical and acoustic levels are capable of detecting differences in accordance with expectations of prior research. Additionally, machine-learning algorithms predict clinical diagnosis surprisingly well.

3.1 Results: Acoustic-Level Hypotheses

For each measure, we performed an ANOVA with respect to diagnosis and found that 25 out of 41 measures were significant at the (Benjamini-Hochberg multiple comparison adjusted) 0.05 level. Hypotheses 7 and 8 in Table 2 and Figure 2 in Supplementary Materials deal specifically with AFE measures. These show that PNFA patients do exhibit significantly longer vowel and consonant durations, as the literature linking PNFA with apraxia of speech would predict. Furthermore, SD and bvFTD patients have significantly shorter pauses than controls, which is consistent with the hypothesis that some patients with these diagnoses exhibit press of speech.

3.2 Results: Lexical-Level Hypotheses

There were several lexical-level differences between diagnostic groups. We checked for significant differences (hereafter, "significant features") with respect to diagnosis while using the Benjamini-Hochberg test for multiple comparisons (Benjamini and Hochberg, 1995). (We use this adjustment for all multiple comparisons). There were several more lexical level differences based on the HTs than one would predict by chance. For example, 11 of the 14 POS features were significant ($p \leq .05$) including verbs, nouns, adjectives and adverbs. For LIWC features, 22 of 81 features were statistically significant at the p

		(A) FTLD vs AD vs Controls	(B) AD vs SD vs PNFA vs bvFTD vs Control	(C) FTLD vs AD	(D) AD vs Controls
1.	Random diagnosis	33%	20%	50%	50%
2.	Naïve learner (always picks largest class in training set)	63%	27%	77%	50%
3.	**Our method**	**80%**	**61%**	**88%** **Sens/Spec AD .58/0.77** **Sens/Spec FTLD .95/.89**	**88%** $\kappa = .64$ **/Spec AD .83/.90** **Sens/Spec Controls .92/.86**
4.	Radiologists in Klöppel at el. (2008) using MRI data			69% Sens/Spec AD .64/.71	89% Sensi/Spec AD .88/.90
5.	Frontal Behavioral Inventory in Blair at el. (2007)			75%	
6.	Neuropsychiatric inventory in Blair at el. (2007).			54%	
7.	NINCDS-ARDA criteria in Lopez at el. (1990)				$\kappa = .36 - .65$
8.	DSM-III criteria in Kukull at el. (1990)				$\kappa = .55$
9.	NINCDS criteria in Kukull at el. (1990)				$\kappa = .64$
10.	ECRDC criteria in Kukull at el. (1990)				$\kappa = .37$

Table 3. Accuracy, sensitivity and specificity for Layered Perceptron learned models for FTLD subtypes. (Accuracy of a random and naïve learner id 33% and 43% respectively)

<= 0.05 level, with $p \leq 0.005$ for 17 of them. As to the question of whether the profile differences correspond meaningfully to existing literature, Table 2 shows which literature-generated hypotheses were supported. See Figure 3 in Supplementary Materials which show the means and standard error for each diagnostic class on a particular feature.

3.3 Machine Learning Results

Using cross-validation, we tested the ability of machine learning methods to produce algorithms that could synthesize lexical-level and acoustic-level profiles and then identify the clinician diagnosis.

We tried several different machine-learning algorithms and found that performance was roughly the same. See Table 3 for the performance of the Multi-layered Perceptron algorithm, which was slightly superior. Performance was measured across several different diagnostic problems (e.g., FTLD vs AD vs Controls (Column A), AD vs Controls (Column D), etc.). For purposes of rough comparison, Table 3 also provides diagnostic performance of other methods, including radiologists using MRI data.

In evaluating machine learning results, we wished to compare model performance against various benchmarks. The two easiest such benchmark are random guessing (see Table 3 Row 1: given N diagnostic alternatives, one has a 1 / N chance of correctly guessing) and *naïve learner guessing*, (see Table 3 Row 2) which always chooses the most frequent (i.e., modal) diagnosis found in the training sample. The row labeled "Our method" corresponds to the accuracy of models generated from lexical and acoustic features using AT. For this case, HT results differs from AT in accuracy by only 2-3% for all prediction problems. Note that our method is at least equal to the accuracies, sensitivities, specificities, and *kappa*'s of the other clinical benchmarks in most cases. See Table 4, which shows the performance on distinguishing FTLD subtypes. For more detail on machine learning results see Peintner et al (2008).

4 DISCUSSION

The accuracy of the best machine learned diagnostic model was 88% in the binary classifications of AD versus FTLD, and AD versus Controls (Table 3). Acoustic and lexical level differences are detectable despite the present level of ASA inaccuracy. Although diagnosis should never be made on the basis of one source of information, our pilot data show that automatic computer-based analyses of spontaneous speech show promise as diagnostic aids by detecting the at times subtle differences that characterize these neurodegenerative disorders.

Inferences drawn from these results are subject to a variety of assumptions and limitations. Perhaps the biggest limitation is the small number of research participants. Larger samples will be needed in order to make valid generalizations to the population. Small samples increase the probability of Type I and II Errors and decrease power in testing for normality. That said, many of our hypothesized linguistic differences based on prior research were confirmed. Additionally, low N in each group entailed that test sets in each fold were small. Though it is remarkable in our pilot study that we obtained classification accuracy on par with clinical judgment, a larger sample size is required to make a rigorously valid claim about on par accuracy.

Statistically minded readers may question our use of parametric statistics (ANOVA) in feature selection because we have not tested the normality assumption. There are too few observations in each group to test for normality of residuals with any power. In future work with a larger sample we should perform such a test. Alternatively, on the present data we could use the non-parametric Kruskal-Wallis test as a stand in for ANOVA.

Additionally, such readers may question our use of the Benjamini-Hochberg (BH) adjustment which controls false discovery rate over a more stringent correction for familywise error rate such as Bonferoni or Holm. Our rationale was that an occasional false positive (5% if we have a 5% false positive rate) among our total set of positives isn't a big concern. As our focal aim was machine learning, scientific discovery, was a secondary concern. Thus, we were less interested in the question "was there *any* difference between the groups". We were more interested in *which* features showed a difference. Better to have a small proportion of false positives than to miss true positives. In addition, because the false negative rate criterion is less stringent about false positives, the BH procedure tends to have greater power than multiple comparison approaches that control the familywise error rate.

The success of our methods is surprising given (1) we have performed no customization of "off the shelf" LFE and machine learning techniques; (2) models were trained on a relatively small number of subjects; (3) speech samples were short (3-5 minutes). Larger speech samples, larger N and more tailored tools (e.g. language models) will enable lower word error rate, higher accuracy and finer discrimination amongst and within diagnostic types. It also suggests that this can be accomplished without training the system to the voice of each subject.

The results also draw significance because the overall approach may be applied to other neurological or psychological disorders. Many such disorders have characteristic lexical or acoustic profiles. For example, Jarrold (2011) and Stirman et al (2001) have shown that depression is associated with high frequencies of first person words (I, me, I've) and lower frequencies of social and second person words (us,we). Sanchez et al (2011) and Keskinpala (2007) have shown acoustic prosodic features indicative of depression or suicide risk. Our results suggest a very similar study design can be applied to detect these kinds of depression related lexical and acoustic/prosodic profiles.

Our results suggest we may be able train the models to assess specific highly diagnostic language symptoms – such as fluency, circumlocution, and apraxia of speech. This can be particularly important where the inter-rater reliability of given symptoms is poor. We believe that poor inter-rater reliability is mainly caused by the inability to precisely delineate the objective characteristics of these symptoms. Assuming we can get a range of values that characterize a given symptom, we can apply machine learning to identify symptoms in addition to diagnosis.

We view the methods described as analogous to EKG. The EKG trace affords a more quantitative and objective picture of cardiac functioning which complements the stethoscope. Analogously, if scaled-up studies can demonstrate adequate diagnostic accuracy results, then computationally extracted lexico-acoustic profiles may someday augment information provided by current speech and language diagnostic methods which are currently based substantially on subjective clinical judgment. As modern EKG's provide automatic interpretation, our analysis suggests that classification of speech as AD-like or FTLD-like may be possible. The competent physician never relies only the automated diagnosis provided by EKG but also interprets a profile of measures in the context of clinical observation. Our assumption is that the methods outlined above should be used in a way analogously to the EKG.

Accuracy	**bvFTD (Sens/Specif)**	**PNFA**	**SD**
63%	.51 / .58	.54 / .72	.76 / .62

Table 4. Accuracy, sensitivity and specificity for Lay-ered Perceptron learned models for FTLD subtypes. (Accuracy of a random and naïve learner id 33% and 43% respectively)

The results of our hypothesis testing show that differences in feature profiles are generally consistent with what we would expect from the clinical literature. This may be the first of several steps required to provide assurance to clinicians who would prefer to trust a model that had somewhat transparent features to the opaque "black box" models that are often learned. Establishing trust of clinicians is required for wide scale adoption and future work should build on these results.

Our pilot data suggest this approach provides diagnoses of comparable accuracy to other more time intensive or more invasive methods (e.g. neuropsychological testing or imaging). This is a fast, inexpensive, and non-invasive means of obtaining diagnostically useful information. Thus the tool may show most promise as a screening tool to decide which patients need deeper evaluation. Additionally, it may provide objective and quantifiable measures of speech and language symptomatology – a kind of symptomatology for which there are few objective, quantifiable measures.

5 Conclusion

Clinical speech analytics applied to spontaneous speech can detect distinguish between AD, bvFTD, SD PNFA and healthy control groups via lexico-acoustic profiles. Diagnostic accuracy is comparable to other clinical data sources despite speech sample brevity. Accuracy levels suggest the approach offers promise as an additional, objective and easily obtained source of diagnostic information for clinicians.

Reference

Varma A.R., Snowden J.S., Lloyd J.J., Talbot P.R., Mann D.M.A., Neary D. 1999. *Evaluation of the NINCDS-ADRDA criteria in the differentiation of Alzheimer's disease and frontotemporal dementia*, Journal of Neurology, Neurosurgery and Psychiatry, 66: 184-188.

Klöppel, S., Stonnington, C.M., Barnes, J., Chen, F., Chu, C., Good, C.D., Mader, I., Mitchell, L.A., Patel, A.C., Roberts, C.C., Fox, N.C., Jack, R. Jr, Ashburner, J., Frackowiak , RS. 2008. *Accuracy of dementia diagnosis: a direct comparison between radiologists and a computerized method*, Brain, 131(11): 2969–2974.

S. Pestell, M. Shanks, J. Warrington, and A. Venneri. 2000. *Quality of spelling breakdown in Alzheimer's disease is independent of disease progression*, Journal of Clinical and Experimental Neuropsychology, volume 22, pages 599–612.

H. Platel, J. Lambert, F. Eustache, B. Cadet, M. Dary, F. Viader, and B. Lechevalier. 1993. *Characterstics and evolution of writing impairment in Alzheimer's disease*, Journal of Clinical and Experimental Neuropsychology, volume 22, pages 599–612.

K. Forbes, A. Venneri, and M. Shanks. 2002. *Distinct patterns of spontaneous speech deterioration: an early predictor of Alzheimer's disease*, Brain and Cognition, volume 48(2-3): 356–61.

C. Crockford and R. Lesser. 1994. *Assessing functional communication in aphasia: Clinical utility and time demands of three methods*, European Journal of Disorders of Communication, volume 29: 165–182.

Thomas, V., Keselj, N., Cercone, K., Rockwood, E. 2005. *Automatic detection and rating of dementia of Alzheimer type through lexical analysis of spontaneous speech*, IEEE International Conference on Mechatronics and Automation.

Mendez, M.F., Selwood, A., Mastri, A.R., Frey, W.H. 1993. 2nd, *Pick's disease versus Alzheimer's disease: A comparison of clinical characteristics*, Neurology, 43(2): 289–92.

Neary, D., Snowden, J.S., Gustafson, L., Passant, U., Stuss, D., Black, S., Freedman, M., Kertesz, A., Robert, H., Albert, M., Boone, K., Miller, B.L., Cummings, J., Benson, D.F. 1998. *Frontotemporal lobar degeneration: A consensus on clinical diagnostic criteria,* Neurology, 51(6): 1546–54.

Davies, R.R., Hodges, J.R., Kril, J.J., et al. 2005. *The pathological basis of semantic dementia.* Brain, 128(9): 1984–95.

Josephs, K.A., Duffy, J.R., Strand, E.A., et al. 2006. *Clinicopathological and imaging correlates of progressive aphasia and apraxia of speech.* Brain, 129(6): 1385–98.

Bright, P., Moss, H. E., Stamatakis, E. A., & Tyler, L. K. 2008. *Longitudinal studies of semantic dementia: The relationship between structural and functional changes over time*, Neuropsychologia, 46: 2177-2188.

S. Singh, R. Bucks, and J. Cuerden. 2001. *Evaluation of an objective technique for analysing temporal variables in DAT spontaneous speech*, Aphasiology, volume 15(6): 571–584.

Stefanie Abel, Walter Huber, Gary S. Dell. 2009. *Connectionist diagnosis of lexical disorders in aphasia*, Aphasiology, volume 23.

Dilek Hakkani-Tür, Dimitra Vergyri, Gökhan Tür. 2010. *Speech-based automated cognitive status assessment.* Interspeech 2010: pages 258-261.

Maider Lehr, Emily T. Prud'hommeaux, Izhak Shafran and Brian Roark. 2012. *Fully Automated Neuropsychological Assessment for Detecting Mild Cognitive Impairment.* In Proceedings of Interspeech.

Kertesz, A. 1980. *Western Aphasia Battery*, London, Ontario: University of Western Ontario Press.

Stolcke, A., Boakye, K., Cetin, Ö., Janin, A., Magimai-Doss, M., Wooters, C., Zheng, J. 2007. *The SRI-ICSI Spring 2007 meeting and lecture recognition system*, Proc. NIST 2007 Rich Transcription Workshop.

Pennebaker, J.W., Francis, M.E., Booth, R.J. 2001. *Linguistic Inquiry and Word Count (LIWC): LIWC2001*, Mahwah, NJ: Erlbaum Publishers.

Toutanova, K., Klein, D., Manning, C., Singer, Y. 2003. *Feature-rich part-of-speech tagging with a cyclic dependency network*, in Proceedings of HLT-NAACL 2003, pages 252–259.

Grossman, M., Ash, S. 2004. *Primary Progressive Aphasia: A Review,* Neurocase, 10(1): 3–18.

Gorno-Tempini, M.L, Dronkers, N.F., Rankin, K.P., Ogar, J.M., La Phengrasamy, B.A., Rosen, H.J., Johnson, J.K., Weiner, M.W., Miller, B.L, *Cognition and Anatomy in three variants of primary progressive aphasia*, Annals of Neurology, 2004. 55: 335–346.

Samuel A. K. Seddoh, Donald A. Robin, Hyun-Sub Sim, Carlin Hageman, Jerald B. Moon, John W. Folkins. 1996. *Speech Timing in Apraxia of Speech versus Conduction Aphasia,* Journal of Speech and Hearing Research, 39: 590–603.

Edythe A. Strand, E.A., McNeil, M.R. 1996. *Effects of Length and Linguistic Complexity on Temporal Acoustic Measures in Apraxia of Speech,* Journal of Speech and Hearing Research, 39: 1018–33.

Kirrie J. Ballarrd, Ph.D., and Donald A. Robin. 2002. *Assessment of AOS for Treatment Planning,* Seminars in Speech and Language, 23(4): 281–291.

Witten, I.H., Frank, E. 2005. *Data mining: Practical machine learning tools and techniques*, San Francisco: Morgan Kaufmann. Second edition.

Benjamini, Y., Hochberg Y. 1995. *Controlling the False Discover Rate: A Practical and Powerful Approach to Multiple Testing*, Journal of the Royal Statistical Society. Series B *(Methodological)*, 57(1): 289–300.

Saffran, E.M., Berndt, R.S., Schwartz, M.F. 1989. *The quantitative analysis of agrammatic production: procedure and data, Brain and Language*, 37(3): 440–79.

Blair, M., Kertesz, A., Davis-Faroque, N., Hsiung, G.Y.R., Black, S.E., Bouchard, R.W., Gauthier, S., Guzman, D.A., Hogan, D.B., Rockwood, K., Feldman. H. 2007. *Behavioural Measures in Frontotemporal Lobar Dementia and Other Dementias: The Utility of the Frontal Behavioural Inventory and the Neuropsychiatric Inventory in a National Cohort Study,* Dementia and Geriatric Cognitive Disorder, 23: 406-15

Lopez, O. L., Swihart, A. A., Becker, J. T., Reinmuth, O. M., Reynolds, C. F., Rezek, D. L., Daly, F. L. 1990. *Reliability of NINCDS-ADRDA clinical criteria for the diagnosis of Alzheimer's disease,* Neurology, 40: 1517

Kukull, W. A., Larson, E. B., Reifler, B. V., Lampe, T. H., Yerby, M., Hughes, J. 1990. *Interrater reliability of Alzheimer's disease diagnosis*, Neurology, 40(2): 257-60

Peintner, B., Jarrold, W, Vergyri, D., Richey, C., Gorno Tempini, M., and Ogar, J. 2008. *Learning Diagnostic Models Using Speech and Language Measures*, 30th Annual International IEEE EMBS Conference, August 20-24, Vancouver, British Columbia, Canada.

Jarrold, W., Javitz, H.S., Krasnow, R., Peintner, B., Yeh E., Swan, G.E. (2011) *Depression and Self-Focused Language in Structured Interviews with Older Adults* Psychological Reports Oct;109(2):686-700.

Stirman, S.W., & Pennebaker, J.W. (2001). *Word use in the poetry of suicidal and non-suicidal poets.* Psychosomatic Medicine 63, 517-522.

Michelle Hewlett Sanchez, Dimitra Vergyri, Luciana Ferrer,,Colleen Richey, Pablo Garcia, Bruce Knoth, William Jarrold: *Using Prosodic and Spectral Features in Detecting Depression in Elderly-Males.* INTERSPEECH 2011: 3001-3004

H. Kaymaz Keskinpala, T. Yingthawornsuk, D. Mitchell Wilkes, Richard G. Shiavi, R. M. Salomon: Distinguishing high risk suicidal subjects among depressed subjects using mel-frequency cepstrum coefficients and cross validation technique. MAVEBA 2007: 157-160

Supplementary Materials

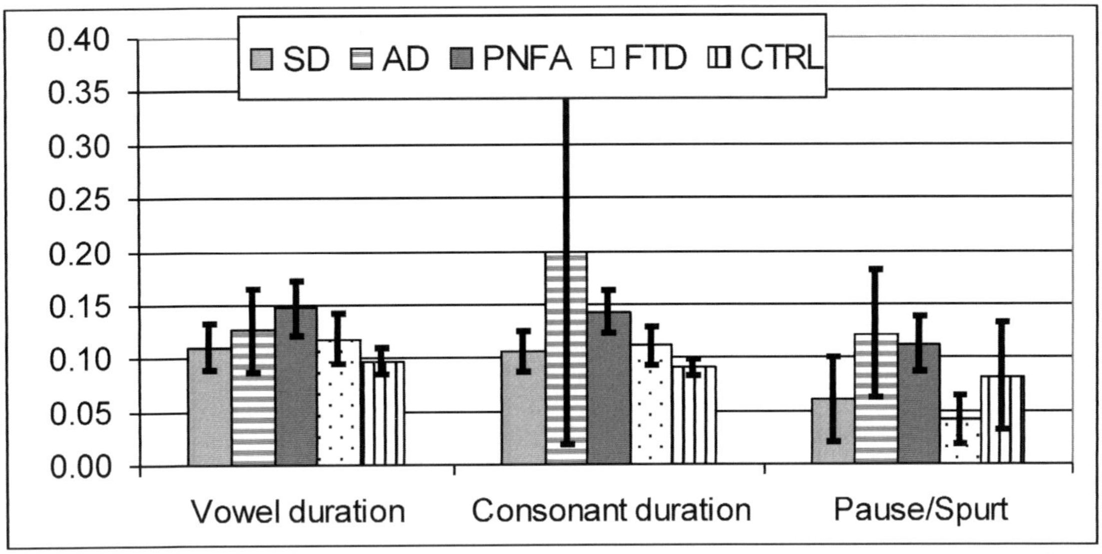

Figure 2. Vowel, consonant, and pause

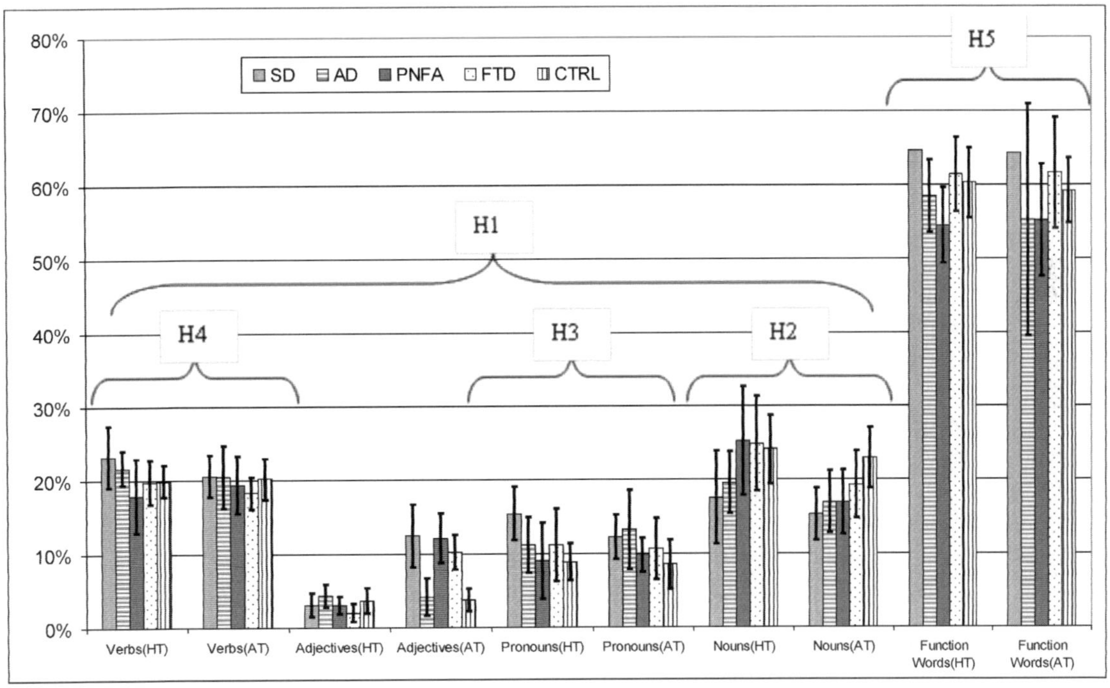

Figure 3. Verb, adjective, pronoun, noun and function word frequencies (H1, H2, H3, H4, H5)

Assessing Violence Risk in Threatening Communications

Kimberly Glasgow
Johns Hopkins University
Applied Physics Laboratory,
and
College of Information Studies,
University of Maryland
kimberly.glasgow@jhuapl.edu

Ronald Schouten
Harvard Medical School,
and
Department of Psychiatry,
Massachusetts General Hospital
rschouten@mgh.harvard.edu

Abstract

Violence risk assessment is an important and challenging task undertaken by mental health professionals and others, in both clinical and nonclinical settings. To date, computational linguistic techniques have not been used in the risk assessment process. However they could contribute to the current threat assessment process by allowing for early detection of elevated risk, identification of risk factors for violence, monitoring of violent intent, and determination of threat level. We analyzed a sample of communications to judges that were referred to security personnel for evaluation as constituting potential threats. We categorized them along multiple dimensions including evidence of mental illness, presence and nature of any threat, and level of threat. While neither word count-based or topic models were able to effectively predict elevated risk, we found topics indicative of persecutory beliefs, paranoid ideation, and other symptoms of Axis I and Axis II disorders.

1 Introduction

Mental health professionals are called upon to assess the risk of violence in many different settings, from the determination of the need for hospitalization or increased treatment to consultations for the criminal justice system (Skeem and Monahan, 2011). These assessments include examination of the verbal content of a subject's communications, primarily for the purpose of detecting symptoms of thought disorder or evidence of impending violent behavior. Language technology is rarely utilized in these efforts, yet it could be a valuable tool for detecting evidence of illness and increased violence risk in verbal and written communications.

We analyzed a unique data set of threatening communications sent to judges. Examination of these written communications indicate that, for this sample, explicit threats are rare, but evidence of mental illness is common. We applied two types of computational methods to the communications in the sample—topic models, and a simple computational text analysis method: LIWC (Pennebaker et al., 2001). The results point towards a useful role for such methods in the analysis of threatening communications, as well as limitations. Advances in language technology methods, as well as the availability of more data, may both be needed to make substantial progress.

2 Violence Risk Assessment and Mental Health Professionals

Assessment of the risk of violence is a task that belongs to a diverse group of mental health professionals (MHPs): those who provide clinical care, forensic MHPs specializing in mental health issues related to the legal system, and those who engage in the even more specialized field of threat assessment. Other disciplines involved in threat assessment include law enforcement, security professionals, and intelligence analysts.

Violence risk assessment is a routine aspect of the work of mental health professionals treating

Workshop on Computational Linguistics and Clinical Psychology: From Linguistic Signal to Clinical Reality, pages 38–45,
Baltimore, Maryland USA, June 27, 2014. ©2014 Association for Computational Linguistics

people with mental illness. While violence against others on the part of people with diagnoses of mental illness is far less prevalent than is popularly thought, the increased risk attributable to these illnesses is barely statistically significant (Steadman et al., 1998; Swanson et al., 1990). This increased risk is largely attributable to a small group of individuals who have a history of childhood or adult antisocial behavior in combination with substance use disorders and psychotic illness (Elbogen and Johnson, 2009).

2.1 Methods and Practice of Violence Risk Assessment

Treating clinicians are responsible for evaluating their patients to determine if they pose a risk of violence and adjusting treatment accordingly, or arranging for hospitalization, as needed. The risk of violence, as evidenced by threats or attempts to harm self or others, are two of the bases for hospitalizing people with mental illness against their will. This assessment primarily relies upon information obtained through interviewing and observing the patient, as well as information from collateral sources when it is available. The patient's language is taken into account largely as a part of the mental status examination, in which attention is paid to the content and form of the patient's thoughts, which are characteristically disrupted in certain illnesses. Clinicians look at many factors to determine if someone poses a risk of violence, but a patient's written communications is typically not one of them.

MHPs who practice in the field of forensic mental health do so as an even larger component of their work. Many are routinely asked to assess the risk of violence in both the civil and criminal justice systems. In the civil justice system, for example, they may be called upon as expert witnesses in civil commitment proceedings or as consultants on such matters. In the criminal justice system, they may be asked to assess the risk of violence in conjunction with the issuance of restraining orders, determination of conditions of bail and probation, and sentencing. While judges make the ultimate decisions, they generally rely highly upon the clinical judgment of MHPs with regard to diagnosis and assessment of the risk of violence.

In recent years, a number of tools have been introduced to assist in the assessment of violence risk, such at the HCR-20 (Webster et al., 1982), COVR (Monahan et al., 2006), and VRAG (Quinsey et al., 1998). None of these instruments consider linguistic factors. They utilize actuarial determinations of violence risk. These instruments do not provide strict cutoff scores that differentiate between nonviolent and violent individuals. Rather, they serve as adjunct tools to clinical judgment. As a result, the current best practice in violence risk assessment consists of structured clinical judgment, a process in which actuarial risk assessments are combined with clinical judgment to reach a determination regarding a specific individual's risk.

Whereas treating clinicians primarily rely upon examination of the patient in assessing the risk of violence, forensic MHPs are expected to go beyond the clinical examination and incorporate information from a variety of collateral sources, such as medical and mental health records, psychological testing, legal documents, police reports, and criminal histories in order to increase the objectivity and "scientific" basis of their opinion. As in clinical care, language is an important part of the mental status examination. More detailed review of the evaluee's communications is more common in forensic work, as it may provide insight into the writer's emotional state, motivation, and intention, as well as thought processes. The content, syntax, and grammar of communications, as well as the page layout, variations in font size, use of color, and graphics may all be considered in assessing for presence of a mental disorder and indications of violence risk.

2.2 Threat Assessment

Threat assessment is a discipline that relates to, yet is separate from, clinical violence risk assessment. Meloy, et al. distinguish between the two fields, noting that violence risk assessment is consultative in nature, and generally aimed at assisting legal decision-making and managing a particular individual over the long term. They note that threat assessment is operational, rather than consultative, in nature and is aimed at protecting victims by determining the level of risk that they face at a given moment in time (Meloy and Hoffmann, 2013). Although the emphasis is different, both take into account the likelihood that a given individual will act in a violent fashion. Threat assessment goes beyond the determination of risk of physical violence and extends to insider threats such as sabotage, espionage, hacking, harassment, and attacks on reputation. Language assumes an even greater role in the analysis of threat than it does in violence risk assessment.

The Risk Assessment Guideline Elements for Violence (RAGE-V) produced by the Association of Threat Assessment Professionals lists a wide range of behaviors and risk factors to be considered in assessing the threat of violence. It contains no reference to the analysis of written materials or communications, other than suicide notes. (Available at www.atapworldwide.org).

3 The Language of Threat

Analysis of language is an important aspect of threat assessment and has traditionally been utilized in much the same manner as in forensic evaluations. That is, it has largely involved ad hoc, impressionistic assessments of communications. Efforts towards a more methodical approach to linguistic analysis of threatening communications have been made. However, many of these still rely primarily on human judgment of content. Smith and Shuy describe closely examining language as evidence for clues to race, ethnicity, or gender of a perpetrator, for identifying false allegations, and for related law enforcement tasks (Smith and Shuy, 2002). Scalora describes analyzing threatening language towards members of Congress in terms of several thematic areas relating to presence and types of demands (such as policy changes or personal favors) (Scalora et al., 2003), and Calhoun (Calhoun, 1998) examines threatening or inappropriate communications and assaults against federal judicial officials based upon factors such as the directness or immediacy of the threat.

In other related work, efforts to predict case outcomes for a set of 96 FBI cases involving threatening communications have incorporated interviews and automated text processing (Smith, 2008) Computational methods have also been applied to the communications of terrorist or radical religious extremist groups to detect aggressive or violent intent, using function word categories (Pennebaker et al., 2008) or frame analysis (Sanfilippo, 2010).

4 Data

Our data consisted of 60 documents that were sent to judges in a major metropolitan area in the United States. These documents were genuine, natural, purposeful communications from a sender to at least one judge or court official. They were perceived as threatening, and referred to court security officers for risk assessment. These referrals were usually made by judges, though District Attorneys and Clerks of the Court can also report threats to court security. The documents represented all cases that contained written material (not just verbal threats) from the two largest districts within the purview of the office responsible for trial court security for this region. Judges may refer a potentially threatening communication based on a perceived risk of harm to self, or to the security of the courtroom.

All documents were in English. All documents underwent optical character recognition (OCR), and the output of the OCR process was reviewed to correct errors in the text. Handwritten portions of documents were manually transcribed.

Each document was manually annotated for the presence of atypical formatting or text features, (e.g., the inclusion of magazine cut-out words or images, or the use of unusual bolding or italics, centering, or large point size in text), or presence of handwritten comments in addition to the text. These documents include legal documents, letters, faxes, cards, and other printed materials, as well as hard copies of emails.

Documents were also coded for indications of psychotic symptoms, Axis I mental disorders such as mania, depression, anxiety and psychotic disorders, or Axis II disorders such as personality disorders, developmental disabilities or autism spectrum disorders, utilizing the multi-axial diagnostic scheme contained in the Diagnostic and Statistical Manual of Mental Disorders (DSM-IV-TR) (American Psychiatric Association, 2000). Psychotic symptoms are characteristic of a number of Axis I disorders, but were coded separately due to their special significance in the conveyance and determination of violence risk. Where indications of one of these types of disorders were present, the strength of the evidence was rated as significant, or very compelling. Forty-eight of the 60 documents showed significant or very compelling indications of at least one of these disorders.

A high, medium, or low judgment for risk of violence was made in the manner common in threat assessment practice, i.e., an overall impression based upon the intensity of emotion conveyed, the presence of paranoid ideation directed toward the

Indications of Mental Illness	Psychotic	Axis I Disorder	Axis II Disorder
Absent	34	24	29
Present	26(7,19)	36(15,21)	31(3,28)

Table 1: Indications of mental illness appeared in most of the threatening communications. When indications were present, these were shown as counts of total number of document, and further broken down into counts of (very compelling, significant).

recipient, and specificity and nature of any threat. This annotation was performed by one of the authors, who is a board-certified forensic psychiatrist with over 20 years' experience in both violence risk assessment and clinical practice.

The presence of an actual threat in the document, and the nature of that threat, were also recorded. Interestingly, while all documents were referred out of concern for the personal safety of at least one judge or court official, in or outside the courtroom, only a minority of the documents threatened violence. Just three of the 60 documents made clear threats of violence, while another five contained vague or ambiguous threats. Fewer than half (26) contained threats of any kind, and most of these were threats to take legal action. Other documents expressed threats to reputation – they purported to "expose" or embarrass the judge in some way. Some threatened to file an ethics complaint. Other threats were more fanciful and clearly outside the power of the author to effect. For example, they threatened to report the judge to a non-existent "people's committee," or threatened punishment from God. Some documents contained more than one threat.

Type of Threat	No. of Documents
None	34
Violence	8 (3 clear, 5 vague)
Legal Action	16
Ethics Complaint	4
Reputation	8
Other	2

Table 2: Actual threats of violence are uncommon. Most communications do not contain a threat.

Based on application of the standard threat assessment methods described above to each document, the perceived risk was rated low for two-thirds of the documents (41), moderate for 18, and high for only one document. These methods consisted of examining each document in isolation. Where two or more communications were available from a single sender, the documents were examined individually, with an effort to isolate each document from its companions, in order to maintain a focus on language used in the document itself, and enable clearer comparison with the automated methods used later.

In the actual practice of threat assessment, if multiple documents were attributed to a single sender, and the case was not referred for assessment until after multiple documents had been received, the documents would be assessed together as a pattern of communications. Our approach more closely parallels the situation faced in assessing anonymous threatening communications, where knowledge of personal, historical, or clinical factors of the sender is not available. Assessment in these circumstances must rely more heavily on linguistic factors of the communications (Simons and Tunkel, 2013).

The fact that a single assessor reviewed all the documents is a limitation of the current study, which can be addressed in future work.

This research was approved as exempt by the Partners Institutional Review Board, with the provisions that the confidentiality of materials and the privacy of individuals be protected.

5 Methods

The potential for computational text analytic methods to contribute to violence risk assessment and threat assessment has been noted (Meloy and Hoffmann, 2013). We apply two such methods, LIWC and topic models, to our sample of threatening communications.

Word count-based methods, such as LIWC (Linguistic Inquiry and Word Count) are widely used. LIWC's central premise is that words people use reveal their psychological or emotional state, and may provide insight into their perceptions and intentions. LIWC has been applied to assessing text for a range of psychological phenomena (Pennebaker et al., 2001), and recently has been used for detecting indications of deception, and of aggression and hostility in the communications of terrorist groups (Pennebaker et al., 2008; Chung and Pennebaker, 2011).

LIWC is organized into a set of dozens of categories that contain words and word stems. These may be grammatical categories such as prepositions or pronouns, or they may be more psychologically informed categories such as "anger" (attack, battle, angry, enemy, violent, etc.). LIWC calculates the percentage of words in a document that belong in each of its categories.

We also employ topic models, which are probabilistic models for illuminating an underlying semantic or thematic structure within a set of documents (Blei and Lafferty, 2009). As an unsupervised method, a topic model is not based on some predetermined set of associated words, as is LIWC, with its dozens of categories for function words, emotion words, and so on. Instead the topics emerge based on the statistical properties of the documents themselves. This is a consequence of documents that are about different things typically using different words with different frequencies.

When the most frequent words in a topic cohere, it is relatively simple to infer what the topic is "about." For example, applying topic modeling to over twenty years of the Yale Law Journal yielded topics appear to relate to various areas of the law, such as labor (labor, workers, employees, union, employer) and contract law (contract, liabilities, parties, contracts, party, creditors) (Blei, 2012).

To help avoid overtraining the model, location names were removed from the documents. Names of individuals were replaced with tokens for last name (LN), male first name (MFN), female first name (FFN), or middle initial (MI). References to famous historical figures (e.g., Abraham Lincoln, Hitler, Winston Churchill) were not altered.

We run a Latent Dirichlet Allocation topic model (Blei, Ng, and Jordan 2003) using MALLET (McCallum, 2002) (McCallum 2002) on the set of threatening communications. In addition to ignoring the standard English stopwords in our documents, we also ignore a small set of extremely common words in the documents (district, court, judge), the "LN" (last name) token, and the months of the year.

Despite the relatively small size of our document corpus, a number of intriguing topics emerge. We observe topics relating to corruption, misconduct and ethics, conspiracy or other delusional beliefs, and family and community relationships.

6 Findings

Expressions of Anger and Negative Emotion and Violence Risk Expression of anger and negative emotions has long been considered a factor in violence risk assessment and threat assessment. It has been observed that acts of targeted violence commonly arise from a grievance on the part of the perpetrator, such as a perceived injustice (Calhoun and Weston, 2003). Chung and Pennebaker also find significantly elevated rates of anger words in the language of Al Qaeda leaders compared to controls (Pennebaker et al., 2008). In our threatening communications to judges, however, we do not observe a comparable effect with respect to perceived violence risk. Words reflecting anger, death, or negative emotions are not used more frequently in documents that indicate elevated risk. Nor do they vary significantly across documents reflecting Axis I, Axis II, or psychotic symptoms.

This may reflect a limitation of any tool such as LIWC that uses word lists to capture emotion. The expressive capacity of natural language is much greater. For example, one threatening communication that contained no terms from LIWC's anger, death, or negative emotion categories, called others "animals" and "CRIMINAL TRASH!", who would be "held accountable" for their actions.

Themes Induced through Topic Modeling Unsurprisingly, given that these threatening communications were sent to judges, often by litigants, terms referencing the judicial system appear prominently in many topics. A closer look reveals themes relating to claims of judicial misconduct or ethical violations, conspiracies and fundamentally sinful or evil acts ("malum in se"). Such topics are suggestive of symptoms such as persecutory beliefs, paranoid ideation, hyperreligiosity, and hypermorality that can be found in both Axis I and Axis II disorders. Tellingly, these themes emerged from the corpus, not from an a-priori categorization of terms.

Not all topics show potential links to detectable psychopathology. Another topic relates to family and emotional attachment, and may be indicative of child custody or child welfare issues. Topics

Risk Level	Number of Documents	Anger	Death	Negative Emotion
Elevated	19	1.22 (1.02)	0.21 (0.40)	2.42 (1.35)
Low	41	1.06 (0.74)	0.20 (0.40)	2.50 (1.45)
All	60	1.11 (0.83)	0.20 (0.40)	2.47 (1.45)

Table 3: Threatening communications judged to show an elevated risk cannot be distinguished from low risk documents, based on LIWC categories of anger, death, or negative emotion. Means and standard deviations based on LIWC scores are reported.

from this 10-topic LDA include

- *Relationships, family, and community:* love children years told thing drug wife family conviction make date person community felony simply letter dss
- *Conspiracy and injustice:* criminal filed order attorney trial conspiracy federal justice conduct made constitutional dr se abuse malum
- *Misconduct, ethics:* judicial complaints appointed justice case attorneys federal commission attorney misconduct ethical conduct complaint respect integrity.

Efforts to build predictive models for identifying documents containing indications of Axis I, Axis II, or psychotic symptoms based solely on topic distributions were not entirely successful. For example, a logistic regression model using features based on a 10-topic LDA outperformed chance on a test set at predicting presence of Axis I symptoms, achieving excellent recall, but low precision. This may have been due to the small size of the document collection. Additionally, the overlap of symptoms between Axis I and Axis II may have lead to topics that do not effectively distinguish between them.

7 Discussion

It is not surprising that judges can be the object of considerable ire and attention directed at them by disappointed litigants, family members, or others who have concerns about legal and social issues. They sit at the apex of a system that resolves interpersonal conflicts and administers justice, but with no shortage of disappointed parties.

Because of the important role they play in our society, judges are normally accorded considerable respect and deference. The majority of disappointed litigants use socially acceptable means of redressing their grievances, e.g. appealing the decision, seeking other legal remedies, or more rarely, filing complaints of judicial misconduct. Others express their disagreement and disappointment in a more direct fashion, either by choice or because they cannot restrain themselves from doing so, in some cases by communicating implied or direct threats to judges. In doing so, they cross the boundary of respect for judges and the legal system that prevents the majority of litigants from personalizing and pursuing their grievances.

Some such communications are referred by their recipients to a protective service responsible for the court in question. The ensuing threat assessment process yields a determination of the level and type of violence risk, and the need for any protective measures. The majority of the communications referred for examination are determined to represent low risk of violence. Others, however, are considered to represent significant risk of harm and to require actions to eliminate or diminish the threat.

Since the office responsible for court security has not yet cataloged its threatening communications, we cannot ensure that this sample is perfectly representative of all threatening communications received by the courts. Plans to implement such a database are under development. In addition, we do not have a sample of communications to judges that the recipients themselves did not find sufficiently threatening to refer for assessment, nor do we know the prevalence of such communications.

This pilot study represents an attempt to use computational linguistic analysis to explore what aspects of written communications to judges result in the perception of threat and the determination of risk level. We analyzed a sample of documents referred by their recipients as potentially threatening. In this sample we found evidence of direct or implied threat of violence in a small minority of examples. An expert rater categorized only one communication as indicating a high level of threat. Evidence of mental illness on the part of the senders was found in the majority of examples (80 percent).

Possible explanations for the disparity between the universal perceptions of threat by recipients and expert assessment of threat may include a combination of the following:

1. The very act of sending an argumentative or hostile communication to a judge represents a breach of normative behavior, and suggests that the sender may have difficulty controlling hostile impulses and maintaining appropriate boundaries.

2. The popular belief that mental illness is associated with a high risk of violence may increase the likelihood that communications containing evidence of psychotic beliefs and other forms of disordered thinking, but no evidence of threat, get referred by court personnel for further investigation.

3. Over-assessment of mental illness by the expert rater, in spite of efforts to be conservative in those ratings.

4. Under-assessment of violence risk by the expert rater, however it should be noted that documents spanned a period from 1995 to 2013 and there have been no episodes of violence against judges in that jurisdiction to date. Whether that represents the true level of actual risk or the successful efforts of court security personnel in managing the threat cannot be determined.

The purpose of the current pilot study was to explore if language technology could be used to identify those aspects of a communication that render it threatening to its recipients or correlate with expert assessment of the level of violence threat they present. We applied these tools to a relatively small group of 60 written communications sent to judges. A single forensic psychiatrist, experienced in threat and violence risk assessment, rated each document individually for the study factors. The results were promising, yet not dispositive, with regard to the ability of language technology to identify those factors that render a communication "threatening," are predictive of increased risk, or indicative of mental illness.

The next steps for this work include examination of a larger number of communications referred for assessment of possible increased risk of violence. Communications addressed to other public figures, as well as organizations and their personnel, can be analyzed and compared to those received by judges. Progress on automating the extraction of text features that were manually annotated, including distinctive orthographic features (contextually inappropriate use of capitalization and emphasis), and number and titles of recipients would be valuable. In addition, it will be important to have the presence of indicators of mental illness and level of risk, rated independently by multiple experts in the field of threat assessment in a two part process. First, the documents will be rated in the absence of any contextual information. Second, evaluators will be provided with additional information regarding the individual's background and asked to rerate the communications.

8 Conclusion

Mental health professionals are asked to assess the risk of violence on a regular basis and in a wide variety of settings. The accuracy and reliability of this complex and challenging task increases with the amount of information available to the evaluator. To date, those charged with conducting these assessments have not utilized automated approaches for linguistic analysis to inform their assessments. The results of this pilot study suggest that such analysis may be a useful addition to the traditional tools currently used in violence threat assessment. The availability of such a tool could increase the accuracy and objectivity of currently applied threat assessment methods. However, more data is needed to train and build models, and fully test their utility. Supervised machine learning approaches, or more sophisticated topic models, may be needed to tackle the complexities of supporting violence risk assessment through language technology.

Acknowledgments We thank the anonymous reviewers and Jordan Boyd-Graber for their insightful comments.

References

American Psychiatric Association. 2000. *Diagnostic*

and statistical manual of mental disorders: DSM-IV-TR®. American Psychiatric Pub.

David M. Blei and John D. Lafferty. 2009. Topic models. *Text mining: classification, clustering, and applications*, 10:71.

David M Blei. 2012. Probabilistic topic models. *Communications of the ACM*, 55(4):77–84.

F Calhoun and S Weston. 2003. Contemporary threat management. *San Diego, CA: Specialized Training Services*.

Frederick S Calhoun. 1998. *Hunters and howlers: Threats and violence against federal judicial officials in the United States, 1789-1993*. Number 80. US Department of Justice, US Marshals Service.

Cindy K Chung and James W Pennebaker. 2011. Using computerized text analysis to assess threatening communications and behavior. *Threatening communications and behavior: Perspectives on the pursuit of public figures*, page 332.

E. B. Elbogen and S. C. Johnson. 2009. The intricate link between violence and mental disorder: Results from the national epidemiologic survey on alcohol and related conditions. *Archives of General Psychiatry*, 66(2):152–161, February.

Andrew Kachites McCallum. 2002. Mallet: A machine learning for language toolkit.

J. Reid Meloy and Jens Hoffmann. 2013. *International Handbook of Threat Assessment*. Oxford University Press.

John Monahan, Henry J Steadman, Paul S Appelbaum, Thomas Grisso, Edward P Mulvey, Loren H Roth, Pamela Clark Robbins, Stephen Banks, and Eric Silver. 2006. The classification of violence risk. *Behavioral sciences & the law*, 24(6):721–730.

James W Pennebaker, Martha E Francis, and Roger J Booth. 2001. Linguistic inquiry and word count: LIWC 2001. *Mahway: Lawrence Erlbaum Associates*, page 71.

James W Pennebaker, Cindy K Chung, et al. 2008. Computerized text analysis of al-qaeda transcripts. *A content analysis reader*, pages 453–465.

Vernon L. Quinsey, Grant T. Harris, Marnie E. Rice, and Catherine A. Cormier. 1998. *Violent offenders: Appraising and managing risk.* American Psychological Association.

Antonio P. Sanfilippo. 2010. *Content Analysis for Proactive Protective Intelligence*. Pacific Northwest National Laboratory.

Mario J Scalora, Jerome V Baumgartner, Mary A Hatch Maillette, Christmas N Covell, Russell E Palarea, Jason A Krebs, David O Washington, William Zimmerman, and David Callaway. 2003. Risk factors for approach behavior toward the US congress. *Journal of threat assessment*, 2(2):3555.

André Simons and Ronald Tunkel. 2013. The assessment of anonymous threatening communications. *International Handbook of Threat Assessment*, pages 195–213.

Jennifer L Skeem and John Monahan. 2011. Current directions in violence risk assessment. *Current Directions in Psychological Science*, 20(1):38–42.

S Smith and R Shuy. 2002. Forensic psycholinguistics: using language analysis for identifying and assessing offenders. *FBI Law Enforcement Bulletin*, 71(4):1621.

S Smith. 2008. From violent words to violent deeds: assessing risk from FBI threatening communication cases. *Stalking, Threatening, and Attacking Public Figures: a psychological and behavioral analysis*, page 435455.

H. J. Steadman, E.P. Mulvey, J. Monahan, and et al. 1998. Violence by people discharged from acute psychiatric inpatient facilities and by others in the same neighborhoods. *Archives of General Psychiatry*, 55(5):393–401, May.

Jeffrey Swanson, Charles Holzer, Vijay Ganju, and Robert Jono. 1990. Violence and psychiatric disorder in the community: evidence from the epidemiologic catchment area surveys. *Hospital & community psychiatry*, 41(7):761–770, July. PMID: 2142118.

Christopher D Webster, Kevin S Douglas, Derek Eaves, and Stephen D Hart. 1982. Assessing risk for violence, version 2 (hcr-20). *Sigma*, 1993:1997.

Detecting linguistic idiosyncratic interests in autism using distributional semantic models

Masoud Rouhizadeh[†], **Emily Prud'hommeaux**[°], **Jan van Santen**[†], **Richard Sproat**[§]
[†]Center for Spoken Language Understanding, Oregon Health & Science University
[°]Center for Language Sciences, University of Rochester
[§] Google, Inc.
{rouhizad,vansantj}@ohsu.edu, emilypx@gmail.com, rws@xoba.com

Abstract

Children with autism spectrum disorder often exhibit idiosyncratic patterns of behaviors and interests. In this paper, we focus on measuring the presence of idiosyncratic interests at the linguistic level in children with autism using distributional semantic models. We model the semantic space of children's narratives by calculating pairwise word overlap, and we compare the overlap found within and across diagnostic groups. We find that the words used by children with typical development tend to be used by other children with typical development, while the words used by children with autism overlap less with those used by children with typical development and even less with those used by other children with autism. These findings suggest that children with autism are veering not only away from the topic of the target narrative but also in idiosyncratic semantic directions potentially defined by their individual topics of interest.

1 Introduction

Autism spectrum disorder (ASD) is a neurodevelopmental disorder characterized by impaired communication and social behavior. One of the core deficits associated with ASD is an intense preoccupation with a restricted set of interests (American Psychiatric Association, 2000; American Psychiatric Association, 2013), which can often be observed in an individual's tendency to perseverate on specific, idiosyncratic topics of conversation. Because this symptom is explicitly mentioned among the diagnostic criteria for ASD used in the DSM-IV and DSM-5, many diagnostic instruments (Lord et al., 2002; Rutter et al., 2003) require a qualitative assessment of this phenomenon. Instances of perseveration on a particular topic in the spontaneous spoken language of children with ASD, however, are not typically explicitly counted in a clinical setting, making comparisons with typically developing children difficult to quantify.

Expert manual analysis of conversations and narratives of individuals with ASD has shown that children and teenagers with autism include significantly more bizarre and irrelevant content in their narratives (Loveland et al., 1990; Losh and Capps, 2003) and introduce more abrupt topic changes in their conversations (Lam et al., 2012) than their typically developing peers. Automatic detection of poor topic maintenance has also been explored using techniques originally developed for information extraction (Rouhizadeh et al., 2013). There has been little work, however, in annotating the precise direction of the departure from a target topic. Thus, it is not clear whether children with ASD are instigating similar topic changes or pursuing idiosyncratic directions in their narratives and conversations consistent with their restricted interests.

In this paper, we attempt to automatically identify topic changes and idiosyncratic interests expressed in the language of children with ASD by measuring the semantic similarity of narrative retellings produced by children with and without ASD. We first use word overlap measures to calculate the semantic similarity between every possible pair of narratives. We then build three pairwise comparison matrices: one comparing pairs of typically developing (TD) children; one comparing pairs of children with ASD; and a third com-

Workshop on Computational Linguistics and Clinical Psychology: From Linguistic Signal to Clinical Reality, pages 46–50,
Baltimore, Maryland USA, June 27, 2014.

paring pairs consisting of one child with ASD and one child with TD. We calculate the significance of the differences between the pairs in the three matrices using the Monte Carlo method to shuffle the diagnosis label of each child.

We find that TD children share the greatest word overlap with one another, while children with ASD have significantly less word overlap with TD children and even less word overlap with other ASD children. These results indicate that TD children tend to adhere to the target topic in the narrative retellings, while children with ASD often stray from the target topic. Furthermore, the fact that the word choices of an individual child with ASD seem not to resemble the word choices of other children with ASD suggests that when a child with ASD chooses to abandon the target topic, he or she does so in an idiosyncratic way. Although these results are only indirect indications of the presence of restricted interests, the work presented here highlights the potential of computational language analysis methods for improving our understanding of the social and linguistic deficits associated with the disorder.

2 Data

Participants in this study included 39 children with typical development (TD) and 21 children with autism spectrum disorder (ASD). ASD was diagnosed via clinical consensus according to the DSM-IV-TR criteria (American Psychiatric Association, 2000) and the established threshold scores on two diagnostic instruments: the Autism Diagnostic Observation Schedule (ADOS) (Lord et al., 2002), a semi-structured series of activities designed to allow an examiner to observe behaviors associated with autism; and the Social Communication Questionnaire (SCQ) (Rutter et al., 2003), a parental questionnaire. None of the children in this study met the criteria for a language impairment, and there were no significant between-group differences in age (mean=6.3) or full-scale IQ (mean=115.5).

The narrative retelling task analyzed here is the Narrative Memory subtest of the NEPSY (Korkman et al., 1998), a large and comprehensive battery of tasks that test neurocognitive functioning in children. The NEPSY Narrative Memory (NNM) subtest is a narrative retelling test in which the subject listens to a brief narrative about a boy and his dog and then must retell the narrative to the examiner. Under standard administration, the NNM free recall score is calculated by counting how many from a set of 17 story elements were used in a retelling. Following the free recall portion of the test is the cued recall task, in which the examiner then asks the subject to provide answers to questions about all of the story elements that were omitted in the retelling.

The NNM was administered to each participant in the study, and each participant's retelling was recorded and transcribed. The responses for the cued recall portion of the subtest were not included in this work presented here. There was no significant difference between the two diagnostic groups in the standard NNM free recall score.

3 Methods

We expect that two different retellings of the same source will lie in the same lexico-semantic space. As a result, they should include high percentage of overlapping words. When a pair of retellings has a low word overlap measure, it could be that one or both retellings include intrusions from unrelated topics. An alternative explanation is that the subjects recalled a non-overlapping set of story elements or simply a small set of story elements. However, since we did not find any significant difference between the TD and ASD groups in the standard narrative recall score, we infer that a low percentage of word overlap indicates a difference in topic between the two retellings.

3.1 Word overlap measures

In order to calculate the similarity between a pair of narratives i and j, we use type and token overlap measures based on the Jaccard similarity coefficient. Token similarity is defined as the size of intersection of the words (i.e., the actual number of tokens in common) in narratives i and j relative to the size of the union of the words in the two narratives (i.e., summing over all tokens in both narratives, the maximum number of instances of that token in either narrative). Type similarity is defined as the size of intersection of the types (i.e., unique words) in narratives i and j relative to the size of the union of the types in the two narratives. For instance, for the following set of words i and j:

$i = \{a, b, c, d, c\}$
$j = \{a, c, e, c, a, a\}$,

the token intersection is equal to {a, c, c} and

	Group Means		
	TD.TD	TD.ASD	ASD.ASD
Type Overlap	.23	.17	.13
Token Overlap	.19	.14	.11

Table 3: Word overlap pairwise group means

the token union is {a, a, a, c, c, b, e, d}. The token overlap similarity between the two sets i and j is therefore 3/8. The type intersection of i and j is equal to {a, c} and the type union is {a, c, b, e, d}, yielding a type overlap similarity of 2/5.

3.2 Pairwise similarity matrix

We next build a similarity matrix for the type and token overlap measures, comparing every possible pair of children. Every child in the TD and ASD groups is compared to the children in his own group (TD.TD and ASD.ASD), as well as the children in the other group (TD.ASD). The pairwise similarity matrix is diagonally symmetrical, and we thus consider only the top right section of the matrix above the diagonal in our analysis.

3.3 Monte Carlo permutation

Since we may not have enough information to make an assumption that the pairwise similarity measures of all children are from a particular distribution, we utilize a non-parametric procedure, the Monte Carlo permutation approach, which is widely used in non-standard significance testing situations.

Given the three sub-matrices in the similarity matrix described above (TD.TD, TD.ASD, and ASD.ASD), we first calculate for each pair of sub-matrices (e.g., TD.TD vs ASD.ASD) three statistics that compare all cells in one submatrix with the cells in other submatrices: the difference between the means, t-statistics (using the Welch Two Sample t-test), and w-statistics (using the Wilcoxon rank sum test). We label these observed values *observed-mean*, *observed-t*, and *observed-w*. We next take a large random sample with replacement from all possible permutations of the data by shuffling the diagnosis labels of the children 1000 times, and then calculate each of the three above statistics for each shuffle. Finally, we determine the number of times the observed values exceed the values generated by the 1000 shuffles.

4 Results

The comparison of the group means of each of the three sub-matrices described in Section 3.2 show that TD children have the greatest overlap with each other; children with ASD have less word overlap with TD children than TD children have with one another and even less word overlap with other ASD children. The group means of both type and token overlap are summarized in Table 3. In addition, examples of overlapping and non-overlapping terms between the groups are provided in Tables 1 and 2 respectively.

The level plot of the pairwise token overlap is shown in figure 1. We see that the TD.TD sub-matrix has the lightest color, indicating higher overlap, followed by TD.ASD. The ASD.ASD submatrix has the darkest color, indicating low word overlap.

In the next step, we determine the significance of the group mean differences. As described in Section 3.3, using the Monte Carlo permutation to test the significance of the following comparisons: TD.TD vs ASD.ASD, TD.TD vs TD.ASD, and TD.ASD vs ASD.ASD. The results of these signif-

Group	Top 10 overlapping words
TD.TD	*shoe, tree, climb, ladder, fall, Pepper, Jim, dog, sister, branch*
TD.ASD	*shoe, tree, Jim, climb, dog, ladder, Pepper, fall, branch, sister*
ASD.ASD	*shoe, tree, Jim, dog, climb, Pepper, ladder, branch, boy, run*

Table 1: Top 10 overlapping words between the groups

Group	Examples of non-overlapping words
TD.TD	*coconut, couch, jew, lie, picture, spike, stuff, t-rex, tight, watch*
TD.ASD	*arm, bottom, cousin, doctor, eat, fruit, giant, meat, push, sense*
ASD.ASD	*bite, bridge, crunch, donut, gadget, lizard, microphone, sell, table, vision*

Table 2: Examples of non-overlapping words between the groups

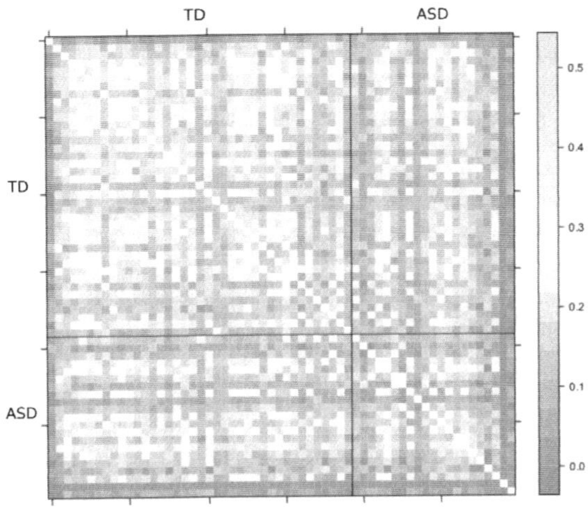

Figure 1: Level plot of the pairwise token overlap (lighter colors indicate higher overlap)

icance tests are summarized in table 4, and in all cases the differences are significant at $p < 0.05$.

5 Conclusions and future work

The methods presented for comparing the lexical choices made by children with and without ASD while generating a narrative retelling demonstrate the utility of language analysis for revealing diagnostically interesting information. The low rates of word overlap between retellings produced by children with ASD and those produced by typically developing children suggest that the children with ASD are having difficulty maintaining the target topic. Furthermore, the low overlap between pairs of children with ASD suggests that children with ASD are not straying from the topic in similar ways but are instead exploring topics that are of idiosyncratic interest.

These findings can be potentially used for diagnostic purposes in combinations of other applications of speech and language processing for automated narrative retelling assessment (Lehr et al., 2013), detection of off-topic words (Rouhizadeh et al., 2013), and pragmatic deficits (Prud'hommeaux and Rouhizadeh, 2012). From a clinical standpoint, diagnostic measures utilizing these methods for automated evaluation of disordered language could be very useful in diagnosis and planning interventions.

One major focus of our future work will be to manually annotate the narrative retellings used in this study to determine the frequency of topic departures and the nature of these departures. Given the vocabulary differences seen here, we expect to find not only that children with ASD are abandoning the topic of the source narrative more frequently than children with typical development but also that the topics they choose to pursue are related to their own individual specific interests.

A second area we hope to explore is the use of external resources, such as WordNet, to expand the set of terms used to calculate word overlap. It is perfectly reasonable to expect that people will use synonyms and paraphrases in their narrative retellings. It is therefore possible that children with autism are discussing the appropriate topic but choosing unusual words within that topic space in their retellings, which could be consistent with the type of atypical language often observed in children with ASD. By considering semantic overlap rather than simple word overlap, we may be able to distinguish instances of atypical language from true examples of poor topic maintenance.

Third, we are also interested in applying the analysis described above to a set of retellings from seniors with and without mild cognitive impairment, a frequent precursor to dementia. Like children with ASD, seniors with dementia are also more likely to include irrelevant information in

overlap	*statistic*	***p-values***		
		TD.TD vs ASD.ASD	TD.TD vs TD.ASD	TD.ASD vs ASD.ASD
Type Overlap	Means	.004	.042	.008
	t.test	.009	.012	.008
	Wilcoxon test	.004	.002	.002
Token Overlap	Means	.012	.034	.028
	t.test	.014	.022	.022
	Wilcoxon test	.012	.002	.002

Table 4: Monte Carlo significance test results

their narrative retellings. These intrusions, however, are often informed by real-world knowledge, and thus may not result in a decrease in measures of word overlap with narratives produced by unimpaired individuals.

Finally, we plan to apply our methods to the output of an automatic speech recognition (ASR) system rather than manual transcripts. Although the ASR output is likely to contain many errors, the fact that our methods focus on content words may make them robust to the sorts of function word recognition errors typically produced by ASR systems.

Acknowledgments

This work was supported in part by NSF grant #BCS-0826654, and NIH NIDCD grants #R01-DC007129 and #1R01DC012033-01. Any opinions, findings, conclusions or recommendations expressed in this publication are those of the authors and do not necessarily reflect the views of the NSF or the NIH.

References

American Psychiatric Association. 2000. *DSM-IV-TR: Diagnostic and Statistical Manual of Mental Disorders*. American Psychiatric Publishing, Washington, DC.

American Psychiatric Association. 2013. *Diagnostic and statistical manual of mental disorders (5th ed.)*. American Psychiatric Publishing, Washington, DC.

Marit Korkman, Ursula Kirk, and Sally Kemp. 1998. *NEPSY: A developmental neuropsychological assessment*. The Psychological Corporation, San Antonio.

Yan Grace Lam, Siu Sze, and Susanna Yeung. 2012. Towards a convergent account of pragmatic language deficits in children with high-functioning autism: Depicting the phenotype using the pragmatic rating scale. *Research in Autism Spectrum Disorders*, 6(2):792–797.

Maider Lehr, Izhak Shafran, Emily Prud'hommeaux, and Brian Roark. 2013. Discriminative joint modeling of lexical variation and acoustic confusion for automated narrative retelling assessment. In *Proceedings of the Conference of the North American Chapter of the Association for Computational Linguistics: Human Language Technologies*.

Catherine Lord, Michael Rutter, Pamela DiLavore, and Susan Risi. 2002. *Autism Diagnostic Observation Schedule (ADOS)*. Western Psychological Services, Los Angeles.

Molly Losh and Lisa Capps. 2003. Narrative ability in high-functioning children with autism or asperger's syndrome. *Journal of Autism and Developmental Disorders*, 33(3):239–251.

Katherine Loveland, Robin McEvoy, and Belgin Tunali. 1990. Narrative story telling in autism and down's syndrome. *British Journal of Developmental Psychology*, 8(1):9–23.

Emily Prud'hommeaux and Masoud Rouhizadeh. 2012. Automatic detection of pragmatic deficits in children with autism. In *Proceedings of the 3rd Workshop on Child, Computer and Interaction (WOCCI)*.

Masoud Rouhizadeh, Emily Prud'hommeaux, Brian Roark, and Jan van Santen. 2013. Distributional semantic models for the evaluation of disordered language. In *Proceedings of the Conference of the North American Chapter of the Association for Computational Linguistics: Human Language Technologies*.

Michael Rutter, Anthony Bailey, and Catherine Lord. 2003. *Social Communication Questionnaire (SCQ)*. Western Psychological Services, Los Angeles.

Quantifying Mental Health Signals in Twitter

Glen Coppersmith   Mark Dredze   Craig Harman
Human Language Technology Center of Excellence
Johns Hopkins University
Balitmore, MD, USA

Abstract

The ubiquity of social media provides a rich opportunity to enhance the data available to mental health clinicians and researchers, enabling a better-informed and better-equipped mental health field. We present analysis of mental health phenomena in publicly available Twitter data, demonstrating how rigorous application of simple natural language processing methods can yield insight into specific disorders as well as mental health writ large, along with evidence that as-of-yet undiscovered linguistic signals relevant to mental health exist in social media. We present a novel method for gathering data for a range of mental illnesses quickly and cheaply, then focus on analysis of four in particular: post-traumatic stress disorder (PTSD), depression, bipolar disorder, and seasonal affective disorder (SAD). We intend for these proof-of-concept results to inform the necessary ethical discussion regarding the balance between the utility of such data and the privacy of mental health related information.

1 Introduction

While mental health issues pose a significant health burden on the general public, mental health research lacks the quantifiable data available to many physical health disciplines. This is partly due to the complexity of the underlying causes of mental illness and partly due to longstanding societal stigma making the subject all but taboo. Lack of data has hampered mental health research in terms of developing reliable diagnoses and effective treatment for many disorders. Moreover, population-level analysis via traditional methods is time consuming, expensive, and often comes with a significant delay.

In contrast, social media is plentiful and has enabled diverse research on a wide range of topics, including political science (Boydstun et al., 2013), social science (Al Zamal et al., 2012), and health at an individual and population level (Paul and Dredze, 2011; Dredze, 2012; Aramaki et al., 2011; Hawn, 2009). Of the numerous health topics for which social media has been considered, mental health may actually be the most appropriate. A major component of mental health research requires the study of behavior, which may be manifest in how an individual acts, how they communicate, what activities they engage in and how they interact with the world around them including friends and family. Additionally, capturing population level behavioral trends from Web data has previously provided revolutionary capabilities to health researchers (Ayers et al., 2014). Thus, social media seems like a perfect fit for studying mental health in both individual and overall trends in the population. Such topics have already been the focus of several studies (Coppersmith et al., 2014; De Choudhury et al., 2014; De Choudhury et al., 2013d; De Choudhury et al., 2013b; De Choudhury et al., 2013c; Ayers et al., 2013).

What can we expect to learn about mental health by studying social media? How does a service like Twitter inform our knowledge in this area? Numerous studies indicate that language use, social expression and interaction are telling indicators of mental health. The well-known Linguistic Inquiry Word Count (LIWC), a validated tool for the psychometric analysis of language data (Pennebaker et al., 2007), has been repeatedly used to study language associated with all types of disorders (Resnik et al., 2013; Alvarez-Conrad et al., 2001; Tausczik and Pennebaker, 2010). Furthermore, social media is by nature *social*, which means that social patterns, a critical part of mental health and illness, may be readily observable in raw Twitter data. Thus, Twitter and other social media provide

Workshop on Computational Linguistics and Clinical Psychology: From Linguistic Signal to Clinical Reality, pages 51–60,
Baltimore, Maryland USA, June 27, 2014. ©2014 Association for Computational Linguistics

a unique quantifiable perspective on human behavior that may otherwise go unobserved, suggesting it as a powerful tool for mental health researchers.

The main vehicle for studying mental health in social media has been the use of surveys, e.g., depression battery (De Choudhury, 2013) or personality test (Schwartz et al., 2013), to determine characteristics of a user coupled with analyzing their corresponding social media data. Work in this area has mostly focused on depression (De Choudhury et al., 2013d; De Choudhury et al., 2013b; De Choudhury et al., 2013c), and the number of users is limited by those that can complete the appropriate survey. For example, De Choudhury et al. (2013d) solicited Twitter users to take the CES-D and to share their public Twitter profile, analyzing linguistic and behavioral patterns. While this type of study has produced high quality data, it is limited in size (by survey respondents) and scope (to diagnoses which have a battery amenable to administration over the internet).

In this paper we examine a range of mental health disorders using *automatically derived* samples from large amounts of Twitter data. Rather than rely on surveys, we automatically identify self-expressions of mental illness diagnoses and leverage these messages to construct a labeled data set for analysis. Using this dataset, we make the following contributions:

- We demonstrate the effectiveness of our automatically derived data by showing that statistical classifiers can differentiate users with four different mental health disorders: depression, bipolar, post traumatic stress disorder and seasonal affective disorder.
- We conduct a LIWC analysis of each disorder to measure deviations in each illness group from a control group, replicating previous findings for depression and providing new findings for bipolar, PTSD and SAD.
- We conduct an open-vocabulary analysis that captures language use relevant to mental health beyond what is captured with LIWC.

Our results open the door to a range of large scale analysis of mental health issues using Twitter.

2 Related Work

For a good retrospective and prospective summary of the role of social media in mental health research, we refer the reader to De Choudhury (2013). De Choudhury identifies ways in which NLP has and can be used on social media data to produce what the relevant mental health literature would predict, both at an individual level and a population level. She proceeds to identify ways in which these types of analyses can be used in the near and far term to influence mental health research and interventions alike.

Differences in language use have been observed in the personal writing of students who score highly on depression scales (Rude et al., 2004), forum posts for depression (Ramirez-Esparza et al., 2008), self narratives for PTSD (He et al., 2012; D'Andrea et al., 2011; Alvarez-Conrad et al., 2001), and chat rooms for bipolar (Kramer et al., 2004). Specifically in social media, differences have previously been observed between depressed and control groups (as assessed by internet-administered batteries) via LIWC: depressed users more frequently use first person pronouns (Chung and Pennebaker, 2007) and more frequently use negative emotion words and anger words on Twitter, but show no differences in positive emotion word usage (Park et al., 2012). Similarly, an increase in negative emotion and first person pronouns, and a decrease in third person pronouns, (via LIWC) is observed, as well as many manifestations of literature findings in the pattern of life of depressed users (e.g., social engagement, demographics) (De Choudhury et al., 2013d). Differences in language use in social media via LIWC have also been observed between PTSD and control groups (Coppersmith et al., 2014).

For population-level analysis, surveys such as the Behavioral Risk Factor Surveillance System (BRFSS) are conducted via telephone (Centers for Disease Control and Prevention (CDC), 2010). Some of these surveys cover relatively few participants (often in the thousands), have significant cost, and have long delays between data collection and dissemination of the findings. However, De Choudhury et al. (2013c) presents a promising population-level analysis of depression that highlights the role of NLP and social media.

3 Data

All data we obtain is public, posted between 2008 and 2013, and made available from Twitter via their application programming interface (API). Specifically, this does **not** include any data that has

Genuine Statements of Diagnosis
In loving memory my mom, she was only 42, I was 17 & taken away from me. I was diagnosed with having P.T.S.D LINK
So today I started therapy, she diagnosed me with anorexia, depression, anxiety disorder, post traumatic stress disorder and wants me to
@USER The VA diagnosed me with PTSD, so I can't go in that direction anymore
I wanted to share some things that have been helping me heal lately. I was diagnosed with severe complex PTSD and... LINK
Disingenuous Statements of Diagnosis
"I think I'm I'm diagnosed with SAD. Sexually active disorder" -anonymous
LOL omg my bro the "psychologist" just diagnosed me with seasonal ADHD AHAHAHAAAAAAAAAAA IM DYING.
The winter blues: Yesterday I was diagnosed with seasonal affective disorder. Now, this sounds a lot more dramat... LINK

Table 1: Examples found via regular expression keyword search for diagnosis tweets.

been marked as 'private' by the author or any direct messages.

Diagnosed Group We seek users who publicly state that they have been diagnosed with various mental illnesses. Users may make such a statement to seek support from others in their social network, to fight the taboo of mental illness, or perhaps as an explanation of some of their behavior. Tweets were obtained using regular expressions on a large multi-year health related collection, e.g. "I was diagnosed with X." We searched for four conditions: depression, bipolar disorder, post traumatic stress disorder (PTSD) and seasonal affective disorder (SAD). The matched diagnosis tweets were manually labeled as to whether the tweet contained a genuine statement of a mental health diagnosis. Table 1 shows examples of both genuine statements of diagnosis and disingenuous statements (often jokes or quotes).

Next, we retrieved the most recent tweets (up to 3200) for each user with a genuine diagnosis tweet. We then filtered the users to remove those with fewer than 25 tweets and those whose tweets were not at least 75% in English (measured using the Compact Language Detector[1]). These filtering steps left us with users that were considered positive examples. Table 2 indicates the number of users and tweets found for each of the mental health categories examined. We manually examined and annotated only half the diagnosis statements for depression – indicating there are likely 800-900 depression users available via these automatic methods from our collection, compared to the 117 obtained via the methods of De Choudhury et al. (2013d). Additionally, we emphasize the low cost and effort of our automated effort as compared to their crowdsourced survey methods. The difference in collection methods also suggests that the two have a reasonable chance of being complementary. This is especially significant when considering disorders with lower incidence rates than depression (arguably the highest), where respondents to crowdsourced surveys or self-stated diagnoses alike are rare.

This method is similar in spirit to that of De Choudhury et al. (2013c), where they inferred a tweet-level classifier for depression from user-level labels (specifically, tweets from the past three months from users scoring highly on CES-D for the positive class and conversely for the negative).

Control Group To build models for analysis and to validate the data, we also need a sample of the general population to use as an approximation of community controls. We follow a similar process: randomly select 10k usernames from a list of Twitter users who posted to a separate random historical collection within a selected two week window, downloaded the 3200 most recent tweets from these users, and apply our two filters: at least 25 tweets and 75% English. This yields a control group of 5728 random users, whose 13.7 million tweets were used as negative examples.

Caveats Our method for finding users with mental health diagnoses has significant caveats: **1)** the method may only capture a subpopulation of each disorder (i.e., those who are speaking publicly about what is usually a very private matter), which may not truly represent all aspects of the population as a whole. **2)** This method in no way verifies whether this diagnosis is genuine (i.e., people are not always truthful in self-reports). However, given the stigma often associated with mental illness, it seems unlikely users would tweet that they are diagnosed with a condition they do not have. **3)** The control group is likely contami-

[1]https://code.google.com/p/cld2/

	Match	Users	Tweets
Bipolar	6k	394	992k
Depression	5k	441	1.0m
PTSD	477	244	573k
SAD	389	159	421k
Control	10k	5728	13.7m

Table 2: Number of users **match**ing the diagnosis regular expression, **users** labeled with genuine diagnoses and **tweets** retrieved from diagnosed users for each mental health condition.

nated by the presence of users that are diagnosed with the various conditions investigated. We make no attempt to remove these users, and if we assume that the prevalence of each disorder in the general population is similar in our control groups, we likely have hundreds of such diagnosed users contaminating our control training data. **4)** Twitter users are not an entirely representative sample of the population as a whole. Despite these caveats, we find that this method yielded promising results as discussed in the next sections.

Comorbidity Since some of these disorders have high comorbidity, there are some users in more than one class (e.g., those that state a diagnosis for PTSD and depression): Bipolar and depression have 19 users in common (4.8% of the bipolar users, 4.3% of the depression users), PTSD and depression share 10 (4.0% of PTSD, 2.2% of depression), and bipolar and PTSD share 9 (2.2% of bipolar, 3.6% of PTSD). Two users state diagnosis of bipolar, PTSD and depression (less than 1% of each set). No users stated diagnoses of both SAD and any other condition investigated.

4 Methods

We quantify various aspects of each user's language usage and pattern of life via automated methods, extracting features for subsequent machine learning. We use these to (1) replicate previous findings, (2) build classifiers to separate diagnosed from control users, and (3) introspect on those classifiers. Introspection here shows us what quantified signals in the content the classifiers base their decision on, and thus we can gain intuition about what signals are present in the content relevant to mental health.

4.1 Linguistic Inquiry Word Count (LIWC)

LIWC provides clinicians with a tool for gathering quantitative data regarding the state of a patient from the patient's writing (Pennebaker et al., 2007). Previous work has found signal in the 'positive affect' and 'negative affect' categories of the LIWC when applied to social media (including Twitter), so we examine their correlations separately, as well as in the context of other LIWC categories (De Choudhury et al., 2013a). In all, we examine some of the LIWC categories directly (*Swear*, *Anger*, *PosEmo*, *NegEmo*, *Anx*) and combine pronoun classes by linguistic form: *I* and *We* classes are combined to form *Pro1*, *You* becomes *Pro2* and *SheHe* and *They* become *Pro3*. Each of these classes provides one feature used by subsequent machine learning and our other analyses.

4.2 Language Models (LMs)

Language models are commonly used to estimate how likely a given sequence of words is. Generally, an n-gram language model refers to a model that examines strings of up to n words long. This is less than ideal for applications in social media: spelling errors, shortenings, space removal, and other aspects of social media data (especially Twitter) confounds many traditional word-based approaches. Thus, we employ two LMs, first a traditional 1-gram LM (ULM) that examines the probability of each whole word. Second, a character 5-gram LM (CLM) to examine sequences of up to 5 characters.

LMs model the likelihood of sequences from training data. In our case, we build one of each model from the positive class (tweets from one class of diagnosed users – e.g., PTSD), yielding ULM^+ and CLM^+. We also build one of each model from the negative class (control users), yielding ULM^- and CLM^-. We score each tweet by computing these probabilities and classifying it according to which model has a higher probability (e.g., for a given tweet, is $\text{ULM}^+ > \text{ULM}^-$?).

4.3 Pattern of Life Analytics

For brevity, we only briefly discuss the pattern of life analytics, since they do not depend on significant NLP. They examine how correlates found to be significant in the mental health literature may manifest and be measured in social media data. These are all imperfect proxies for the findings from the literature, but our experiments will demonstrate that they do collectively provide information relevant to mental health.

For each of the following analytics we extract one feature to use in subsequent machine learning. Social engagement has been correlated with

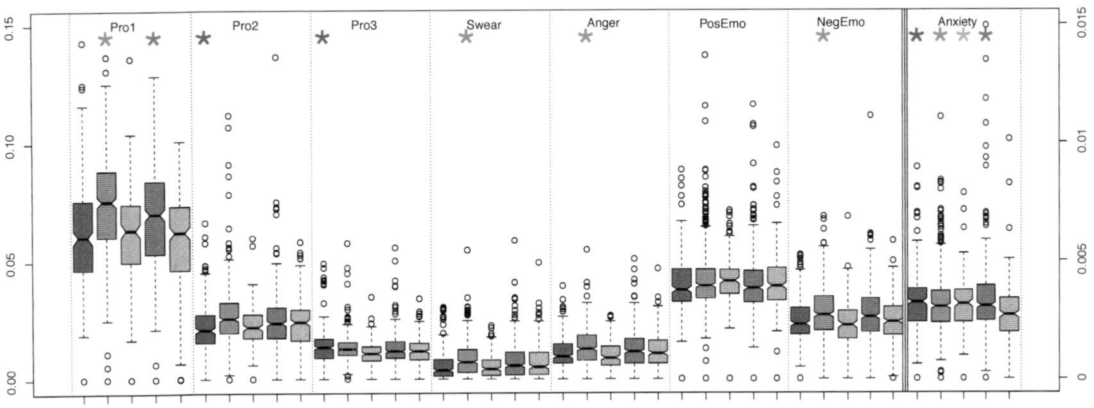

Figure 1: Box and whiskers plot of proportion of tweets each user has (y-axis) matching various LIWC categories. Each bar represents one LIWC category for one condition – PTSD in purple, depression in blue, SAD in orange, bipolar in red and control in gray. *Anxiety* occurs an order of magnitude less often than the others, so its proportion is on the right y-axis (and thus not comparable to the others). Statistically significant deviations from control users are denoted by asterisks.

positive mental health outcomes (Greetham et al., 2011; Berkman et al., 2000; Organization, 2001; De Choudhury et al., 2013d), which is difficult to measure directly so we examine various ways in which this may be manifest in a user's tweet stream: *Tweet rate* measures how often a twitter user posts (a measure of overall engagement with this social media platform) and *Proportion of tweets with @mentions* measures how often a user posts 'in conversation' (for lack of better terms) with other users. *Number of @mentions* is a measure of how often the user in question engages other users, while *Number of self @mentions* is a measure of how often the user responds to mentions of themselves (since users rarely include their own username in a tweet). To estimate the size of a user's social network, we calculate *Number of unique users @mentioned* and *Number of users @mentioned at least 3 times*, respectively.

For each of the following analytics, we calculate the proportion of a user's tweets that the analytic finds evidence in: *Insomnia* and sleep disturbance is often a symptom of mental health disorders (Weissman et al., 1996; De Choudhury et al., 2013d), so we calculate the proportion of tweets that a user makes between midnight and 4am according to their local timezone. *Exercise* has also been correlated with positive mental health outcomes (Penedo and Dahn, 2005; Callaghan, 2004), so we examine tweets mentioning one of a small set of exercise-related terms. We also use an English *sentiment* analysis lexicon from Mitchell et al. (2013) to score individual tweets according to the presence and valence of sentiment words. We apply no thresholds, so any tweet with a sentiment score above 0 was considered *positive*, below 0 was considered *negative*, and those with score 0 were considered to have *no sentiment*. Thus we use the proportion of *Insomnia*, *Exercise*, *Positive Sentiment* and *Negative Sentiment* tweets as features in subsequent machine learning and analysis.

5 Results

We present three types of experiments to evaluate the quality and character of these data, and to demonstrate some quantifiable mental health signals in Twitter. First, we validate our method for obtaining data by replicating previous findings using LIWC. Next, we build classifiers to distinguish each group from the control group, demonstrating that there is useful signal in the language of each group, and compare these classifiers. Finally, we analyze the correlations between our analytics and classifiers to uncover relationships between them and derive insight into quantifiable and relevant mental health signals in Twitter.

Validation First, we provide some validation for our novel method for gathering samples. We demonstrate that language use, as measured by LIWC, is statistically significantly different between control and diagnosed users. Figure 1 shows the proportion of tweets from each user that scores positively on various LIWC categories (i.e., have at least one word from that category). Box-and-whiskers plots (Tukey, 1977)[2] summarize a distribution of observations and ease com-

[2]For a modern implementation see Wickham (2009).

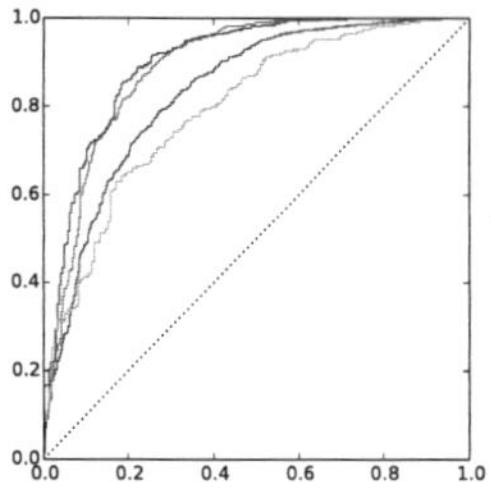

False Alarm:	**0.1**	**0.2**
Bipolar	0.64	0.82
Depression	0.48	0.68
PTSD	0.67	0.81
SAD	0.42	0.65

Figure 2: ROC curves for separating diagnosed from control users, compared across disorders: bipolar in red, depression in blue, PTSD in purple, SAD in orange. The precision (diagnosed, correctly labeled) for each disorder at false alarm (control, labeled as diagnosed) rates of 10% and 20% are shown to the right of the ROC curve. Chance performance is indicated by the dotted black line.

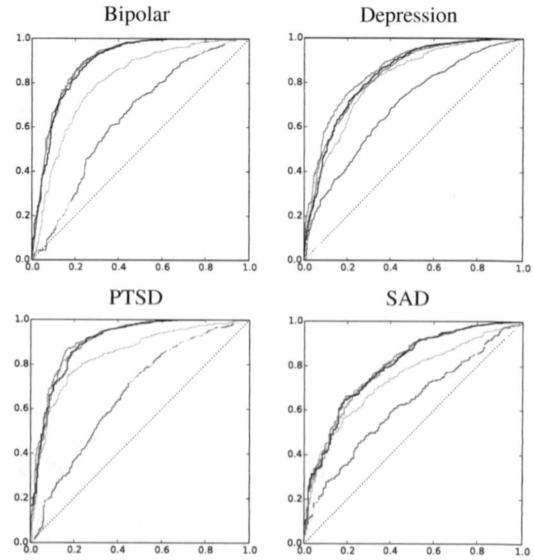

Figure 3: ROC curves of performance of individual analytics for each disorder: LIWC in blue, pattern of life in yellow, CLM in red, ULM in green, all in black. Chance performance is indicated by the dotted black line.

parison between them (here, each observation is the proportion of a user's tweets that score positively on LIWC). The median of the distribution is the black horizontal line in the middle of the bar, the bar covers the inter quartile range (where 50% of the observations lie), the whiskers are a robust estimate of the extent of the data, with outliers plotted as circles beyond the whiskers. An approximation of statistical significance is indicated by the pinched in notches on each bar. If the notches on the bars do not overlap, the differences between those distributions is different (α<0.05, 95% confidence interval). Each bar is colored according to diagnosis, and each group of 5 bars notes the scores for one LIWC category. Differences that reach statistical significance from the control group are noted with asterisks (e.g., *Pro1*, *Swear*, *Anger*, *NegEmo* and *Anxiety* are statistically significantly different for the depression group). Importantly, this replicates previous findings of significant differences between depressed users (according to an internet-administered diagnostic battery): significant increases are expected in *NegEmo*, *Anger*, *Pro1* and *Pro3* and no change in *PosEmo*, given all previous work (Park et al., 2012; Chung and Pennebaker, 2007; De Choudhury et al., 2013d). We replicate all these findings except the increase in *Pro3* (which only De Choudhury et al. (2013d) found), which validates our data collection methods.

Classification We next explore the ability of the various analytics to separate diagnosed from control users and assess performance on a leave-one-out cross-validation task. We train a log linear classifier on the features described in §4 using scikit-learn (Pedregosa et al., 2011).

The receiver operating characteristic (ROC) curves in Figures 2 and 3 demonstrate performance of the various classifiers at the task of separating diagnosed from control groups. In all cases, the correct detections (or hits) are on the y-axis and the false detections (or false alarms) are on the x-axis. Figure 2 compares performance across diagnoses, one line per disorder.

Figure 3 shows one plot per mental health condition, with the performance of the various analytics, individually and in concert as individual ROC curves. A few trends emerge – **1)** All analytics show some ability to separate the classes, indicating they are finding useful signals. **2)** The LMs provide superior performance to the other analytics, indicating there are more signals present in the language than are captured by LIWC and pattern-of-life analytics. For readability we do not show the performance of all combinations of analytics, but they perform as expected: any set of them perform equal to or better than their individual components. Taken together, this indicates that there is information relevant to separating diagnosed users from controls in all the analytics discussed here. Furthermore, this highlights that there remains significant signals to be uncovered and understood in the language of social media.

These trends also allow us to compare the disorders as manifest in language usage, though this tends to raise more questions than it answers. Generally, the pattern-of-life analytics and LIWC are on par, but this is decidedly not true for depression, where pattern-of-life seems to perform especially poorly, and for SAD, where pattern-of-life seems to perform especially well. This indicates that the depression users have patterns-of-life that look more similar to the controls than is the case for the other disorders (perhaps especially surprising given the inclusion of the sentiment lexicon) and that there may be significant correlation between pattern-of-life factors and SAD.

5.1 Analytic Introspection

To examine correlations between the analytics and the linguistic content they depend on, we scored a random subset of 1 million tweets from control users with each of the linguistic analytics, and plot their Pearson's correlation coefficients (r) in Figure 4. A simple overlap of wordlists is not sufficient to assess the true utility of these methods since it does not take into account the frequency of occurrence of each word, nor the correlation between these words in real data (e.g., does a classifier based on the LIWC category *Swear* provide redundant information to the sentiment analysis). Each row and column in Figure 4 represents one of the 17 analytics, in the same order. Colors denote Bonferroni-corrected Pearson's r for statistically significant correlations between the analytic on the row and column. Correlations that do not reach statistical significance are in aquamarine (corresponding to r=0). Excluded for brevity is a sanity check of a χ^2 test between the analytics to assert they were scoring significantly differently.

The strong correlations between the various LIWC analytics, notably *Swear*, *Anger* and *NegEmo*, likely indicates that the analytics are triggered by the same word(s) – in this case profanity. Similarly for LIWC's *PosEmo* and the sentiment lexicon – 'happy' for example. The correlation between CLM for various diagnoses is particularly intriguingly, as it is in line with known patterns of comorbidity: major depressive disorder, PTSD, and bipolar all have observed comorbidity (Brady et al., 2000; Campbell et al., 2007; McElroy et al., 2001) while SAD is currently considered a specifier of major depressive disorder or bipolar disorder (American Psychiatric Association, 2013; Lurie et al., 2006), without published findings indicating comorbidity. Indeed our small

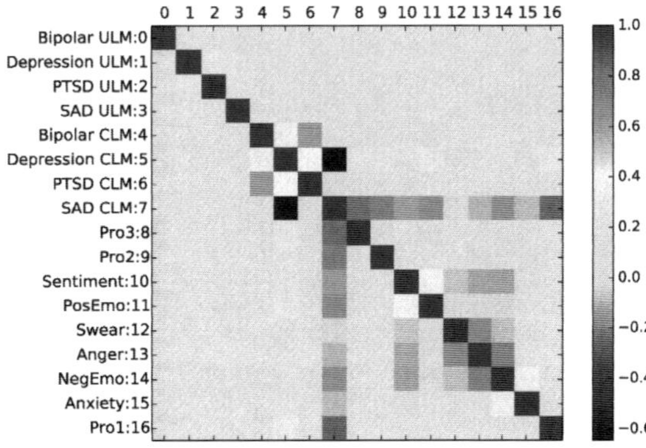

Figure 4: Pearson's r correlations between various analytics, color indicates the strength of statistically significant correlations, or 0 (aquamarine) otherwise. Bonferroni corrected, each comparison is significant only if α<0.0002). Rows and columns represent the analytics in the same order, so the diagonal is self-correlation.

sample dataset follows the same trends, where we observed users with multiple diagnoses exist within depression, PTSD, and bipolar, but none exist with SAD. The correlation observed is too large to be solely attributed to those users shared between the groups, though (correlations at most $r = 0.05$ would be attributable to that alone). Furthermore, when taken in combination with the different patterns exhibited by the groups as seen in Figure 1, this correlation is not solely attributable to LIWC categories either. At its core, these correlations seem to suggest that similar language is employed by users diagnosed with these occasionally comorbid disorders, and dissimilar language by users with SAD. This should be taken as merely suggestive of the type of analysis one could do, though, since the literature does not present a strong and clear prediction for the comorbidity and exhibited symptoms (to include language use).

Interestingly, the lack of (or negative) correlation between most of the analytics again highlights the complexity of the mental illnesses and the divergent signals it presents. Additionally, the lack of correlation between ULM and the other models is to be expected, since they are basing their scores on significantly more words (or different signals as is the case for CLM). Each one of these analytics is highly imperfect, and often give contradictory evidence, but when combined, the machine learning algorithms are able to sort through the conflicting signals with some success.

Analytic	Example Tweet Text
Bipolar LM	I'm insecure because being around your ex of 4 years little sister, makes me feel a slight bit uncomfortable. Ok.
Depression LM	Pain has a weird way of working. You're still the same person from before the pain, but that person is underneath & doesn't come out.
PTSD LM	Don't wanna get out my bed but I really need to get up & prepare myself for work
Sentiment(+)	NAME is absolutely unbelievable, he just gets better and better every time I see him. The best play in the world, no doubt about it.
Sentiment(-)	I hate losing people in my life. I try so hard to not let it happen
PosEmo	Wowee...that was a hectic day... Got more done than expected but so glad to be in bed now. Grateful for my supportive husband & loving pooch
Functioning	if i had a dollar for all the grammatical errors ive ever typed, my college tuition, book cost, and dorm rent would be paid in full
NegEmo	My tooth hurts, my neck hurts, my mouth hurts, my toungue hurts, my head hurts...kill me now.
Anx	don't stress over someone who is going to stress over you..
Anger	Ugly n arrogant sums everytin up.shdnt hv ffd her seff

Table 3: Example high scoring tweets from each analytic.

6 Conclusion

We demonstrate quantifiable signals in Twitter data relevant to bipolar disorder, major depressive disorder, post-traumatic-stress disorder and seasonal affective disorder. We introduce a novel method for automatic data collection and validate its veracity by **1)** replicating observations of significant differences between depressed and control user groups and **2)** constructing classifiers capable of separating diagnosed from control users for each disorder. This data allows us to demonstrate equivalent differences in language use (according to LIWC) for bipolar, PTSD, and SAD. Furthermore, we provide evidence that more information relevant to mental health is encoded in language use in social media (above and beyond that captured by methods based on the mental health literature). By examining correlations between the various analytics investigated, we provide some insight into what quantifiable linguistic information is captured by our classifiers. We finally demonstrate the utility of examining multiple disorders simultaneously and other larger analyses, difficult or impossible with other methods.

Crucially, we expect that these novel data collection methods can provide complementary information to existing survey-based methods, rather than supplant them. For many disorders rarer than depression (which has comparatively high incidence rates), we suspect that finding any data will be a challenge, in which case combining these methods with the existing survey collection methods may be the best way to obtain sufficient amounts of data for statistical analyses.

Since the LMs take more information into account when modeling the language usage of diagnosed and control users, it is unsurprising that they outperform LIWC and pattern-of-life analyses alone, but this is evidence of as-of-yet undiscovered linguistic differences between diagnosed and control users for all disorders investigated. Uncovering and interpreting these signals can be best accomplished through collaboration between NLP and mental health researchers.

Naturally, some caveats come with these results: while identifying genuine self-statements of diagnosis in Twitter works well for some conditions, others exist for which there were few or no diagnoses stated. For Alzheimer's, the demographic with the majority of diagnoses does not frequently use Twitter (or likely any social media). Eating disorders are also elusive via this method, though related automatic methods (e.g., using disorder-related hashtags) may address this. Finally, those willing to publicly reveal a mental health diagnosis may not be representative of the population suffering from that mental illness.

All these experiments, taken together, indicate that there are a diverse set of quantifiable signals relevant to mental health observable in Twitter. They indicate that individual- and population-level analyses can be made cheaper and more timely than current methods, yet there remains as-of-yet untapped information encoded in language use – promising a rich collaboration between the fields of natural language processing and mental health.

Acknowledgments: The authors would like to thank Kristy Hollingshead for thoughtful comments and contributions throughout this research.

References

Faiyaz Al Zamal, Wendy Liu, and Derek Ruths. 2012. Homophily and latent attribute inference: Inferring latent attributes of Twitter users from neighbors. In *Proceedings of the International AAAI Conference on Weblogs and Social Media (ICWSM)*.

Jennifer Alvarez-Conrad, Lori A. Zoellner, and Edna B. Foa. 2001. Linguistic predictors of trauma pathology and physical health. *Applied Cognitive Psychology*, 15(7):S159–S170.

American Psychiatric Association. 2013. *Diagnostic Statistical Manual 5*. American Psychiatric Association.

Eiji Aramaki, Sachiko Maskawa, and Mizuki Morita. 2011. Twitter catches the flu: Detecting influenza epidemics using twitter. In *Empirical Natural Language Processing Conference (EMNLP)*.

John W. Ayers, Benjamin M. Althouse, Jon-Patrick Allem, J. Niels Rosenquist, and Daniel E. Ford. 2013. Seasonality in seeking mental health information on google. *American journal of preventive medicine*, 44(5):520–525.

John W. Ayers, Benjamin M. Althouse, and Mark Dredze. 2014. Could behavioral medicine lead the web data revolution? *Journal of the American Medical Association (JAMA)*, February 27.

Lisa F. Berkman, Thomas Glass, Ian Brissette, and Teresa E. Seeman. 2000. From social integration to health: Durkheim in the new millennium? *Social Science & Medicine*, 51(6):843–857, September.

Amber Boydstun, Rebecca Glazier, Timothy Jurka, and Matthew Pietryka. 2013. Examining debate effects in real time: A report of the 2012 React Labs: Educate study. *The Political Communication Report*, 23(1), February. [Online; accessed 25-February-2014].

Kathleen T. Brady, Therese K. Killeen, Tim Brewerton, and Sylvia Lucerini. 2000. Comorbidity of psychiatric disorders and posttraumatic stress disorder. *Journal of Clinical Psychiatry*.

Patrick Callaghan. 2004. Exercise: a neglected intervention in mental health care? *Journal of Psychiatric and Mental Health Nursing*, 11:476–483.

Duncan G. Campbell, Bradford L. Felker, Chuan-Fen Liu, Elizabeth M. Yano, JoAnn E. Kirchner, Domin Chan, Lisa V. Rubenstein, and Edmund F. Chaney. 2007. Prevalence of depression-PTSD comorbidity: Implications for clinical practice guidelines and primary care-based interventions. *Journal of General Internal Medicine*, 22(6):711–718.

Centers for Disease Control and Prevention (CDC). 2010. Behavioral risk factor surveillance system survey data.

Cindy Chung and James Pennebaker. 2007. The psychological functions of function words. *Social communication*, pages 343–359.

Glen A. Coppersmith, Craig T. Harman, and Mark Dredze. 2014. Measuring post traumatic stress disorder in Twitter. In *Proceedings of the International AAAI Conference on Weblogs and Social Media (ICWSM)*.

Wendy D'Andrea, Pearl H. Chiu, Brooks R. Casas, and Patricia Deldin. 2011. Linguistic predictors of post-traumatic stress disorder symptoms following 11 September 2001. *Applied Cognitive Psychology*, 26(2):316–323, October.

Munmun De Choudhury, Scott Counts, and Eric Horvitz. 2013a. Major life changes and behavioral markers in social media: Case of childbirth. In *Proceedings of the ACM Conference on Computer Supported Cooperative Work and Social Computing (CSCW)*.

Munmun De Choudhury, Scott Counts, and Eric Horvitz. 2013b. Predicting postpartum changes in emotion and behavior via social media. In *Proceedings of the ACM Annual Conference on Human Factors in Computing Systems (CHI)*, pages 3267–3276. ACM.

Munmun De Choudhury, Scott Counts, and Eric Horvitz. 2013c. Social media as a measurement tool of depression in populations. In *Proceedings of the Annual ACM Web Science Conference*.

Munmun De Choudhury, Michael Gamon, Scott Counts, and Eric Horvitz. 2013d. Predicting depression via social media. In *Proceedings of the International AAAI Conference on Weblogs and Social Media (ICWSM)*.

Munmun De Choudhury, Andres Monroy-Hernandez, and Gloria Mark. 2014. " narco" emotions: Affect and desensitization in social media during the mexican drug war.

Munmun De Choudhury. 2013. Role of social media in tackling challenges in mental health. In *Proceedings of the 2nd International Workshop on Socially-Aware Multimedia*, pages 49–52.

Mark Dredze. 2012. How social media will change public health. *IEEE Intelligent Systems*, 27(4):81–84.

Danica Vukadinovic Greetham, Robert Hurling, Gabrielle Osborne, and Alex Linley. 2011. Social networks and positive and negative affect. *Procedia - Social and Behavioral Sciences*, 22:4–13, January.

Carleen Hawn. 2009. Take Two Aspirin And Tweet Me In The Morning: How Twitter, Facebook, And Other Social Media Are Reshaping Health Care. *Health Affairs*, 28(2):361–368.

Qiwei He, Bernard P. Veldkamp, and Theo de Vries. 2012. Screening for posttraumatic stress disorder using verbal features in self narratives: A text mining approach. *Psychiatry Research*.

Adam D. I. Kramer, Susan R. Fussell, and Leslie D. Setlock. 2004. Text analysis as a tool for analyzing conversation in online support groups. In *Proceedings of the ACM Annual Conference on Human Factors in Computing Systems (CHI)*.

Stephen J. Lurie, Barbara Gawinski, Deborah Pierce, and Sally J. Rousseau. 2006. Seasonal affective disorder. *American family physician*, 74(9).

Susan L. McElroy, Lori L. Altshuler, Trisha Suppes, Paul E. Keck, Mark A. Frye, Kirk D. Denicoff, Willem A. Nolen, Ralph W. Kupka, Gabriele S. Leverich, Jennifer R. Rochussen, A. John Rush Rush, and Robert M. Post Post. 2001. Axis I psychiatric comorbidity and its relationship to historical illness variables in 288 patients with bipolar disorder. *American Journal of Psychiatry*, 158(3):420–426.

Margaret Mitchell, Jacqueline Aguilar, Theresa Wilson, and Benjamin Van Durme. 2013. Open domain targeted sentiment. In *Proceedings of the 2013 Conference on Empirical Methods in Natural Language Processing*, pages 1643–1654.

World Health Organization. 2001. The world health report 2001 - Mental health: New understanding, new hope. Technical report, Genf, Schweiz.

Minsu Park, Chiyoung Cha, and Meeyoung Cha. 2012. Depressive moods of users portrayed in Twitter. In *Proceedings of the ACM SIGKDD Workshop on Healthcare Informatics (HI-KDD)*.

Michael J. Paul and Mark Dredze. 2011. You are what you tweet: Analyzing Twitter for public health. In *Proceedings of the International AAAI Conference on Weblogs and Social Media (ICWSM)*.

Fabian Pedregosa, Gaël Varoquaux, Alexandre Gramfort, Vincent Michel, Bertrand Thirion, Olivier Grisel, Mathieu Blondel, Peter Prettenhofer, Ron Weiss, Vincent Dubourg, Jake Vanderplas, Alexandre Passos, David Cournapeau, Matthieu Brucher, and Matthieu Perrot Édouard Duchesnay. 2011. scikit-learn: Machine learning in Python. *The Journal of Machine Learning Research*, 12:2825–2830.

Frank J. Penedo and Jason R. Dahn. 2005. Exercise and well-being: a review of mental and physical health benefits associated with physical activity. *Current Opinion in Psychiatry*, 18(2):189–193, March.

James W. Pennebaker, Cindy K. Chung, Molly Ireland, Amy Gonzales, and Roger J. Booth. 2007. *The development and psychometric properties of LIWC2007*.

Nairan Ramirez-Esparza, Cindy K. Chung, Ewa Kacewicz, and James W. Pennebaker. 2008. The psychology of word use in depression forums in English and in Spanish: Testing two text analytic approaches. In *Proceedings of the International AAAI Conference on Weblogs and Social Media (ICWSM)*.

Philip Resnik, Anderson Garron, and Rebecca Resnik. 2013. Using topic modeling to improve prediction of neuroticism and depression. In *Proceedings of the 2013 Conference on Empirical Methods in Natural*, pages 1348–1353.

Stephanie S. Rude, Eva-Maria Gortner, and James W. Pennebaker. 2004. Language use of depressed and depression-vulnerable college students. *Cognition & Emotion*, 18(8):1121–1133, December.

H. Andrew Schwartz, Johannes C. Eichstaedt, Margaret L. Kern, Lukasz Dziurzynski, Stephanie M. Ramones, Megha Agrawal, Achal Shah, Michal Kosinski, David Stillwell, Martin E. P. Seligman, and Lyle H. Ungar. 2013. Personality, gender, and age in the language of social media: The open-vocabulary approach. *PLOS One*, 8(9).

Yla R. Tausczik and James W. Pennebaker. 2010. The psychological meaning of words: LIWC and computerized text analysis methods. *Journal of Language and Social Psychology*, 29(1):24–54.

John W. Tukey. 1977. Box-and-whisker plots. *Exploratory Data Analysis*, pages 39–43.

Myrna M. Weissman, Roger C. Bland, Glorisa J. Canino, Carlo Faravelli, Steven Greenwald, Hai-Gwo Hwu, Peter R. Joyce, Eile G. Karam, Chung-Kyoon Lee, Joseph Lellouch, Jean-Pierre Lépine, Stephen C. Newman, Maritza Rubio-Stipec, J. Elisabeth Wells, Priya J. Wickramaratne, Hans-Ulrich Wittchen, and Eng-Kung Yeh. 1996. Cross-national epidemiology of major depression and bipolar disorder. *Journal of the American Medical Association (JAMA)*, 276(4):293–299.

Hadley Wickham. 2009. *ggplot2: elegant graphics for data analysis*. Springer.

Applying prosodic speech features in mental health care: An exploratory study in a life-review intervention for depression

Sanne M.A. Lamers
University of Twente
Psychology, Health, & Technology
the Netherlands
s.m.a.lamers@utwente.nl

Khiet P. Truong
University of Twente
Human Media Interaction
the Netherlands
k.p.truong@utwente.nl

Bas Steunenberg
UMC Utrecht
the Netherlands
b.steunenberg@umcutrecht.nl

Franciska de Jong
University of Twente
Human Media Interaction
the Netherlands
f.m.g.dejong@utwente.nl

Gerben J. Westerhof
University of Twente
Psychology, Health, & Technology
the Netherlands
g.j.westerhof@utwente.nl

Abstract

The present study aims to investigate the application of prosodic speech features in a psychological intervention based on life-review. Several studies have shown that speech features can be used as indicators of depression severity, but these studies are mainly based on controlled speech recording tasks instead of natural conversations. The present exploratory study investigated speech features as indicators of depression in conversations of a therapeutic intervention. The changes in the prosodic speech features pitch, duration of pauses, and total duration of the participant's speaking time were studied over four sessions of a life-review intervention for three older participants. The ecological validity of the dynamics observed for prosodic speech features could not be established in the present study. The changes in speech features differed from what can be expected in an intervention that is effective in decreasing depression and were inconsistent with each other for each of the participants. We suggest future research to investigate changes within the intervention sessions, to relate the changes in feature values to the topical content of the speech, and to relate the speech features directly to depression scores.

1 Introduction

Depression is a mood disorder that is mainly characterized by a sad mood or the loss of in terest and pleasure in nearly all activities in a period of at least two weeks (American Psychiatric Association, 2000). Depression disorders are the leading cause of disability and contribute largely to the burden of disease in middle- and high-income countries worldwide (Üstun et al., 2004). In 2012, more than 350 million people around the world suffered from depression symptoms (World Health Organization, 2012). To decrease the onset of depression disorders, early psychological interventions, i.e., psychological methods targeting behavioral change to reduce limitations or problems (Vingerhoets, Kop, & Soons, 2002), aiming at adults with depression symptoms or mild depression disorders are necessary. Meta-analytic findings show that psychological interventions reduce the incidence of depression disorders by 22%, indicating that prevention of new cases of depression disorders is indeed possible (Cuijpers et al., 2008).

To evaluate the effectiveness of interventions for depression and changes during the interventions, reliable and valid measures of depression severity are necessary. Depression severity is mostly measured by self-report questionnaires such as the Center for Epidemiologic Studies Depression scale (CES-D; Radloff, 1977), the Hamilton Depression Rating Scale (HAM-D; Hamilton, 1960), and the Beck Depression Inventory (Beck, Steer, & Brown, 1996). These self-report questionnaires often include items on mood and feelings. Moreover, questionnaire items may cover physical depression symptoms such as sleep disturbances, changes in weight

Workshop on Computational Linguistics and Clinical Psychology: From Linguistic Signal to Clinical Reality, pages 61–68,
Baltimore, Maryland USA, June 27, 2014.

and appetite, and loss in energy. However, in some target groups such as older adults these items can confound with health problems and physical diseases, which increase in old age. For these reasons, there is a need for valid and objective measures of depression severity. Not only to assess depression severity before and after therapy, but also to detect the dynamics during the therapy (Elliot, 2010).

1.1 Computational linguistics, speech analysis, and mental health care

It is commonly assumed and confirmed in several studies that emotions and mood can influence the speaking behavior of a person and the characteristics of the sound in speech (Kuny & Stassen, 1993; Scherer, Johnstone, & Klasmeyer, 2003). Already in 1954, Moses concluded that the voice and speech patterns of psychiatric patients differed from those of people without a psychiatric diagnosis. Clinicians observe the speech of depressed patients frequently as uniform, monotonous, slow, and with a low voice (Kuny & Stassen, 1993). A review by Sobin and Sackeim (1997) showed that depressed people differ from normal and other psychiatric groups on psychomotor symptoms such as speech. The speech of depressed patients is characterized by a longer pause duration, that is, an increased amount of time between speech utterances as well as by a reduced variability in mean vocal pitch.

More recently these insights have led to collaborative and multidisciplinary work between researchers from the fields of computational linguistics and mental health care. With the growing availability of models and algorithms for automated natural language processing that can be put to use in clinical scenarios, depression can now increasingly be measured based on the characteristics of the language used by patients, such as the frequency of verbal elements in a narrative that express a certain mood or sentiment (Pennebaker & Chung, 2011), and acoustic speech features. Because vocal acoustic features such as pause durations and pitch are biologically based, it has even been argued that they can serve as biomarkers of depression severity (Mundt et al., 2012). As a consequence, speech features such as pitch and pause durations can be used to estimate the severity of a depression.

To date, several studies investigated the validity of several speech features as indicators of depression. Indeed, the speech features pitch and speech loudness correlate significantly with global depression scores during recovery (Kuny & Stassen, 1993; Stassen, Kuny, & Hell, 1998). After recovery from depression, the speech pause time of depressed adults was no longer elongated (Hardy et al., 1984). These results indicate that prosodic speech features are valid measures of depression.

However, these studies have the limitation that the speech analyses are based on the recording of controlled speech based on tasks such as counting and reading out loud. Such speech recording tasks take place under ideal voice recording conditions (Cannizzaro, Harel, Reilly, Chappell, & Snyder, 2004), while speech analysis is more difficult when conducted outside a controlled setting, because of so-called noisy channel effects (Janssen, Tacke, de Vries, van den Broek, Westerink, Haselager, & IJsselsteijn, 2013). Moreover, controlled speech tasks are cognitively less demanding than free speech tasks (Alpert et al., 2011). This evokes the question whether speech features are also ecological valid, i.e., whether they can be used as indicators of depression severity, when measured during natural conversations instead of during the recording of controlled speech tasks (Bronfenbrenner, 1977).

A study on speech samples from video recordings of structured interviews revealed promising results: speaking rate and pitch variation, but not the percentage of pauses, showed a large correlation with depression rating scores (Cannizaro, Harel, Reilly, Chappell, & Snyder, 2004). Additional studies on the ecological validity of using prosodic speech features as indicator for depression are necessary.

1.2 Speech features as mood markers in a life-review intervention

In the present study the speech of older adults will be measured in four sessions of a psychological intervention, combining knowledge in the fields of computational linguistics and psychological interventions in mental health care. Because psychological interventions of depression have shown to be effective (e.g., Cuijpers, van Straten, & Smit, 2006) and are broadly implemented in mental health care, the measurement of speech features in psychological interventions is a promising application for the field of computational linguistics. For example, speech features can be used to provide direct feedback to both the therapist and patient on the severity and changes in severity of depression during the psychological intervention. Clinicians do not have the ability to differentiate precisely the duration of for example the patient's utterances and pauses (Alpert et al. 2001). There is also ample evidence that text mining techniques based on the frequency of certain terms can be applied to narratives from patients in order to monitor changes in mood (Pennebaker & Chung, 2011), and a recent study has shown that machines can better recognize certain emotions than lay people (Janssen et al., 2013), underlining once again the added value of automated speech analysis. To pave the way for future applications that would enable the use of speech features as a direct feedback mechanism, the first step is to gain more knowledge on the patterns in speech features and on how changes in these features can be considered as meaningful signals of patterns in psychological interventions.

The psychological intervention in the present study is based on life-review: the structured recollection of autobiographical memories. Depressed people have difficulties in retrieving specific, positive memories. Their autobiographical memory is characterized by more negative and general memories (e.g., Williams et al., 2007), for example memories that reflect a period or recurrent event (e.g., the period of a marriage) rather than a specific event (e.g., the ceremony on the wedding day). The present life-review course targets the recollection of specific, positive memories in older adults with depression symptoms. In four weekly sessions, the interviewer stimulates the recollection by asking questions on the depressed person's childhood, adolescence, adulthood and life in general. An advantage of life-review in comparison to other therapies such as Cognitive Behavioral Therapy, is that it fits in with a natural activity of older adults to recollect memories and tell stories about their lives (Bluck & Levine, 1998). Life-review has shown to be an effective method to decrease depression symptoms (Korte, Bohlmeijer, Cappeliez, Smit, & Westerhof, 2012; Pinquart & Forstmeier, 2012) and is considered an evidence-based intervention for depression in older adults (Scogin, Welsh, Hanson, Stump, & Coates, 2005).

Our study is one of the first to investigate prosodic speech features during a psychological intervention. The study is exploratory and aims to gain insight into the ecological validity of prosodic speech features in a psychological life-review intervention. The life-review intervention offers the opportunity to investigate the prosodic speech features over time. Life-review is highly suitable to investigate speech features during an intervention, since the speech from the recall of autobiographical memories provides strong prosodic speech changes (Cohen, Hong, & Guevara, 2010) and the expression of emotions characterized by speech characteristics is stronger after open and meaning-questions as compared to closed and fact-questions (Truong, Westerhof, Lamers, & de Jong, under review). Our paper is a first step to gain insight into the methods that are necessary to evaluate the application of prosodic speech features in mental health care. In the present study into the role of prosodic speech features, vocal pitch and pause duration will be investigated in three participants across all four weekly sessions. Because the life-review intervention is effective in decreasing depression symptoms (Korte et al., 2011; Serrano, Latorre, Gatz, & Montanes, 2004), we expect that the prosodic features change accordingly. Therefore, we hypothesize (a) an increase in average vocal pitch, (b) an increase in the variation in vocal pitch, (c) a decrease in average pause duration, (d) a decrease in the ratio between the total pause time and total speech time (pause speech ratio), and (e) an increase in the ratio between the participant's speech and total duration of the session (speech total duration ratio) during the intervention.

2 Method

In this section we will describe the methodology applied in the design of the psychological interventions during which the research data sets were generated, the procedure for selecting the participants and the corresponding data sets, the data preparations steps and the analyses performed.

2.1 Intervention 'Precious memories'

The life-review intervention 'Precious memories' (Bohlmeijer, Serrano, Cuijpers, & Steunenberg, 2007) targets the recollection of specific, positive memories. The intervention is developed for older adults with depression symptoms living in a nursing home. Each of the four weekly sessions focuses on a different theme: childhood, adolescence, adulthood, and life in general. The sessions are individual and guided by a trained interviewer. The sessions take place at the participant's home and last approximately 45 minutes. Each of the sessions is structured by fourteen main questions that stimulate the participant to recollect and tell specific positive memories about his or her life. The interviewers are instructed to ask for lively details about each of the positive memories of the participants, for example the colors, smells and people that were involved in the memory. Table 1 shows an example question for each of the four sessions.

Session	Example question
1: Childhood	Can you remember an event in which your father or mother did something when you were a child that made you very happy?
2: Adolescence	Do you remember a special moment of getting your first kiss or falling in love with someone?
3: Adulthood	What has been a very important positive experience in your life between the ages of 20 and 60?
4: Life in general	What is the largest gift you ever received in your life?

Tabel 1. Example questions for the four sessions of the life-review intervention 'Precious memories'

2.2 Procedure and participants

Participants with depression symptoms were recruited in nursing homes in the area of Amsterdam, the Netherlands. Participation in the life-review intervention was voluntary. Three participants were selected for whom audio recordings of the four sessions were available, which resulted in a dataset of twelve life-review sessions. The three participants (below labeled as P1, P3 and P5) were females with an age between 83 and 90 years. The educational background varied from low to high and the marital status from married to never married. The participants signed an informed consent form for the use of the audio-tapes for scientific purposes.

2.3 Data preparation and analysis

All acoustic features were automatically extracted with Praat (Boersma, 2001). Because the speech of both the interviewer and the participants were recorded on one mixed audio channel, some manual interventions had to be applied in order to determine the segments in which the participant is talking. First, for each session, the segments in which the participant is the main speaker were selected. These so-called 'turns' were then labeled in more detail; utterances produced by the interviewer were marked and discarded in the speech analysis. For each turn, mean pitch, standard deviation pitch, pause duration, the ratio between total pause time and total speech time, and the ratio between total speech time and total duration of the session were extracted. Pause durations were automatically extracted by applying silence detection where the minimal silence duration was set at 500 ms. All features were normalized per speaker by transforming the raw feature values to z-scores (mean and standard deviation were calculated over all 4 sessions, $z = ((x\text{-}m)/sd)$). The ratio between total speech time and total duration time was not normalized because this feature was calculated over a whole session instead of a turn. Subsequently, averages over all turns per session were taken in order to obtain one value per session.

3 Results

The results of the prosodic speech features over the four sessions of the life-review intervention are graphically presented separately for each feature, in the Figures 1 to 5. We hypothesized an increase in the average pitch during the intervention. As shown in Figure 1, the patterns in average pitch during the intervention differs across the three participants. Only in Participant 3, the pattern is in line with our expectations, showing an increase in the sessions 3 and 4. In both Participant 1 and 5, there was a decrease in average pitch in the sessions 3 and 4.

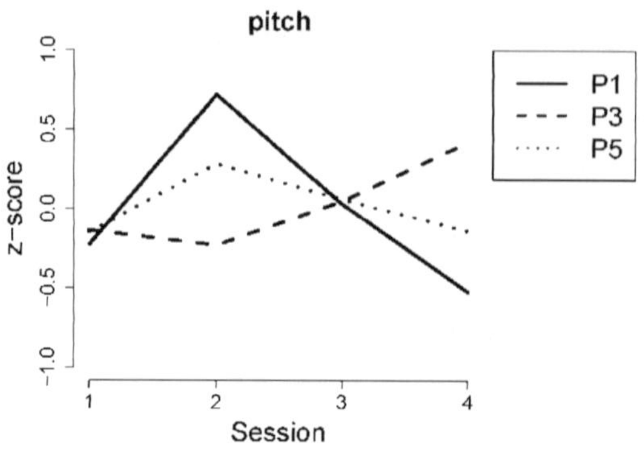

Figure 1. Average pitch of the participants (P1,P3,P5) during the four sessions.

We expected the variation in pitch to increase during the intervention. Figure 2 shows the participants' patterns of the standard deviation of pitch during the intervention. The changes in standard deviation do not confirm our hypothesis. Although the speech of Participant 3 shows an increase in session 4, the standard deviation is lower in session 4 than in session 1 of the intervention. The standard deviation of Participant 5 is relatively stable during the intervention. Participant 1 mainly shows a large variation in pitch in session 2.

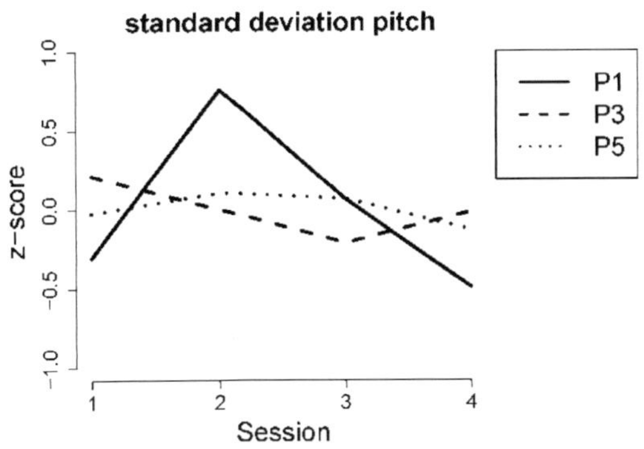

Figure 2. Standard deviation in pitch of the participants (P1,P3,P5) during the four sessions.

It was hypothesized that the average pause duration would decrease during the four sessions of the intervention. Figure 3 shows that the average pause duration was relatively stable over the first three sessions in all three participants. Only in Participant 1 the average pause duration decreased in session 4, in line with our expectations.

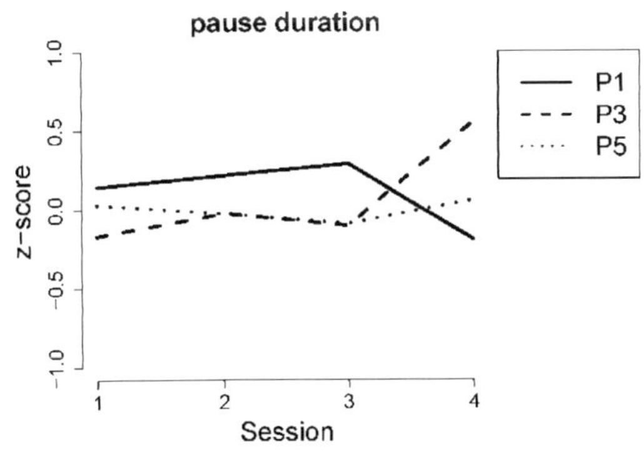

Figure 3. Pause duration of the participants (P1,P3,P5) during the four sessions.

In agreement with our hypothesis on average pause duration, we also expected a decrease during the intervention in the ratio between the total pause time and total speech time. Although there was a large decrease in the pause speech ratio of Participant 1 between the sessions 2 and 3, the ratio in session 4 was similar to the pause speech ratio in the first session (see Figure 4). In both Participant 2 and 3, the ratio was relatively stable in the sessions 1 to 3, but in session 4 the pause speech ratio showed an increase in Participant 3 and a slight decrease in Participant 2.

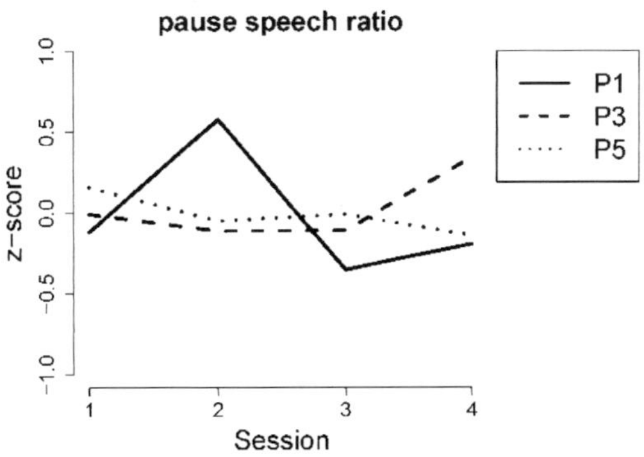

Figure 4. Pause speech ratio of the participants (P1,P3,P5) during the four sessions.

Last, we investigated the ratio between the participant's speech and total duration of the session. We hypothesized an increase in the speech total duration ration during the intervention. Figure 5 shows the differences between the participants in the speech total duration ratio over the four sessions. The ratio is relatively stable, and high, in Participant 5. The ratio in both Participant 1 and 3 in general decreases during the intervention, with a lower speech total duration ratio in session 4 as compared to session 1.

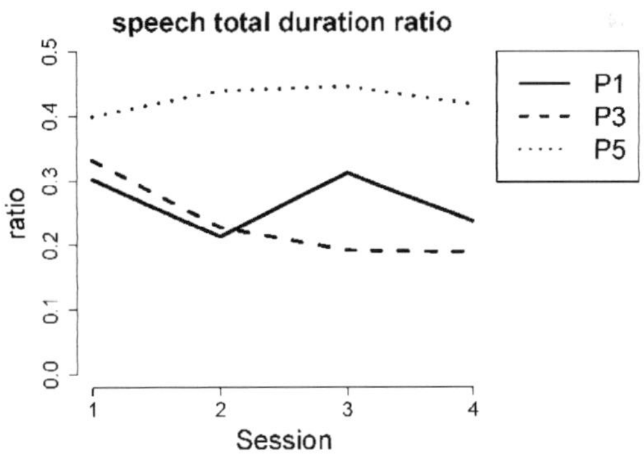

Figure 5. Speech total duration ratio of the participants (P1,P3,P5) during the four sessions.

4 Conclusion

The aim of the present study was to investigate the suitability of applying an analysis of prosodic speech features in the speech recordings collected in psychological intervention based on life-review. Because several studies have shown that speech features can be used as indicators of depression severity (e.g., Kuny & Stassen, 1993; Stassen, Kuny, & Hell, 1998), the application of speech analyses in mental health care is promising. However, the measurement of speech features is often based on speech recording tasks and the ecological validity within psychological interventions is not yet established. The study is a first exploratory step to gain insight into the ecological validity of prosodic speech features in a psychological life-review intervention.

We expected to measure a change during the intervention in the prosodic speech features that could be related to depression symptoms, and hypothesized an increase in average pitch and pitch variation, a decrease in average pause duration, and an increase in the amount of speech by the participant during the intervention. However, we could not establish the ecological validity of these speech indicators in the present study. In general, the patterns of the prosodic speech indicators differ from our expectations. The dynamics in the speech indicators was different from what can be expected in an intervention that is effective in decreasing depression (Korte et al., 2011; Serrano et al., 2004). Moreover, the speech indicators were inconsistent with each other for the participants in the pool. For example, Participant 3 showed an increase in pitch during the intervention, which indicates a decrease in depression, and an increase in average pause duration and pause speech ratio, which indicates an increase in depression.

Taken together, the findings from the present study indicate that the prosodic speech features that have been validated for controlled settings, are not directly applicable for the spontaneous type of conversation that is typical for a mental health care setting. More research is needed to establish the ecological validity of prosodic speech features such as pitch, pauses, and speech duration as indicators of depression severity. A few suggestions can be made. First, each of the four sessions in the life-review intervention in the present study focused on a different theme. Although we aimed to evaluate the development of the speech features during the intervention, the differences across the session may be the consequence of differences in session theme. Moreover, not all parts of the session consisted of life-review, and participants were talking about a variety of subjects, for example about their caregivers. The goal of the life-review intervention is to stimulate the retrieval of specific positive memories. In a next step, we aim to select the parts in which the participant is recollecting such memories and to evaluate the patterns in prosodic speech features only for these parts.

Second, the prosodic speech indicators were averaged per session to provide a clear overview of the changes over the four sessions. However, changes can also occur within the session. For example, vocal pitch may increase during the session, which would indicate a decrease in depression symptoms. Furthermore, within each session, the interaction between the interviewer and participant may play a role. For instance, when the interviewer speaks with a higher pitch and more variation in pitch, the participant may unconsciously take over some of this speaking behavior. We suggest future studies to investigate not only the average session, but to include changes during the session the interviewer's speech features.

Third, the present research was conducted in line with the assumption that life-review is effective as an intervention for mood disorder, as is shown in several studies (Korte et al., 2011; Serrano et al., 2004). However, we due to lack of data on depression severity we do not know whether the life-review intervention was fully effective for the participants in the present study. To validate the patterns prosodic speech features as a reliable indicator for depressions that can be used in mental health care, it is necessary to demonstrate that the dynamics in speech features can be related directly to changes in depression scores. As argued in earlier studies, in order to conclude that speech features correlate significantly with global depression scores during recovery (Kuny & Stassen, 1993; Stassen, Kuny, & Hell, 1998), these correlations need to be investigated in psychological interventions.

In sum, the study of how prosodic speech features such as pitch and pauses relate to the kind of spoken narratives that play a role in mental health care settings is a promising field. However, the ecological validity of prosodic speech features could not be established in the present study. More research based on larger data samples the establishment of a direct relation to depression scores is necessary before the techniques from the field of computational linguistics can be applied as a basis for the collection of indicators that can be used in psychological interventions in a meaningful and effective way.

References

Alpert, M., Pouget, E. R., & Silva, R. R. (2001). Reflections of depression in acoustic measures of the patient's speech. *Journal of Affective Disorders, 66*, 59-69.

American Psychiatric Association (2000). *Diagnostic and statistical manual of mental disorders* (4th ed., text rev.). Washington, DC: Author.

Beck, A. T., Steer, R. A., & Brown, G. K. (1996). *Manual for the Beck Depression Inventory-II.* San Antoinio, TX: Psychological Corporation.

Bluck, S., & Levine, L. J. (1998). Reminiscence as autobiographical memory: A catalyst for reminiscence theory development. *Ageing and Society, 18*, 185-208.

Boersma, P. (2001). Praat, a sysem for doing phonetics by computer. *Glot International, 5*(9/10), 341-345.

Bohlmeijer, E. T., Serrano, J., Cuijpers, P., & Steunenberg, B. (2007). *Dierbare herinneringen. Protocol voor life-review bij ouderen met depressieve klachten in verzorgings- en verpleeghuizen* [Precious memories. Protocol for life-review in older people with depressive symptoms in nursing homes].

Bronfenbrenner, U. (1977). Toward an experimental ecology of human development. *American Psychologist, 32*, 513-531.

Cannizzaro, M., Harel, B., Reilly, N., Chappell, P., & Snyder, P. J. (2004). Voice acoustical measurement of the severity of major depression. *Brain and Cognition, 56*, 30-35.

Chien, J.-T., & Chueh, C-H. (2010). Joint acoustic and language modeling for speech recognition. *Speech Communication, 52*, 223-235.

Cohen, A. S., Hong, S. L., & Guevara, A. (2010). Understanding emotional expression using prosodic analysis of natural speech: refining the methodology. *Journal of Behavioral Therapy & Experimental Psychiatry, 41*, 150-157.

Cuijpers, P., van Straten, A., Smit, F. (2006). Psychological treatment of late-life depression: A meta-analysis of randomized controlled trials. *International Journal of Geriatric Psychiatry, 21*, 1139-1149.

Cuijpers, P., van Straten, A., Smit, F., Mihalopoulos, C., & Beekman, M. D. (2008). Preventing the onset of depressive disorders: a meta-analytic review of psychological interventions. *American Journal of Psychiatry, 165*, 1272-1280.

Elliot, R. (2010). Psychotherapy change process research: Realizing the promise. *Psychotherapy Research, 20*, 123-135.

Hamilton, M. (1960). A rating scale for depression. *Journal of Neurology, Neurosurgery, & Psychiatry, 23*, 56-62.

Hardy, P., Jouvant, R., & Widlöcher, D. (1984). Speech pause time and the retardation rating scale for depresstion (ERD): towards a reciprocal validation. *Journal of Affective Disorders, 6*, 123-127.

Janssen, J. H., Tacke, P., de Vries, J. J. G., van den Broek, E. L., Westerink, J. H. D. M., Haselager, P., & IJsselsteijn, W. A. (2013). Machines outperform laypersons in recognizing emotions elicited by autobiographical recollection. *Human-Computer Interaction, 28*, 479-517.

Koolagudi, S. G., & Sreenivasa, K. S. (2012). Emotion recognition from speech: a review. *International Journal of Speech Technology, 15*, 99-117.

Korte, J., Bohlmeijer, E. T., Cappeliez, P., Smit, F., & Westerhof G. J. (2012). Life-review therapy for older adults with moderate depressive symptomatology: A pragmatic randomized controlled trial. *Psychological Medicine, 42*, 1163-1172.

Kuny, S., & Stassen, H. H. (1993). Speaking behavior and voice sound characteristics in depressive patients during recovery. *Journal of Psychiatric Research, 27*, 289-307.

Moses, J. P. (1954). *The voice of neurosis.* Oxford, UK: Grune and Stratton.

Mundt, J. C., Vogel, A. P., Feltner, D. E., & Lenderking, W. R. (2012). Vocal acoustic biomarkers of depression severity and treatment response. *Biological Psychiatry, 72*, 580-587.

Pennebaker, J. W. and Chung, C. K. (2011). Expressive Writing and its Links to Mental and Physical Health. In H. S. Friedman (Ed.), *Oxford Handbook of Health Psychology*. New York, NY: Oxford University Press, 417-437.

Pinquart, M., & Forstmeier, S. (2012). Effects of reminiscence interventions on psychosocial outcomes: A meta-analysis. *Aging & Mental Health, 16*, 514-558.

Radloff, L. S. (1977). The CES-D Scale: A Self-Report Depression Scale for Research in the General Population. *Applied Psychological Measurement, 1*, 385-401.

Scherer, K. R., Johnstone, T., & Klasmeyer, G. (2003). Vocal expression of emotion. In R. J. Davidson, K. R. Scherer, & H. Goldsmith (Eds.), *Handbook of the Affective Sciences* (pp. 433–456). New York and Oxford: Oxford University Press.

Scogin, F., Welsh, D., Hanson, A., Stump, J., & Coates, A. (2005). Evidence-based psychotherapies for depression in older adults. *Clinical Psychology: Science and Practice, 12*, 222-237.

Serrano, J., Latorre, J., Gatz, M., & Montanes, J. (2004). Life review therapy using autobiographical retrieval practice for older adults with depressive symptomatology. *Psychology & Aging, 19*, 272-277.

Sobin, C., & Alpert, M. (1999). Emotion in speech: the acoustic attributes of fear, anger, sadness, and joy. *Journal of Psycholinguistic Research, 28*, 347-365.

Sobin, C., & Sackeim, H. A. (1997). Psychomotor symptoms of depression. *American Journal of Psychiatry, 154, 4-17.*

Stassen, H. H., Kuny, S., & Hell, D. (1998). The speech analysis approach to determining onset of improvement under antidepressants. *European Neuropsychopharmacology, 8*, 303-310.

Truong, K., Westerhof, G. J., Lamers, S. M. A., & de Jong, F. (under review). Towards modeling expressed emotions in oral history interviews: using verbal and non-verbal signals to track personal narratives. *Literary and Linguistic Computing*.

Üstün, T. B., Ayuso-Mateos, J. L., Chatterji, S., Mathers, C., & Murray, C. J. L. (2004). Global burden of depressive disorders in the year 2000. *British Journal of Psychiatry, 184*, 386-392.

Vervedis, D., & Kotropoulos, C. (2006). Emotional speech recognition: Resources, features, and methods. *Speech Communication, 48*, 1162-1181.

Vingerhoets, A. J. J. M., Kop, P. F. M., & Soons, P. H. G. M. (2002). *Psychologie in de gezondheidszorg: een praktijkoriëntatie [Psychology in health care: a practical orientation]*. Houten, the Netherlands: Bohn Stafleu van Loghum.

Williams, J. M., Barnhofer, T., Crane, C., Herman, D, Raes, F., Watkins, E., & Dalgleish, T. (2007). Autobiographical memory specificity and emotional disorder. *Psychological Bulletin, 133*, 122-148.

World Health Organization. (2012). Depression Fact Sheet. Retrieved at March, 5, 2014: www.who.int/mediacentre/factsheets/fs369/en/

Challenges in Automating Maze Detection

Eric Morley
CSLU
OHSU
Portland, OR 97239
morleye@gmail.com

Anna Eva Hallin
Department of Communicative
Sciences and Disorders
New York University
New York, NY
ae.hallin@nyu.edu

Brian Roark
Google Research
New York, NY 10011
roarkbr@gmail.com

Abstract

SALT is a widely used annotation approach for analyzing natural language transcripts of children. Nine annotated corpora are distributed along with scoring software to provide norming data. We explore automatic identification of *mazes* – SALT's version of disfluency annotations – and find that cross-corpus generalization is very poor. This surprising lack of cross-corpus generalization suggests substantial differences between the corpora. This is the first paper to investigate the SALT corpora from the lens of natural language processing, and to compare the utility of different corpora collected in a clinical setting to train an automatic annotation system.

1 Introduction

Assessing a child's linguistic abilities is a critical component of diagnosing developmental disorders such as Specific Language Impairment or Autism Spectrum Disorder, and for evaluating progress made with remediation. Structured instruments ("tests") that elicit brief, easy to score, responses to a sequence of items are a popular way of performing such assessment. An example of a structured instrument is the CELF-4, which includes nineteen multi-item subtests with tasks such as object naming, word definition, reciting the days of the week, or repeating sentences (Semel et al., 2003). Over the past two decades, researchers have discussed the limitations of standardized tests and how well they tap into different language impairments. Many have advocated the potential benefits of language sample analysis (LSA) (Johnston, 2006; Dunn et al., 1996). The analysis of natural language samples may be particularly beneficial for language assessment in ASD, where pragmatic and social communication issues are paramount yet may be hard to assess in a conventional test format (Tager-Flusberg et al., 2009).

At present, the expense of LSA prevents it from being more widely used. Heilmann (2010), while arguing that LSA is not too time-consuming, estimates that each minute of spoken language takes five to manually transcribe and annotate. At this rate, it is clearly impractical for clinicians to perform LSA on hours of speech. Techniques from natural language processing could be used to build tools to automatically annotate transcripts, thus facilitating LSA.

Here, we evaluate the utility of a set of annotated corpora for automating a key annotation in the de facto standard annotation schema for LSA: the Systematic Analysis of Language Transcripts (SALT) (Miller et al., 2011). SALT comprises a scheme for coding transcripts of recorded speech, together with software that tallies these codes, computes scores describing utterance length and error counts, among a range of other standard measures, and compares these scores with normative samples. SALT codes indicate bound morphemes, several types of grammatical errors (for example using a pronoun of the wrong gender or case), and *mazes*, which are defined as "filled pauses, false starts, and repetitions and revisions of words, morphemes and phrases" (Miller et al., 2011, p. 48).

Mazes have sparked interest in the child language disorders literature for several reasons. They are most often analyzed from a language processing perspective where the disruptions are viewed as a consequence of monitoring, detecting and repairing language, potentially including speech errors (Levelt, 1993; Postma and Kolk, 1993; Rispoli et al., 2008). Several studies have found that as grammatical complexity and utterance length increase, the number of mazes increases in typically developing children and children with language impairments (MacLachlan and

Workshop on Computational Linguistics and Clinical Psychology: From Linguistic Signal to Clinical Reality, pages 69–77,
Baltimore, Maryland USA, June 27, 2014.

Chapman, 1988; Nippold et al., 2008; Reuterskiöld Wagner et al., 2000; Wetherell et al., 2007). Mazes in narrative contexts have been shown to differ between typical children and children with specific language impairment (MacLachlan and Chapman, 1988; Thordardottir and Weismer, 2001), though others have not found reliable group differences (Guo et al., 2008; Scott and Windsor, 2000). Furthermore, outside the potential usefulness of looking at mazes in themselves, mazes always have to be detected and excluded in order to calculate other standard LSA measures such as mean length of utterance and type or token counts. Mazes also must be excluded when analyzing speech errors, since some mazes are in fact self-corrections of language or speech errors.

Thus, automatically delimiting mazes could be clinically useful in several ways. First, if mazes can be automatically detected, standard measures such as token and type counts can be calculated with ease, as noted above. Automatic maze detection could also be a first processing step for automatically identifying errors: error codes cannot appear in mazes, and certain grammatical errors may be easier to identify once mazes have been excised. Finally, after mazes have been identified, further analysis of the mazes themselves (e.g. the number of word in mazes, and the placement of mazes in the sentence) can provide supplementary information about language formulation abilities and word retrieval abilities (Miller et al., 2011, p. 87-89).

We use the corpora included with the SALT software to train maze detectors. These are the corpora that the software uses to compute reference counts. These corpora share several characteristics we expect to be typical of clinical data: they were collected under a diverse set of circumstances; they were annotated by different groups; the annotations ostensibly follow the same guidelines; and the annotations were not designed with automation in mind. We will investigate whether we can extract usable generalizations from the available data, and explore how well the automated system performs, which will be of interest to clinicians looking to expedite LSA.

2 Background

Here we provide an overview of SALT and maze annotations. We are not aware of any attempts to automate maze detection, although maze detection closely resembles the well-established task of *edited word detection*. We also provide an overview of the corpora included with the SALT software, which are the ones we will use to train maze detectors.

2.1 SALT and Maze Annotations

The approach used in SALT has been in wide use for nearly 30 years (Miller and Chapman, 1985), and now also exists as a software package[1] providing transcription and coding support along with tools for aggregating statistics for manual codes over the annotated corpora and comparing with age norms. The SALT software is not the focus of this investigation, so we do not discuss it further.

Following the SALT guidelines, speech should be transcribed orthographically and verbatim. The transcript must include and indicate: the speaker of each utterance, partial words or stuttering, overlapping speech, unintelligible words, and any non-speech sounds from the speaker. Even atypical language, for example neologisms (novel words) or grammatical errors (for example 'her went') should be written as such.

There are three broad categories of SALT annotations: indicators of 1) certain bound morphemes, 2) errors, and 3) *mazes*. In general, verbal suffixes that are visible in the surface form (for example -ing in "going") and clitics that appear with an unmodified root (so for example -n't in "don't", but not the -n't in "won't") must be indicated. SALT includes various codes to indicate grammatical errors including, but not limited to: overgeneralization errors ("goed"), extraneous words, omitted words or morphemes, and inappropriate utterances (e.g. answering a yes/no question with "fight"). For more information on these standard annotations, we refer the reader to the SALT manual (Miller et al., 2011).

Here, we are interested in automatically delimiting mazes. In SALT, filled pauses, repetitions and revisions are included in the umbrella term "mazes" but the manual does not include definitions for any of these categories. In SALT, mazes are simply delimited by parentheses; they have no internal structure, and cannot be nested. Contiguous spans of maze words are delimited by a single set of parentheses, as in the following utterance:

(1) (You have you have um there/'s only) there/'s ten people

[1] `http://www.saltsoftware.com/`

To be clear, we define the task of automatically applying maze detections as taking unannotated transcripts of speech as input, and then outputting a binary tag for each word that indicates whether or not it is in a maze.

2.2 Edited Word Detection

Although we are not aware of any previous work on automating maze detection, there is a well-established task in natural language processing that is quite similar: edited word detection. The goal of edited word detection is to identify words that have been revised or deleted by the speaker, for example 'to Dallas' in the utterance 'I want to go to Dallas, um I mean to Denver.'. Many investigations have approached edited word detection from what Nakatani et al. (1993) have termed 'speech-first' perspective, meaning that edited detection is performed with features from the speech signal in addition to a transcript. These approaches, however, are not applicable to the SALT corpora, because they only contain transcripts. As a result, we must adopt a *text-first* approach to maze detection, using only features extracted from a transcript.

The text-first approach to edited word detection is well established. One of the first investigations taking a text-first approach was conducted by Charniak and Johnson (2001). There, they used boosted linear classifiers to identify edited words. Later, Johnson and Charniak (2004) improved upon the linear classifiers' performance with a tree adjoining grammar based noisy channel model. Zwarts and Johnson (2011) improve the noisy channel model by adding in a reranker that leverages features extracted with the help of a large language model.

Qian and Liu (2013) have developed what is currently the best-performing edited word detector, and it takes a text-first approach. Unlike the detector proposed by Zwarts and Johnson, Qian and Liu's does not rely on any external data. Their detector operates in three passes. In the first pass, filler words ('um', 'uh', 'I mean', 'well', etc.) are detected. In the second and third passes, edited words are detected. The reason for the three passes is that in addition to extracting features (mostly words and part of speech tags) from the raw transcript, the second and third steps use features extracted from the output of previous steps. An example of such features is adjacent words from the utterance with filler words and some likely edited words removed.

3 Overview of SALT Corpora

We explore nine corpora included with the SALT software. Table 1 has a high level overview of these corpora, showing where each was collected, the age ranges of the speakers, and the size of each corpus both in terms of transcripts and utterances. Note that only utterances spoken by the child are counted, as we throw out all others.

Table 1 shows several divisions among the corpora. We see that one group of corpora comes from New Zealand, while the majority come from North America. All of the corpora, except for Expository, include children at very different stages of language development.

Four research groups were responsible for the transcriptions and annotations of the corpora in Table 1. One group produced the CONVERSATION, EXPOSITORY, NARRATIVESSS, and NARRATIVESTORYRETELL corpora. Another was responsible for all of the corpora from New Zealand. Finally, the ENNI and GILLAMNT corpora were transcribed and annotated by two different groups. For more details on these corpora, how they were collected, and the annotators, we refer the reader to the SALT website at `http://www.saltsoftware.com/resources/databases.html`.

Some basic inspection reveals that the corpora can be put into three groups based on the median utterance lengths, and the distribution of ut-

Table 1: Description of SALT corpora

Corpus	Transcripts	Utterances	Age Range	Speaker Location
CONVERSATION	584	82,643	2;9 – 13;3	WI & CA
ENNI	377	56,108	3;11 – 10;0	Canada
EXPOSITORY	242	4,918	10;7 – 15;9	WI
GILLAMNT	500	40,102	5;0 – 11;11	USA
NARRATIVESSS	330	16,091	5;2 – 13;3	WI & CA
NARRATIVESTORYRETELL	500	14,834	4;4 – 12;8	WI & CA
NZCONVERSATION	248	25,503	4;5 – 7;7	NZ
NZPERSONALNARRATIVE	248	20,253	4;5 – 7;7	NZ
NZSTORYRETELL	264	2,574	4;0 – 7;7	NZ

terance[2] lengths, following the groups Figure 1, with the EXPOSITORY and CONVERSATION corpora in their own groups. Note that the counts in Figure 1 are of all of the words in each utterance, including those in mazes. We see that the corpora in Group A have a modal utterance length ranging from seven to ten words. There are many utterances in these corpora that are shorter or longer than the median length. Compared to the corpora in Group A, those in Group B have a shorter modal utterance length, and fewer long utterances. In Figure 1, we see that the CONVERSATION corpus consists mostly of very short utterances. At the other extreme is the EXPOSITORY corpus, which resembles the corpora in Group A in terms of modal utterance length, but which generally contains longer utterances than any of the other corpora.

4 Maze Detection Experiments

4.1 Maze Detector

We carry out our experiments in automatic maze detection using a statistical maze detector that learns to identify mazes from manually labeled data using features extracted from words and automatically predicted part of speech tags. The maze detector uses the feature set shown in Table 2. This set of features is identical to the ones used by the 'filler word' detector in Qian and Liu's disfluency detector (2013). We also use the same clas-

[2] All of these corpora are reported to have been segmented into *c-units*, which is defined as "an independent clause with its modifiers" (Miller et al., 2011).

Table 2: Feature templates for maze word detection, following Qian and Liu (2013). We extract all of the above features from both words and POS tags, albeit separately. t_0 indicates the current word or POS tag, while t_{-1} is the previous one and t_1 is the following. The function $I(a, b)$ is 1 if a and b are identical, and otherwise 0. y_{-1} is the tag predicted for the previous word.

Category	Features
Unigrams	$t_{-2}, t_{-1}, t_0, t_1, t_2$
Bigrams	$t_{-1}t_0, t_0t_1$
Trigrams	$t_{-2}t_{-1}t_0, t_{-1}t_0t_1, t_0t_1t_2$
Logic Unigrams	$I(t_i, t_0), I(p_i, p_0)$; $-4 \leq i \leq 4; i \neq 0$
Logic Bigrams	$I(t_{i-2}t_{i-1}, t_{-1}t_0)$ $I(t_it_{i+1}, t_0t_{i+1})$; $-4 \leq i \leq 4; i \neq 0$
Predicted tag	y_{-1}

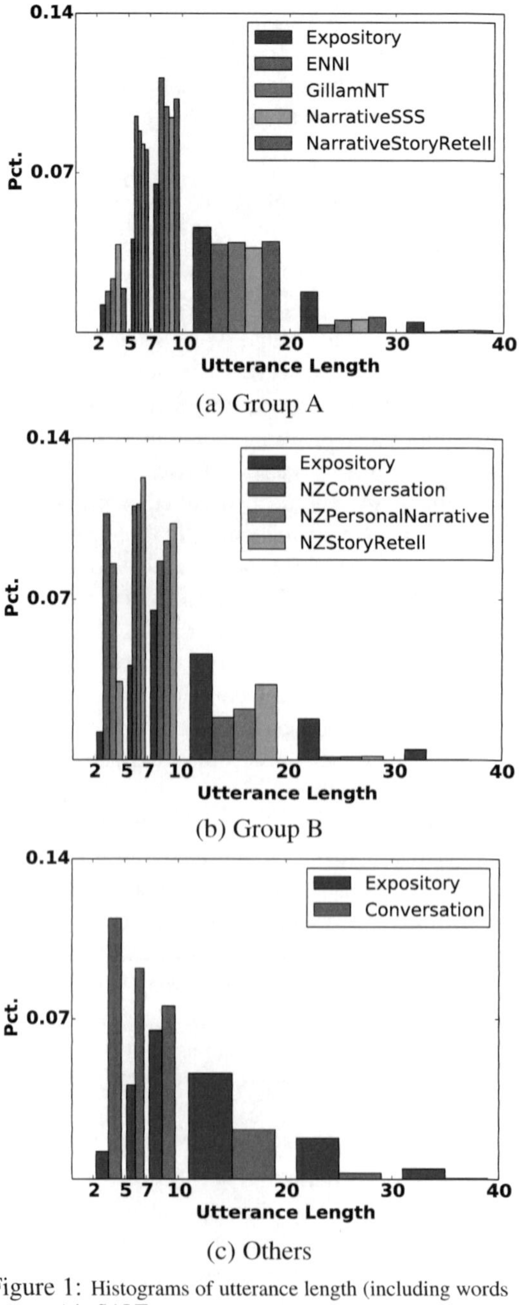

(a) Group A

(b) Group B

(c) Others

Figure 1: Histograms of utterance length (including words in mazes) in SALT corpora

sifier as the second and third steps of their system: the Max Margin Markov Network 'M3N' classifier in the pocketcrf toolkit (available at `http://code.google.com/p/pocketcrf/`). The M3N classifier is a kernel-based classifier that is able to leverage the sequential nature the data in this problem (Taskar et al., 2003). We use the following label set: S-O (not in maze); S-M (single word maze); B-M (beginning of multi-word maze); I-M (in multi-word maze); and E-M (end of multi-word maze). The M3N classifier allows us to set a unique penalty for each pair of confused labels, for example penalizing an erroneous prediction of S-O (failing to identify maze words) more heavily than spurious predictions of maze words (all -M labels). This ability is particularly useful for maze detection because maze words are so infrequent compared to words that are not in mazes.

4.2 Evaluation

We split each SALT corpus into training, development, and test partitions. Each training partition contains 80% of the utterances the corpus, while the development and test partitions each contain 10% of the utterances. We use the development portion of each corpus to set the penalty matrix system to roughly balance precision and recall.

We evaluate maze detection in terms of both *tagging* performance and *bracketing* performance, both of which are standard forms of evaluation for various tasks in the Natural Language Processing literature. *Tagging* performance captures how effectively maze detection is done on a word-by-word basis, while *bracketing* performance describes how well each maze is identified in its entirety. For both tagging and bracketing performance, we count the number of true and false positives and negatives, as illustrated in Figure 2. In tagging performance, each word gets counted once, while in bracketing performance we compare the predicted and observed maze spans. We use these counts to compute the following metrics:

$$\text{(P)recision} = \frac{tp}{tp + fp}$$

$$(R)ecall = \frac{tp}{tp + fn}$$

$$\text{F1} = \frac{2PR}{P + R}$$

Note that partial words and punctuation are both ignored in evaluation. We exclude punctuation because punctuation does not need to be included in mazes: it is not counted in summary statistics (e.g. MLU, word count, etc.), and punctuation errors are not captured by the SALT error codes. We exclude partial words because they are always in mazes, and therefore can be detected trivially with a simple rule. Furthermore, because partial words are excluded from evaluation, the performance metrics are comparable across corpora, even if they vary widely in the frequency of partial words.

For both space and clarity, we do not present the complete results of every experiment in this paper, although they are available online[3]. Instead, we present the complete baseline results, and then report F1 scores that are significantly better than the baseline. We establish statistical significance by using a randomized paired-sample test (see Yeh (2000) or Noreen (1989)) to compare the baseline system (system A) and the proposed system (system B). First, we compute the difference d in F1 score between systems A and B. Then, we repeatedly construct a random set of predictions for each input item by choosing between the outputs of system A and B with equal probability. We compute the F1 score of these random predictions, and if it exceeds the F1 score of the baseline system by at least d, we count the iteration as a success. The significance level is at most the number of successes divided by one more than the number of trials (Noreen, 1989).

4.3 Baseline Results

For each corpus, we train the maze detector on the training partition and test it on the development partition. The results of these runs are in Table 3, which also includes the rank of the size of each corpus (1 = biggest, 9 = smallest). We see immediately that our maze detector performs far better on some corpora than on others, both in terms of tagging and bracketing performance. We note that maze detection performance is not solely determined by corpus size: tagging performance is substantially worse on the largest corpus (CONVERSATION) than the small-

[3] `http://bit.ly/1dtFTPl`

Figure 2: Tagging and bracketing evaluation for maze detection. TP = True Positive, FP = False Positive, TN = True Negative, FN = False Negative

Pred.	(	and then it	)	oh		and then it	(	um	)	put his wings out .
Gold	(	and then it		oh	)	and then it	(	um	)	put his wings out .
Tag		TP ×3		FN		TN ×3		TP		TN ×4
Brack.		FP, FN						TP		

Corpus	Size Rank	Tagging P	Tagging R	Tagging F1	Bracketing P	Bracketing R	Bracketing F1
CONVERSATION	1	0.821	0.779	0.800	0.716	0.729	0.723
ENNI	2	0.923	0.882	0.902	0.845	0.837	0.841
EXPOSITORY	8	0.703	0.680	0.691	0.620	0.615	0.618
GILLAMNT	3	0.902	0.907	0.904	0.827	0.843	0.835
NARRATIVESSS	6	0.781	0.768	0.774	0.598	0.679	0.636
NARRATIVESTORYRETELL	7	0.799	0.774	0.786	0.627	0.671	0.649
NZCONVERSATION	4	0.832	0.835	0.838	0.707	0.757	0.731
NZPERSONALNARRATIVE	5	0.842	0.835	0.838	0.707	0.757	0.731
NZSTORYRETELL	9	0.905	0.862	0.883	0.773	0.780	0.776

Table 3: Baseline maze detection performance on development sections of SALT corpora: corpus-specific models

est (NZSTORYRETELL).

4.4 Generic Model

We train a generic model for maze detection on all of the training portions of the nine SALT corpora. We use the combined development sections of all of the corpora to tune the loss matrix for balanced precision and recall. We then test the resulting model on the development section of each SALT corpus, and evaluate in terms of tagging and bracketing accuracy.

We find that the generic model performs worse than the baseline in terms of both tagging and bracketing performance on six of the nine corpora corpora. The generic model significantly improves tagging (F1=0.925, $p \leq 0.0022$) on the NZSTORYRETELL corpus, but the improvement in bracketing performance is not significant ($p \leq 0.1635$). There is improvement of both tagging (F1=0.805, $p \leq 0.0001$) and bracketing (F1=0.677, $p \leq 0.0025$) performance on the NARRATIVESSS corpus. The generic model does not perform better than the baseline corpus-specific models on any other corpora.

The poor performance of the generic model is somewhat surprising, as it is trained with far more data than any of the corpus-specific models. In many tasks in natural language processing, increasing the amount of training data improves the resulting model, although this is not necessarily the case if the additional data is noisy or out-of-domain. This suggests two possibilities: 1) the language in the corpora varies substantially, perhaps due to the speakers' ages or the activity that was transcribed; and 2) the maze annotations are inconsistent between corpora.

4.5 Multi-Corpus Models

It is possible that poor performance of the generic model relative to the baseline corpus-specific models can be attributed to systematic differences between the SALT corpora. We may be able to train a model for a set of corpora that share particular characteristics that can outperform the baseline models because such a model could leverage more training data. We first evaluate a model for corpora that contain transcripts collected from children of similar ages. We also evaluate task-specific models, specifically a maze-detection model for story retellings, and another for conversations. These two types of models could perform well if children of similar ages or performing similar tasks produce mazes in a similar manner. Finally, we train models for each group of annotators to see whether systematic variation in annotation standards between research groups could be responsible for the generic model's poor performance.

We train all of these models similarly to the generic model: we pool the training sections of the selected corpora, train the model, then test on the development section of each selected corpus. We use the combined development sections of the selected corpora to tune the penalty matrix to balance precision and recall.

Again, we only report F1 scores that are higher than the baseline model's, and we test whether the improvement is statistically significant. We do not report results where just the precision or just the recall exceeds the baseline model performance, but not F1, because these are typically the result of model imbalance, favoring precision at the expense of recall or vice versa. Bear in mind that we roughly balance precision and recall on the combined development sets, not each corpus's development set individually.

4.5.1 Age-Specific Model

We train a single model on the following corpora: ENNI, GILLAMNT, NARRATIVESSS, and NARRATIVESTORYRETELL. As shown in Table 1, these corpora contain transcripts collected from children roughly aged 4-12. In three of the four corpora, the age-based model performs worse than the baseline. The only exception is NAR-

RATIVESTORYRETELL, for which the age-based model outperforms the baseline in terms of both tagging (F1=0.794, $p \leq 0.0673$) and bracketing (F1=0.679, $p \leq 0.0062$).

4.5.2 Task-Specific Models

We construct two task-specific models for maze detection: one for conversations, and the other for narrative tasks. A conversational model trained on the CONVERSATION and NZCONVERSATION corpora does not improve performance on either corpus relative to the baseline. A model for narrative tasks trained on the ENNI, GILLAMNT, NARRATIVESSS, NARRATIVESTORYRETELL, NZPERSONALNARRATIVE and NZSTORYRETELL corpora only improves performance on one of these, relative to the baseline. Specifically, the narrative task model improves performance on the NARRATIVESSS corpus both in terms of tagging (F1=0.797, $p \leq 0.0005$) and bracketing (F1=0.693, $p \leq 0.0002$).

4.5.3 Research Group-Specific Models

There are two groups of researchers that have annotated multiple corpora: a group in New Zealand, which annotated the NZCONVERSATION, NZPERSONALNARRATIVE, and NZSTORYRETELL corpora; and another group in Wisconsin, which annotated the CONVERSATION, EXPOSITORY, NARRATIVESSS, and NARRATIVESTORYRETELL corpora. We trained research group-specific models, one for each of these groups.

Overall, these models do not improve performance. The New Zealand research group model does not significantly improve performance on any of the corpora they annotated, relative to the baseline. The Wisconsin research group model yields significant improvement on the NARRATIVESSS corpus, both in terms of tagging (F1=0.803, $p \leq 0.0001$) and bracketing (F1=0.699, $p \leq 0.0001$) performance. Performance on the CONVERSATION and EXPOSITORY corpora is lower with the Wisconsin research group model than with the corpus-specific baseline models, while performance on NARRATIVESTORYRETELL is essentially the same with the two models.

5 Discussion

We compared corpus-specific models for maze detection to more generic models applicable to multiple corpora, and found that the generic models performed worse than the corpus-specific ones. This was surprising because the more generic models were able to leverage more training data than the corpus specific ones, and more training data typically improves the performance of data-driven models such as our maze detector. These results strongly suggest that there are substantial differences between the nine SALT corpora.

We suspect there are many areas in which the SALT corpora diverge from one another. One such area may be the nature of the language: perhaps the language differs so much between each of the corpora that it is difficult to learn a model appropriate for one corpus from any of the others. Another potential source of divegence is in transcription, which does not always follow the SALT guidelines (Miller et al., 2011). Two of the idiosyncracies we have observed are: more than three X's (or a consonant followed by multiple X's) to indicate unintelligble language, instead of the conventional X, XX, and XXX for unintelligible words, phrases, and utterances, respectively; and non-canonical transcriptions of what appear to be filled pauses, including 'uhm' and 'umhm'. These idiosyncracies could be straightforward to normalize using automated methods, but doing so requires that they be identified to begin with. Furthermore, although these idiosyncracies may appear to be minor, taken together they may actually be substantial.

Another potential source of variation between corpora is likely in the maze annotations themselves. SALT's definition of mazes, "filled pauses, false starts, and repetitions and revisions of words, morphemes and phrases" (Miller et al., 2011, p. 48), is very short, and none of the components is defined in the SALT manual. In contrast, the Disfluency Annotation Stylebook for Switchboard Corpus (Meteer et al., 1995) describes a system of disfluency annotations over approximately 25 pages, devoting two pages to filled pauses and five to restarts. The Switchboard disfluency annotations are much richer than SALT maze annotations, and we are not suggesting that they are appropriate for a clinical setting. However, between the stark contrast in detail of the two annotation systems' guidelines, and our finding that cross-corpus models for maze detection perform poorly, we recommend that SALT's definition of mazes and their components be elaborated and clarified. This would be of benefit not just to those trying to automate the application of SALT annotations, but also to clinicians who use SALT and depend upon consistently annotated transcripts.

There are two clear tasks for future research that build upon these results. First, maze detection performance can surely be improved. We note, however, that evaluating maze detectors in terms of F1 score may not always be appropriate if such a detector is used in a pipeline. For example, there may be a minimum acceptable level of precision for a maze detector used in a preprocessing step to applying SALT error codes so that maze excision does not create additional errors. In such a scenario, the goal would be to maximize recall at a given level of precision.

The second task suggested by this paper is to explore the hypothesized differences within and between corpora. Such exploration could ultimately result in more rigorous, communicable guidelines for maze annotations, as well as other annotations and conventions in SALT. If there are systematic differences in maze annotations across the SALT corpora, such exploration could suggest ways of making the annotations consistent without completely redoing them.

Acknowledgments

We would like to thank members of the ASD research group at the Center for Spoken Language Understanding at OHSU, for useful input into this study: Jan van Santen, Alison Presmanes Hill, Steven Bedrick, Emily Prud'hommeaux, Kyle Gorman and Masoud Rouhizadeh. This research was supported in part by NIH NIDCD award R01DC012033 and NSF award #0826654. Any opinions, findings, conclusions or recommendations expressed in this publication are those of the authors and do not reflect the views of the NIH or NSF.

References

Eugene Charniak and Mark Johnson. 2001. Edit detection and parsing for transcribed speech. In *Proceedings of the second meeting of the North American Chapter of the Association for Computational Linguistics on Language technologies*, pages 1–9. Association for Computational Linguistics.

Michelle Dunn, Judith Flax, Martin Sliwinski, and Dorothy Aram. 1996. The use of spontaneous language measures as criteria for identifying children with specific language impairment: An attempt to reconcile clinical and research incongruence. *Journal of Speech and Hearing research*, 39(3):643.

Ling-yu Guo, J Bruce Tomblin, and Vicki Samelson. 2008. Speech disruptions in the narratives of english-speaking children with specific language impairment. *Journal of Speech, Language, and Hearing Research*, 51(3):722–738.

John J Heilmann. 2010. Myths and realities of language sample analysis. *SIG 1 Perspectives on Language Learning and Education*, 17(1):4–8.

Mark Johnson and Eugene Charniak. 2004. A tag-based noisy-channel model of speech repairs. In *Proceedings of the 42nd Meeting of the Association for Computational Linguistics (ACL'04), Main Volume*, pages 33–39, Barcelona, Spain, July.

Judith R Johnston. 2006. *Thinking about child language: Research to practice*. Thinking Publications.

Willem JM Levelt. 1993. *Speaking: From intention to articulation*, volume 1. MIT press, Cambridge, MA.

Barbara G MacLachlan and Robin S Chapman. 1988. Communication breakdowns in normal and language learning-disabled children's conversation and narration. *Journal of Speech and Hearing Disorders*, 53(1):2.

Marie W Meteer, Ann A Taylor, Robert MacIntyre, and Rukmini Iyer. 1995. *Dysfluency annotation stylebook for the switchboard corpus*. University of Pennsylvania.

Jon Miller and Robin Chapman. 1985. Systematic analysis of language transcripts. *Madison, WI: Language Analysis Laboratory*.

Jon F Miller, Karen Andriacchi, and Ann Nockerts. 2011. *Assessing language production using SALT software: A clinician's guide to language sample analysis*. SALT Software, LLC.

Christine Nakatani and Julia Hirschberg. 1993. A speech-first model for repair detection and correction. In *Proceedings of the 31st Annual Meeting of the Association for Computational Linguistics*, pages 46–53, Columbus, Ohio, USA, June. Association for Computational Linguistics.

Marilyn A Nippold, Tracy C Mansfield, Jesse L Billow, and J Bruce Tomblin. 2008. Expository discourse in adolescents with language impairments: Examining syntactic development. *American Journal of Speech-Language Pathology*, 17(4):356–366.

Eric W Noreen. 1989. Computer intensive methods for testing hypotheses. an introduction. 1989. *John Wiley & Sons*, 2(5):33.

Albert Postma and Herman Kolk. 1993. The covert repair hypothesis: Prearticulatory repair processes in normal and stuttered disfluencies. *Journal of Speech and Hearing Research*, 36(3):472.

Xian Qian and Yang Liu. 2013. Disfluency detection using multi-step stacked learning. In *Proceedings of the 2013 Conference of the North American Chapter of the Association for Computational Linguistics: Human Language Technologies*, pages 820–825, Atlanta, Georgia, June. Association for Computational Linguistics.

Christina Reuterskiöld Wagner, Ulrika Nettelbladt, Birgitta Sahlén, and Claes Nilholm. 2000. Conversation versus narration in pre-school children with language impairment. *International Journal of Language & Communication Disorders*, 35(1):83–93.

Matthew Rispoli, Pamela Hadley, and Janet Holt. 2008. Stalls and revisions: A developmental perspective on sentence production. *Journal of Speech, Language, and Hearing Research*, 51(4):953–966.

Cheryl M Scott and Jennifer Windsor. 2000. General language performance measures in spoken and written narrative and expository discourse of school-age children with language learning disabilities. *Journal of Speech, Language & Hearing Research*, 43(2).

Eleanor Messing Semel, Elisabeth Hemmersam Wiig, and Wayne Secord. 2003. *Clinical evaluation of language fundamentals*. The Psychological Corporation, A Harcourt Assessment Company, Toronto, Canada, fourth edition.

Helen Tager-Flusberg, Sally Rogers, Judith Cooper, Rebecca Landa, Catherine Lord, Rhea Paul, Mabel Rice, Carol Stoel-Gammon, Amy Wetherby, and Paul Yoder. 2009. Defining spoken language benchmarks and selecting measures of expressive language development for young children with autism spectrum disorders. *Journal of Speech, Language and Hearing Research*, 52(3):643.

Ben Taskar, Carlos Guestrin, and Daphne Koller. 2003. Maximum-margin markov networks. In *Neural Information Processing Systems (NIPS)*.

Elin T Thordardottir and Susan Ellis Weismer. 2001. Content mazes and filled pauses in narrative language samples of children with specific language impairment. *Brain and cognition*, 48(2-3):587–592.

Danielle Wetherell, Nicola Botting, and Gina Conti-Ramsden. 2007. Narrative in adolescent specific language impairment (sli): A comparison with peers across two different narrative genres. *International Journal of Language & Communication Disorders*, 42(5):583–605.

Alexander Yeh. 2000. More accurate tests for the statistical significance of result differences. In *Proceedings of the 18th conference on Computational linguistics-Volume 2*, pages 947–953. Association for Computational Linguistics.

Simon Zwarts and Mark Johnson. 2011. The impact of language models and loss functions on repair disfluency detection. In *Proceedings of the 49th Annual Meeting of the Association for Computational Linguistics: Human Language Technologies*, pages 703–711, Portland, Oregon, USA, June. Association for Computational Linguistics.

Learning Predictive Linguistic Features for Alzheimer's Disease and related Dementias using Verbal Utterances

Sylvester Olubolu Orimaye
Intelligent Health Research Group
School of Information Technology
Monash University Malaysia
sylvester.orimaye@monash.edu

Jojo Sze-Meng Wong
Intelligent Health Research Group
School of Information Technology
Monash University Malaysia
jojo.wong@monash.edu

Karen Jennifer Golden
Jeffrey Cheah School of
Medicine and Health Sciences
Monash University Malaysia
karen.golden@monash.edu

Abstract

Early diagnosis of neurodegenerative disorders (ND) such as Alzheimer's disease (AD) and related Dementias is currently a challenge. Currently, AD can only be diagnosed by examining the patient's brain after death and Dementia is diagnosed typically through consensus using specific diagnostic criteria and extensive neuropsychological examinations with tools such as the Mini-Mental State Examination (MMSE) or the Montreal Cognitive Assessment (MoCA). In this paper, we use several Machine Learning (ML) algorithms to build diagnostic models using syntactic and lexical features resulting from verbal utterances of AD and related Dementia patients. We emphasize that the best diagnostic model distinguished the AD and related Dementias group from the healthy elderly group with 74% F-Measure using Support Vector Machines (SVM). Additionally, we perform several statistical tests to indicate the significance of the selected linguistic features. Our results show that syntactic and lexical features could be good indicative features for helping to diagnose AD and related Dementias.

1 Introduction

Ageing and neurodegeneration can be a huge challenge for developing countries. As ageing population continues to increase, government and health care providers will need to deal with the associated economic and social effects such as an increased dependency ratio, higher need for social protection, and smaller workforce. The significance of this increase and demographic transition is a high prevalence of neurodegenerative diseases such as AD and related Dementias. According to Kalaria et al. (2008), 71% of 81.1 million dementia related cases have been projected to be in the developing countries with annual costs of US$73 billion.

Alzheimer's disease is the most common form of dementia (Ballard et al., 2011). However, early diagnosis of dementia is currently challenging, especially in the earlier stages. Dementias have been typically diagnosed through extensive neuropsychological examinations using a series of cognitive tests containing set questions and images (Williams et al., 2013). For example, the MMSE screening tool is composed of a series of questions and cognitive tests that assess different cognitive abilities, with a maximum score of 30 points. A MMSE score of 27 and above is suggestive of not having a Dementia related disease. The challenge with these cognitive tests is that the accuracy depends on the clinician's level of experience and their ability to diagnose different subtypes of the disease as Dementia disease can be classified further into Alzheimer's disease, Vascular Dementia, Dementia with Lewy bodies (DLB), Mixed dementia, Parkinson's disease, as well as other forms[1].

As such, this paper investigates effective computational diagnostic models for predicting AD and related Dementias using several linguistic features extracted from the transcribed verbal utterances produced by potential patients. The premise is that, neurodegenrative disorders (ND) are characterized by the deterioration of nerve cells that control cognitive, speech and language processes, which consequentially translates to how patients compose verbal utterances. Thus, we proposed the diagnostic models using Machine Learning (ML) algorithms that learn such linguistic features and classify the AD and related Dementias group from the healthy elderly group.

[1] http://www.alz.org/dementia/types-of-dementia.asp

Workshop on Computational Linguistics and Clinical Psychology: From Linguistic Signal to Clinical Reality, pages 78–87,
Baltimore, Maryland USA, June 27, 2014.

2 Related Work

Few ML algorithms have been proposed to automate the diagnosis of Dementias using linguistic features. In a recent study, Williams et al. (2013) experimented with different ML algorithms for learning neuropsychological and demographic data which are then used for the prediction of Clinical Dementia Rating (CDR) scores for different sub-types of Dementia and other cognitive impairments. In that study, four ML algorithms were used comprising of Naïve Bayes (NB), C4.5 Decision Trees (DT), Neural Networks with back-propagation (NN), and Support Vector Machines (SVM). The study reports NB with the highest classification accuracy; however, its accuracy could be biased as the same NB was used for the initial feature selection for all the four ML algorithms. As such, the feature sets would have been optimized for NB.

In another study, Chen and Herskovits (2010) proposed different diagnostic models that distinguished the very mild dementia (VMD) group from the healthy elderly group by using features from structural magnetic-resonance images (MRI) to train seven ML algorithms. Their study reported that both SVM and Bayesian Networks (Bayes Nets) gave the best diagnostic models with the same accuracy of 80%. Similarly, a study by Klöppel et al. (2008) reported a better accuracy with SVM on the scans provided by radiologists. In contrast, we study several linguistic features from the transcribed verbal utterances of AD and related Dementia patients. We emphasize that the proposed diagnostic models do not depend on the complex MRI scan processes but a simple verbal description of familiar activities in order to diagnose the disease.

A closely related work to ours is Garrard et al. (2013) research. The study used Naïve Bayes Gaussian (NBG) and Naïve Bayes multinomial (NBM) to classify textual descriptions into a Dementia group and a healthy elderly group. The Information Gain (IG) feature selection algorithm was used in both cases and both algorithms achieved a better accuracy of up to 90% with features such as low frequency content words and certain generic word components. In this paper, we study more exclusive syntactic and lexical features that could distinguish the AD and related Dementia patients from the healthy group. In addition, we build several models by experimenting with different ML algorithms rather than NB alone.

Similarly, Roark et al. (2011) demonstrated the efficacy of using complex syntactic features to classify mild cognitive impairment (MCI) but not AD and Dementia. Also, de Lira et al. (2011) investigated the significance of lexical and syntactic features from the verbal narratives of AD patients by performing several statistical tests based on 121 elderly participants comprising of 60 AD subjects and 61 healthy subjects. Their lexical features comprised of word-finding difficulties, immediate word repetition of isolated words, word revisions, semantic substitutions, and phonemic paraphasias. For syntactic features, coordinated sentences, subordinated sentences, and reduced sentences were examined. Upon performing and making comparison between the parametric Student's t-test (t) and the non-parametric Mann-Whitney test (U), only word-finding difficulties, immediate repetitions, word revisions, coordinated sentences, and reduced sentences were found to be statistically significant with $p = 0.001$ at a 95% confidence interval (CI). Further post-hoc analysis with the Wald test (Wald X^2) showed that immediate word repetitions, word revisions, and coordinated sentences could be used to distinguish AD patients from the healthy elderly group.

While de Lira et al. (2011) did not perform any evaluation using ML algorithms, we focus on the feasibility of effectively diagnosing AD and related Dementias by learning additional syntactic and lexical features with different ML algorithms. According to Ball et al. (2009), syntactic processing in acquired language disorders such as Aphasia in adults, has shown promising findings, encouraging further study on identifying effective syntactic techniques. Similarly, Locke (1997) emphasized the significance of lexical-semantic components of a language, part of which is observable during utterance acquisition at a younger age. Locke highlighted further that as the lexical capacity increases, syntactic processing becomes automated, hence leading to changes in language. As such, it is almost certain that the effects of a specific language disorder could be observed as changes to the lexical and syntactic processes governing language and verbal utterances.

In this paper, we identify several syntactic and lexical features in addition to the significant features studied by de Lira et al. (2011) and then train five different ML models to predict the likelihood of a patient having Dementia. First, we extract predictive syntactic and lexical features from the existing DementiaBank[2] corpus containing a set of transcribed texts from verbal utterances produced by AD and related Dementia patients living in the United States. The transcribed texts are stored in the CHAT system format in the DementiaBank corpus made available by the School of Medicine of the University of Pittsburgh as part of the TalkBank project[3]. We further extract several lexical and syntactic features from the CHAT format and conduct different statistical tests and then learn and evaluate with different ML algorithms. We emphasize that the best model accuracy reported in our study is comparable to the accuracy reported in Garrard et al. (2013) and outperforms a model using only the three significant features reported in de Lira et al. (2011).

The rest of this paper is organized as follows. We present the methodology used in this study in Section 3. The DementiaBank dataset and the participants are described in Section 3.1 and Section 3.2 respectively. Section 4 discusses the feature extraction process that extracts both the lexical and syntactic features used in this study. In Section 5, we perform statistical tests to understand the significant features. Section 6 performs additional feature selection and make comparison with the statistical test results. We discuss the ML models used in this study in Section 7. Finally, results, discussion and conclusion are presented in Section 8, 9, and 10.

3 Methods

It is common in clinical research to conduct investigation on the actual patients (or subjects). This process can be achieved over a period of time; however, previous research studies have made available series of clinical datasets that reduce the investigation time considerably. Although, this study does not involve direct interaction with actual patients, we focus on understanding the linguistic patterns from the verbal utterances of existing patients. In Section 2, we have discussed those verbal utterances to be present in the transcription files contained in the DementiaBank dataset and we will describe the dataset further in Section 3.1. In this study, our focus is to use the extended syntactic and lexical features from the transcripts and compare to the features established in de Lira et al. (2011) as our baseline. We identified 21 features including the 3 significant features investigated in de Lira et al. (2011). 9 of those features are syntactic, 11 are lexical features, and 1 is a confounding feature (age). We will describe the features in detail in Section 4. Our feature extraction is followed by statistical tests as performed in de Lira et al. (2011). Both the Student's t-test (t) and the Mann-Whitney test (U) are performed and followed by multiple logistic regression (MLR) that shows the most significant features. In addition, we also perform feature selection using the Information Gain algorithm and compare our results to those achieved by MLR. The final ML models are built using SVM, NB, Bayes Net, DT, and NN.

3.1 Datasets

In this study, an existing DementiaBank clinical dataset was used. The dataset was created during a longitudinal study conducted by the University of Pittsburgh School of Medicine on Alzheimer's and related Dementia and funded by the National Institute of Aging[4]. The dataset contains transcripts of verbal interviews with AD and related Dementia patients, including those with MCI. Interviews were conducted in the English language and were based on the description of the Cookie-Theft picture component which is part of the Boston Diagnostic Aphasia Examination (Kaplan et al., 2001). During the interview, patients were given the picture and were told to discuss everything they could see happening in the picture. The patients' verbal utterances were recorded and then transcribed into the CHAT transcription format (MacWhinney, 2000). Thus, in this study, we extract the transcribed patient sentences from the CHAT files and then pre-process the sentences for feature extraction.

3.2 Participants

The participants in the DementiaBank dataset have been categorized into Dementia, Control, and Unknown patient groups. Our study uses only the Dementia and Control groups as we are interested in the binary diagnosis of the AD and related Dementias. Thus, the Dementia group consists of 314 elderly patients with an approximate age range of 49 to 90 years. The group consists of 239 peo-

[2]http://talkbank.org/DementiaBank/

[3]http://www.talkbank.org/browser/index.php

[4]http://www.nia.nih.gov/

ple diagnosed with probable AD; 21 with possible AD; 5 with Vascula Dementia (VD); 43 with MCI; 3 with Memory problem and 4 other people with an unidentified form of dementia. On the other hand, the Control group consists of 242 healthy elderly without any reported diagnosis and with approximate age range of 46 to 81 years. In order to have a balanced number of participants across groups, we reduced the AD and related Dementias group to the first 242 patients consisting of 189 probable AD, 8 possible AD, 37 MCI, 3 memory problems, 4 Vascular dementia, and 1 other participant with an unidentified form of dementia. In addition, some demographic information was made available in the DementiaBank dataset, however, we have only selected age in order to measure the significance of the disease with respect to age.

4 Features Extraction

Several features were extracted from the transcript files. First, we extracted every CHAT symbol in the transcript files and stored them according to their frequencies and positions in each sentence. We emphasize that some CHAT symbols represent both explicit and implicit features that describe the lexical capability of the patient. For example, having the CHAT symbol [//] at a specific position within a sentence implies that the patient was retracing a verbal error that precedes that position and at the same time attempting to make correction, while the CHAT symbol [/] shows the patient making immediate word repetition (MacWhinney, 2000). On the other hand, it is non-trivial to extract the syntactic features without performing syntactic parsing on the sentences. As such, using the Stanford Parser Klein and Manning (2003), we generated the syntactic tree structure of each sentence and extract features as appropriate.

4.1 Syntactic features

As described below, we investigated a number of features that are seen to demand complex syntactic processing, including the three syntactic features (*coordinated*, *subordinated*, and *reduced* sentences) evaluated by de Lira et al. (2011) and the *Dependency distance* feature evaluated by Roark et al. (2011) and Pakhomov et al. (2011). All syntactic features are extracted from the syntactic tree structures produced by the Stanford Parser.

- Coordinated sentences: Coordinated sentences are those whose clauses are combined using coordinating conjunctions. The number of occurrence for this feature per patient narrative is obtained based on the frequency of the coordinating conjunction PoS tag (`CC`) detected in the parse tree structure.
- Subordinated sentences: Subordinated sentences are those that are subordinate to the independent primary sentence to which they are linked. Similarly, the number of occurrence for this feature per patient narrative is obtained based on the frequency of the sub-sentences indicated by the PoS tag (`S`) detected in the parse tree structure.
- Reduced sentences: Following the definition set out by de Lira et al. (2011), this feature represents those subordinated sentences without a conjunction but with nominal verb forms (which are either participles or gerund). To obtain the count for this feature, the frequencies of PoS tags (`VBG` and `VBN`) are used.
- Number of predicates: The number of predicates found in every patient's narrative can be seen as another estimation of the sentence complexity. The predicates are extracted using a rule-based algorithm that locates transitive verbs which are followed by one or more arguments. We emphasize that the importance of predicate-argument structures has been explored in the literature for text classification tasks (Surdeanu et al., 2003; Orimaye, 2013).
- Average number of predicates: The average number of predicates per patient narrative is investigated as well to study its effect.
- Dependency distance: This feature was used in the study of Pakhomov et al. (2011) as a way to measure grammatical complexity in patients with Alzheimer's disease. The distance value is calculated based on the sum of all the dependency distances, in which each dependency distance is the absolute difference between the serial position of two words that participate in a dependency relation.
- Number of dependencies: For a purpose similar as to the syntactic dependency distance, the number of unique syntactic dependency

relations found in every patient's narrative is examined.

- Average dependencies per sentence: We also consider the average number of the unique dependency relations per sentence.

- Production rules: Production rules derived from parse trees has been explored in a number of NLP related classification tasks (Wong and Dras, 2010; Post and Bergsma, 2013). We investigate this feature by counting the number of unique production rules in the context-free grammar form extracted from each patient's narrative.

4.2 Lexical features

The lexical features used in this study include the *revision* and *repetition* features proposed in Croisile et al. (1996) and evaluated in de Lira et al. (2011). The remaining features are additionally investigated lexical features that show better improvement with our models.

- Utterances: The total number of utterances per patient was computed. Each utterance is identified to start from the beginning of a verbal communication to the next verbal pause length, such as punctuation or a CHAT symbol that represents a specific break in communication (Marini et al., 2008). A sentence could have one or more utterances, and an utterance could be one word, a phrase or a clause. It has been identified that utterance acquisitions form a grammatical lexicon for a language (Locke, 1997). Thus, we hypothesize that the absolute number of utterances in a conversation could show the language strength of a potential patient.

- Mean Length of Utterances (MLU): We measure the structural organization of sentences using the MLU. This was computed as the ratio of the total number of words to the number of utterances (Marini et al., 2008). MLU has been specifically used to measure grammar growth in children with Specific Language Impairment (SLI) (Yoder et al., 2011). In this study, we investigate the significance of MLU in determining language disorder in AD and related Dementias.

- Function words: We compute the total number of function words in the patient's narrative. Function words enable sentences to have meaning and they have been studied as an essential attribute to brain and language processing (Friederici, 2011).

- Unique words: We measure the total number of unique words as the absolute word count minus the number of immediate repeated words.

- Word count: This is measured as the absolute word count including repeated words.

- Character length: We measure the absolute character length of the patient's narrative.

- Total sentences: This is the absolute count of sentences in the patient's narrative.

- Repetitions: This is measured as the number of immediate word repetitions in the patient's narrative (de Lira et al., 2011; Croisile et al., 1996).

- Revisions: This feature is measured as the count of pause positions where the patient retraced a preceding error and then made a correction (MacWhinney, 2000; de Lira et al., 2011; Croisile et al., 1996).

- Lexical bigrams: We take into account the number of unique bigrams in a patient's narrative in order to capture repeated bigram patterns.

- Morphemes: To capture the morphology structure of the patient's narrative, we measured the number of morphemes. Each morpheme represents a word or a part of it that cannot be further divided (Creutz and Lagus, 2002).

5 Statistical Evaluation

One of the challenges that we encountered in evaluating the features above is that some features are not normally distributed. An exception to that is the confounding feature "age". For age, it is our assumption that the DementiaBank study was designed to cover normally distributed participants in terms of age range. For the other generated features, it is understandable, since each patient would give specific attributes that show the severity of the disease overtime. As such, we performed one parametric test (Student's t-test (t)) and one non-parametric test (Mann-Whitney test (U)) and then compared the results of the two tests similar to the baseline paper (de Lira et al., 2011). Both results achieved the same results as shown in Table 1; thus, we chose the parametric results for further statistical evaluation.

Further, we conducted a post-hoc test using multiple logistic regression analysis in order to identify specific features that distinguish the AD and related Dementias group from the healthy elderly group. We present the results of the analysis using the Wald test (Wald X^2) and the Odds Ratio or $Exp(B)$ as shown in Table 2. A 95% confidence interval (CI) was computed for both lower and upper bound of $Exp(B)$ and $p < 0.05$ shows statistical significance. All tests performed are two-tailed using the IBM Statistical Package for the Social Sciences (SPSS) version 20.0.0[5].

The result of our analysis is in agreement with the study conducted by de Lira et al. (2011); however, we examined more features in our study. Our analysis shows that the statistically significant syntactic features of the ADAG have *lower* mean compared to the HAG. This indicates that the disease group have difficulties in constructing complex sentences unlike the healthy group. We suggest that effective use of predicates and reduced structures could be of vital importance to appropriately measure healthy language in Alzheimer's disease and related Dementia patients. On the other hand, statistically significant lexical features of the ADAG have *higher* mean compared to the HAG, except for MLU with just 0.91 difference. This makes sense, for example, the disease group performed more immediate word repetitions and made more revisions on grammatical errors in their narrative. More utterances were also noticed with the disease group as they tend to make several pauses resulting from syntactic errors and attempts to correct or avoid those errors in the first place.

The multiple logistic regression analysis indicates that number of utterances, reduced sentences, MLU, revisions, and number of predicates significantly distinguish the disease group from the healthy elderly group leaving out repetitions and average predicates per sentence. Interestingly, repetitions was found to be significant in de Lira et al. (2011), albeit with just 121 patients. In our case, we suspect that repeated words could be less common with both groups given the combined 484 patients, while the absolute count of predicates in a discourse (not at the sentence level) could be more representative of the groups. The confounding feature age was used because of the age difference between ADAG and HAG. The resulting odd ratios OR emphasize the likelihood of having Alzheimer's and the related Dementia diseases when the distinguishing features are used. Lower β values for MLU, predicates, and reduced sentences decreases the likelihood of having Alzheimer's disease and related Dementias.

6 Feature Selection

To further support that the features selected through statistical testing from the previous section (Section 5) are indeed significant, one of the widely adopted metrics for feature selection in the ML-based text classification paradigm — Information Gain (IG) — is explored. We could adopt the feature selection approach taken by Williams et al. (2013), in which the subset of indicative features were selected based on a specific classifier, NB in their case; we chose to use IG instead given that the IG value for each feature is calculated independent of the classifiers and thus reduces the chance of bias in terms of the model performance. By ranking the IG values for each of the extracted features (both lexical and syntactic), the top eight features with the highest IG values are the same as the subset of the eight significant features identified through the statistical tests.

7 Machine Learning Models

In order to conduct an informed comparison with the findings from the previous related work, we evaluate the same four ML models investigated by Williams et al. (2013) which include Support Vector Machines (SVM) with radial basis kernel, Naïve Bayes (NB), J48 Decision Trees (DT), and Neural Networks (NN) with back propagation. In addition, Bayesian Networks (Bayes Nets), which has also been found useful in the work of Chen and Herskovits (2010), is also evaluated. Using the ML models, we performed three sets of experiments[6] to confirm the hypothesis that the identified significant syntactic and lexical features could give effective diagnostic models. First, we experimented with the three significant features reported in de Lira et al. (2011). Second, we performed

[5]`http://www-01.ibm.com/software/analytics/spss/`

[6]`https://github.com/sooril/ADresearch`

	ADAG MEAN(SD)	HAG MEAN(SD)	t	df	p	95% CI(Difference)
Syntactic features						
Coordinated sentences	5.21(3.51)	4.73(3.11)	1.59	482	0.11	-0.11 to 1.07
Subordinated sentences	5.37(3.41)	5.12(2.84)	0.85	482	0.40	-0.32 to 0.81
Reduced Sentences	3.24(2.47)	4.12(2.67)	-3.77	482	<0.000*	-1.34 to -0.42
Number of Predicates	5.77 (3.33)	7.03(3.63)	-3.99	482	<0.000*	-1.89 to -0.64
Avr.Predicates per sentence	0.46(0.19)	0.57(0.23)	-5.48	482	<0.000*	-0.15 to -0.07
Number of Dependencies	104.67(53.76)	104.12(50.20)	0.11	482	0.91	-8.75 to 9.83
Avr.dependency per sentence	8.84(2.71)	8.82(2.47)	0.09	482	0.932	-0.44 to 0.48
Dependency distance	18.57(8.71)	18.12(8.04)	0.59	482	0.56	-1.05 to 1.95
Production rules	128.36(50.68)	126.83(44.68)	0.35	482	0.73	-7.01 to 10.05
Lexical features						
Utterances	43.56(28.22)	32.31(15.42)	5.44	482	<0.000*	7.19 to 15.31
MLU	2.66(1.22)	3.57(1.31)	-7.87	482	<0.000*	-1.13 to -0.68
Function words	59.18(34.82)	58.98(32.46)	0.07	482	0.948	-5.81 to 6.21
Unique words	115.54(60.93)	116.17(55.61)	-0.12	482	0.905	-11.05 to 9.79
Word count	127.28(68.42)	127.25(63.24)	0.005	482	0.996	-11.74 to 11.79
Character length	567.01(303.59)	580.87(292.07)	-0.512	482	0.61	-67.07 to 39.35
Total sentences	13.24(7.03)	12.86(5.29)	0.67	482	0.502	-0.73 to 1.49
Repetitions	1.64(2.44)	0.64(0.99)	5.92	482	<0.000*	0.67 to 1.34
Revision	3.77(4.36)	1.93(2.22)	5.87	482	<0.000*	1.23 to 2.47
Lexical bigrams	104.84 (52.55)	106.79 (50.61)	-0.42	482	0.677	-11.17 to 7.26
Number of Morphemes	104.23(60.73)	107.90(55.74)	-0.694	482	0.488	-14.09 to 6.74

ADAG = Alzheimer's disease and related Dementia group (n=242); HAG = Healthy elderly group (n=242); SD = standard deviation; df = degree of freedom; CI = confidence Interval.

Table 1: Statistical analysis of linguistic features based on Student's t-test.

Features	β	S.E	Wald X^2	p	OR	95% CI of OR
Age	-0.11	0.02	39.53	<0.000*	0.90	0.87 to 0.93
Utterances	-0.03	0.01	5.55	0.018*	0.97	0.95 to 0.99
MLU	0.374	0.137	7.39	0.007*	1.45	1.11 to 1.90
No of Predicates	0.25	0.059	17.64	<0.000*	1.28	1.14 to 1.44
Revisions	-0.143	0.069	4.33	0.037*	0.87	0.76 to 0.99
Reduced Sentences	0.121	0.055	4.89	0.027*	1.129	1.01 to 1.26
Constant	5.23	1.18	19.67	<0.000*	187.25	-

ADAG, n=242; HAG, n = 242; S.E = standard error; OR = Odds ratio or Exp(β); CI = confidence Interval.

Table 2: Multiple logistic regression analysis on significant and confounding features.

an experiment with the eight significant features identified by the parametric test reported in Table 1. Finally, we used the six distinguishing features identified by MLR in Table 2.

Given the relatively small size of the dataset used in this study, we conduct a 10-fold cross validation on each of the ML models by using a balanced data set with 242 instances for each group: the AD and related Dementias group and the healthy (Control) group. Performance of the ML models were measured in terms of *precision*, *recall*, and *F-measure*. All the ML experiments including the IG ranking are conducted using the Weka toolkit[7] with the default settings.

[7]http://www.cs.waikato.ac.nz/ml/weka/

8 Results

The results of the three experiments are shown in Table 3, 4, and 5 respectively. In addition, Table 6 shows a summary of the performance of the best ML model (SVM) for predicting Alzheimer's disease and the related Dementia diseases.

Our results show that SVM gave better F-Measure and recall in most cases compared to other ML algorithms. Interestingly, DT, Bayes Nets, and NB showed better precision on the disease group using the 6 and 8 significant features. Specifically, using the 6 significant features, DT showed 78% precision but 69% recall on the disease group. Similarly, Bayes Nets showed 77% precision but 66% recall on the disease group. Overall, SVM takes the lead as it showed the highest F-Measure of 74% on the disease group with 75% precision and 73% recall.

Model	Precision (ADAG/HAG)	Recall (ADAG/HAG)	F−Measure (ADAG/HAG)
SVM	0.70/0.65	0.59/0.75	0.64/0.70
NB	0.72/0.57	0.34/0.87	0.47/0.69
DT	0.67/0.65	0.62/0.69	0.65/0.67
NN	0.70/065	0.60/0.74	0.64/0.69
Bayes Nets	0.66/0.68	0.71/0.64	0.68/0.66

Table 3: Results of different ML models using the three significant features reported in (de Lira et al., 2011) on both disease and healthy elderly groups.

Model	Precision (ADAG/HAG)	Recall (ADAG/HAG)	F−Measure (ADAG/HAG)
SVM	0.74/0.73	0.73/0.74	0.73/0.74
NB	0.77/0.62	0.46/0.86	0.58/0.72
DT	0.74/0.69	0.66/0.77	0.70/0.73
NN	0.75/0.72	0.69/0.77	0.72/0.74
Bayes Nets	0.75/0.69	0.65/0.78	0.70/0.73

Table 4: Results of different ML models using the eight statistically significant features in Table 1 on both disease and healthy elderly groups.

9 Discussion

The results of our ML experiments and statistical evaluations suggest that using ML algorithms by learning syntactic and lexical features from the verbal utterances of elderly people can help the diagnosis of Alzheimers and the related Dementia diseases. The outcome of our evaluations is similar to the study conducted in de Lira et al. (2011). However, our study identifies more indicative and representative linguistic features compared to de Lira et al. (2011). Furthermore, the results of our statistical evaluation agree with the feature selection results (using IG). That is, all the statistically significant features discussed in Section 5 are also the top ranked features using the IG feature selection algorithm in Section 6. Following the identification of additional linguistic features, we emphasize that the best ML model with six significant linguistic features (age, utterances, MLU, reduced sentences, revisions, and predicates) outperforms a three-feature model (repetitions, revisions, and coordinated sentence). More importantly, unlike de Lira et al. (2011), repetitions and coordinated sentences did not contribute to the accuracy of our diagnostic models. Finally, in comparison to Williams et al. (2013), SVM obtained the highest prediction accuracy, albeit on linguistic features. Moreover, unlike Williams et al. (2013), our feature selection process is independent of the best ML algorithm (SVM) in our case. Again, this avoids unnecessary bias especially in clinical diagnosis. A limitation of this study could be the use of a binary classification between a combined Dementia related diseases group with different subtypes (such as AD, MCI and memory problems) and a control group of healthy participants. Although MCI could sometimes (but not always) be a precursor to AD and Dementia, we suggest that it could be important to exclude patients with MCI and other minor memory problems from the AD and related Dementia patients in future study.

10 Conclusion and Future Work

We have investigated promising diagnostic models for Alzheimer's and the related Dementia diseases using syntactic and lexical features from verbal utterances. We performed statistical and ML evaluations and show that the disease group used less complex sentences than the healthy elderly group. Additionally, following our regression analysis, we show that the disease group makes more grammatical errors and at the same time makes reasonable attempts to correct or avoid those errors in the first place. We also emphasized that utterances, reduced sentences, MLU, revisions, and number of predicates, significantly distinguish the disease group from the healthy elderly group. In the future, we plan to investigate indexical cues, prosodic cues, and semantic cues in order to capture the perspectives in a patient's narrative. Furthermore, we intend to evaluate our models against the MMSE and MoCA diagnostic thresholds on actual AD and Dementia patients in a developing country. More importantly, there is a need to train the diagnostic models on a larger dataset, which

Model	Precision (ADAG/HAG)	Recall (ADAG/HAG)	F−Measure (ADAG/HAG)
SVM	0.75/0.74	0.73/0.76	0.74/0.75
NB	0.79/0.65	0.53/0.86	0.63/0.74
DT	0.78/0.71	0.69/0.76	0.71/0.73
NN	0.74/0.70	0.67/0.76	0.71/0.73
Bayes Nets	0.77/0.70	0.66/0.80	0.71/0.75

Table 5: Results of different ML models using the six statistically significant features in Table 2 on both disease and healthy elderly groups.

Model	Precision	Recall	F−Measure
6-feature	**0.75***	**0.73***	**0.74***
8-feature	0.74	0.73	0.73
3-feature(Baseline)	0.70	0.59	0.64

Table 6: Summary of SVM performance with the best predictive features for diagnosing AD and related Dementias.

could lead to better accuracy. Furthermore, longitudinal studies are recommended in order to improve sample sizes and follow the course of the disease overtime.

References

Martin J Ball, Michael R Perkins, Nicole Müller, and Sara Howard. 2009. *The handbook of clinical linguistics*, volume 56. John Wiley & Sons.

Clive Ballard, Serge Gauthier, Anne Corbett, Carol Brayne, Dag Aarsland, and Emma Jones. 2011. Alzheimer's disease. *The Lancet*, 377(9770):1019 – 1031.

Rong Chen and Edward H Herskovits. 2010. Machine-learning techniques for building a diagnostic model for very mild dementia. *Neuroimage*, 52(1):234–244.

Mathias Creutz and Krista Lagus. 2002. Unsupervised discovery of morphemes. In *Proceedings of the ACL-02 workshop on Morphological and phonological learning-Volume 6*, pages 21–30. Association for Computational Linguistics.

Bernard Croisile, Bernadette Ska, Marie-Josee Brabant, Annick Duchene, Yves Lepage, Gilbert Aimard, and Marc Trillet. 1996. Comparative study of oral and written picture description in patients with alzheimer's disease. *Brain and language*, 53(1):1–19.

Juliana Onofre de Lira, Karin Zazo Ortiz, Aline Carvalho Campanha, Paulo Henrique Ferreira Bertolucci, and Thaís Soares Cianciarullo Minett. 2011. Microlinguistic aspects of the oral narrative in patients with alzheimer's disease. *International Psychogeriatrics*, 23(03):404–412.

Angela D Friederici. 2011. The brain basis of language processing: from structure to function. *Physiological reviews*, 91(4):1357–1392.

Peter Garrard, Vassiliki Rentoumi, Benno Gesierich, Bruce Miller, and Maria Luisa Gorno-Tempini. 2013. Machine learning approaches to diagnosis and laterality effects in semantic dementia discourse. *Cortex*.

Raj N Kalaria, Gladys E Maestre, Raul Arizaga, Robert P Friedland, Doug Galasko, Kathleen Hall, José A Luchsinger, Adesola Ogunniyi, Elaine K Perry, Felix Potocnik, et al. 2008. Alzheimer's disease and vascular dementia in developing countries: prevalence, management, and risk factors. *The Lancet Neurology*, 7(9):812–826.

Edith Kaplan, Harold Goodglass, Sandra Weintraub, Osa Segal, and Anita van Loon-Vervoorn. 2001. *Boston naming test*. Pro-ed.

Dan Klein and Christopher D. Manning. 2003. Accurate unlexicalized parsing. In *Proceedings of the 41st Annual Meeting on Association for Computational Linguistics - Volume 1*, ACL '03, pages 423–430. Association for Computational Linguistics.

Stefan Klöppel, Cynthia M Stonnington, Josephine Barnes, Frederick Chen, Carlton Chu, Catriona D Good, Irina Mader, L Anne Mitchell, Ameet C Patel, Catherine C Roberts, et al. 2008. Accuracy of dementia diagnosisa direct comparison between radiologists and a computerized method. *Brain*, 131(11):2969–2974.

John L Locke. 1997. A theory of neurolinguistic development. *Brain and language*, 58(2):265–326.

Brian MacWhinney. 2000. *The CHILDES Project: The database*, volume 2. Psychology Press.

Andrea Marini, Ilaria Spoletini, Ivo Alex Rubino, Manuela Ciuffa, Pietro Bria, Giovanni Martinotti, Giulia Banfi, Rocco Boccascino, Perla Strom, Alberto Siracusano, et al. 2008. The language of schizophrenia: An analysis of micro and macrolinguistic abilities and their neuropsychological correlates. *Schizophrenia Research*, 105(1):144–155.

Sylvester Olubolu Orimaye. 2013. Learning to classify subjective sentences from multiple domains using extended subjectivity lexicon and subjective predicates. In *Information Retrieval Technology*, pages 191–202. Springer.

Serguei Pakhomov, Dustin Chacon, Mark Wicklund, and Jeanette Gundel. 2011. Computerized assessment of syntactic complexity in alzheimerś disease: A case study of iris murdochś writting. *Behavior Research Methods*, 43(1):136–144.

Matt Post and Shane Bergsma. 2013. Explicit and implicit syntactic features for text classification. In *Proceedings of the 51st Annual Meeting on Association for Computational Linguistics - Volume 2*, ACL '13, pages 866–872, August.

Brian Roark, Margaret Mitchell, John-Paul Hosom, Kristy Hollingshead, and Jeffrey Kaye. 2011. Spoken language derived measures for detecting mild cognitive impairment. *Audio, Speech, and Language Processing, IEEE Transactions on*, 19(7):2081–2090.

Mihai Surdeanu, Sanda Harabagiu, John Williams, and Paul Aarseth. 2003. Using predicate-argument structures for information extraction. In *Proceedings of the 41st Annual Meeting on Association for Computational Linguistics-Volume 1*, pages 8–15. Association for Computational Linguistics.

Jennifer A Williams, Alyssa Weakley, Diane J Cook, and Maureen Schmitter-Edgecombe. 2013. Machine learning techniques for diagnostic differentiation of mild cognitive impairment and dementia. In *Workshops at the Twenty-Seventh AAAI Conference on Artificial Intelligence*.

Sze-Meng Jojo Wong and Mark Dras. 2010. Parser features for sentence grammaticality classification. In *Proceedings of the Australasian Language Technology Association Workshop 2010*, pages 67–75, December.

Paul J Yoder, Dennis Molfese, and Elizabeth Gardner. 2011. Initial mean length of utterance predicts the relative efficacy of two grammatical treatments in preschoolers with specific language impairment. *Journal of Speech, Language, and Hearing Research*, 54(4):1170–1181.

Linguistic and Acoustic Features for Automatic Identification of Autism Spectrum Disorders in Children's Narrative

Hiroki Tanaka, Sakriani Sakti, Graham Neubig, Tomoki Toda, Satoshi Nakamura
Graduate School of Information Science, Nara Institute of Science and Technology
{hiroki-tan, ssakti, neubig, tomoki, s-nakamura}@is.naist.jp

Abstract

Autism spectrum disorders are developmental disorders characterised as deficits in social and communication skills, and they affect both verbal and non-verbal communication. Previous works measured differences in children with and without autism spectrum disorders in terms of linguistic and acoustic features, although they do not mention automatic identification using integration of these features. In this paper, we perform an exploratory study of several language and speech features of both single utterances and full narratives. We find that there are characteristic differences between children with autism spectrum disorders and typical development with respect to word categories, prosody, and voice quality, and that these differences can be used in automatic classifiers. We also examine the differences between American and Japanese children and find significant differences with regards to pauses before new turns and linguistic cues.

1 Introduction

Autism spectrum disorders (ASD) are developmental disorders, first described by Kanner and Asperger in 1943 and 1944 respectively (Kanner, 1943; Asperger, 1944). The American Psychiatric Association defines the two characteristics of ASD as: 1) persistent deficits in social communication and social interaction across multiple contexts, and 2) restricted, repetitive patterns of behavior, interests, or activities (American Psychiatric Association, 2013). In particular, the former deficits in social communication are viewed as the most central characteristic of ASD. Thus, quantifying the degree of social communication skills is a necessary component of understanding the nature of ASD, creating systems for automatic ASD screening, and early intervention methods such as social skills training and applied behaviour analysis (Wallace et al., 1980; Lovaas et al., 1973).

There are a number of studies finding differences between people with ASD and people with typical development (TD). In terms of deficits in social communication, there have been reports describing atypical usage of gestures (Ashley and Inge-Marie, 2010), frequency of eye-contact and laughter (Geraldine et al., 1990), prosody (McCann and Peppe, 2003; Rhea et al., 2005), voice quality (Asgari et al., 2013), delay responses (Heeman et al., 2010), and unexpected words (Rouhizadeh et al., 2013). In this paper, we particularly focus on the cues of ASD that appear in children's language and speech

In the case of language, Newton et al. (2009) analyze blogs of people with ASD and TD, and found that people with ASD have larger variation of usage of words describing social processes, although there are no significant differences in other word categories. In the case of speech, people with ASD tend to have prosody that differs from that of their peers (Kanner, 1943), although McCann and Peppe (2003) note that prosody in ASD is an under-researched area and that where research has been undertaken, findings often conflict. Since then, there have been various studies analyzing and modeling prosody in people with ASD (Daniel et al., 2012; Kiss et al., 2013; Santen et al., 2013; Van et al., 2010). For example, Kiss et al. (2012) find several significant differences in the pitch characteristics of ASD, and report that automatic classification utilizing these features achieves accuracy well above chance level. To our knowledge, there is no previous work integrating both language and speech features to identify differences between people with ASD and TD. However, it has been noted that differences in person-

Workshop on Computational Linguistics and Clinical Psychology: From Linguistic Signal to Clinical Reality, pages 88–96,
Baltimore, Maryland USA, June 27, 2014.

ality traits including introversion/extroversion can be identified using these features (Mairesse et al., 2007).

In this paper, we perform a comprehensive analysis of language and speech features mentioned in previous works, as well as novel features specific to this work. In addition, while previous works analyzed differences between people with ASD and TD, we additionally investigate whether it is possible to automatically distinguish between children with ASD or TD using both language and speech features and a number of classification methods. We focus on narratives, where the children serving as our subjects tell a memorable story to their parent (Davis et al., 2004). Here, the use of narrative allows us to consider not only single-sentence features, but also features considering interaction aspects between the child and parent such as pauses before new turns and overall narrative-specific features such as words per minute and usage of unexpected words. Given this setting, we perform a pilot study examining differences between children with ASD and TD, the possibilities of automatic classification between ASD and TD, and the differences between American and Japanese children.

2 Data Description

As a target for our analysis, we first collected a data set of interactions between Japanese children and their parents. In collecting the data, we followed the procedure used in the creation of the USC Rachel corpus (Mower et al., 2011). The data consists of four sessions: doh (free play), jenga (a game), narrative, and natural conversation. The first child-parent interaction is free play with the parent. The child and parent are given play doh, Mr. Potato Head, and blocks. The second child-parent interaction is a jenga game. Jenga is a game in which the participants must remove blocks, one at a time, from a tower. The game ends when the tower falls. The third child-parent interaction is a narrative task. The child and parent are asked to explain stories in which they experienced a memorable emotion. The final child-parent interaction is a natural conversation without a task. These child-parent interactions are recorded and will enable comparison of the child's interaction style and communication with their parent. Each session continues for 10 minutes. During interaction, a pin microphone and video camera record the speech and video of the child and the parent.

In this paper, we use narrative data of four children with ASD (male: 3, female: 1) and two children with TD (male: 1, female: 1) as an exploratory study. The intelligence quotient (IQ) for all subjects is above 70, which is often used as a threshold for diagnosis of intellectual disability. Each subject's age and diagnosis as ASD/TD is provided in Table 1. In the narrative session, each child and parent speaks "a memorable story" for 5 minutes in turn, and the listener responds to the speaker's story by asking questions. After 5 minutes, the experimenter provides directions to change the turn.

Table 1: Subjects' age and diagnosis

Subject	A1	A2	A3	A4	T1	T2
Age	10	10	10	13	10	12
Diagnosis	ASD	ASD	ASD	ASD	TD	TD

In this paper, we analyze the child-speaking turn of the narrative session in which the parent responds to the child's utterances. All utterances are transcribed based on USC Rachel corpus manual (Mower et al., 2011) to facilitate comparison with this existing corpus. In the transcription manual, if the speaker pauses for more than one second, the speech is transcribed as separate utterances. In this paper, we examine two segment levels, the first treating each speech segment independently, and the second handling a whole narrative as the target. When handling each segment independently, we use a total of 116 utterances for both children with ASD and TD.

3 Single Utterance Level

In this section, we describe language and speech features and analysis of these characteristics towards automatic classification of utterances based on whether they were spoken by children with ASD or TD. We hypothesize that based on the features extracted from the speech signal we are capable to classify children with ASD and TD on a speech segment level, as well as on narrative level after temporally combining all the segment-based decisions.

3.1 Feature Extraction

We extract language and speech features based on those proposed by (Mairesse et al., 2007) and

(Hanson, 1995). Extracted features are summarized in Table 2. We also add one feature not covered in previous work counting the number of occurrences of laughter.

Table 2: Description of language and speech features.

Language	Features
General descriptor	Words per sentence (WPS) Words with more than 6 letters Occurrences of laughter
Sentence structure	Percentage of pronouns, conjunctions, negations, quantifiers, numbers
Psychological proc.	Percentage of words describing social, affect, cognitive, perceptual, and biological
Personal concerns	Percentage of words describing work, achievement, leisure, and home
Paralinguistic	Percentage of assent, disfluencies, and fillers
Speech	**Features**
Pitch	Statistics of sd and cov
Intensity	Statistics of sd and cov
Speech rate	Words per voiced second
Voice quality	Amplitude of a3 Difference of the h1 and the h2 Difference of the h1 and the a3

3.1.1 Language Features

We use the linguistic inquiry and word count (LIWC) (Pennebaker et al., 2007), which is a tool to categorize words, to extract language features. Because a Japanese version of LIWC is not available and there is no existing similar resource for Japanese, we implement the following procedures to automatically establish correspondences between LIWC categories and transcribed Japanese utterances. First, we use Mecab[1] for part-of-speech tagging in Japanese utterances, translate each word into English using the WWWJDIC[2] dictionary, and finally determine the LIWC category corresponding to the English word. Among the language features described in Table 2, we calculate sentence structures, psychological processes, and personal concerns using LIWC, and other features using Mecab. Here, we do not consider language-dependent features and subcategories of LIWC.

[1]https://code.google.com/p/mecab/

[2]http://www.edrdg.org/cgi-bin/wwwjdic/wwwjdic?1C

3.1.2 Speech Features

For speech feature extraction, we use the Snack sound toolkit[3]. Here, we consider fundamental frequency, power, and voice quality, which are effective features according to previous works (McCann and Peppe, 2003; Hanson, 1995). We do not extract mean values of fundamental frequency and power because those features are strongly related to individuality. Thus, we extract statistics of standard deviation (fsd, psd) and coefficient of variation (fcov, pcov) for fundamental frequency and power. We calculate speech rate, which is a feature dividing the number of words by the number of voiced seconds. Voice quality is also computed using: the amplitude of the third formant (a3), the difference between the first harmonic and the second harmonic (h1h2), and the difference between the first harmonic and the third formant (h1a3) (Hanson, 1995).

3.1.3 Projection Normalization

For normalization, we simply project all feature values to a range of [0, 1], where 0 corresponds to the smallest observed value and 1 to the largest observed value across all utterances. For utterance i, we define the value of the jth feature as v_{ij} and define $p_{ij} = \frac{v_{ij} - min_j}{max_j - min_j}$, where p_{ij} is the feature value after normalisation.

3.2 Characteristics of Language and Speech Features

In this section, we report the result of a t-test, principal component analysis, factor analysis, and decision tree using the normalised features. We use R[4] for statistical analysis.

Table 3 shows whether utterances of children with ASD or TD have a greater mean on the corresponding feature. The results indicate that the children with ASD more frequently use words with more than 6 letters (e.g. complicated words), assent (e.g. "uh-huh," or "un" in Japanese), and fillers (e.g. "umm," or "eh" in Japanese) significantly more than the children with TD. In contrast, the children with TD more frequently use the words words categorized as social (e.g. friend), affect (e.g. enjoy), and cognitive (e.g. understand) significantly more than the children with ASD. In addition, there are differences in terms of fundamental frequency variations and voice quality (e.g.

[3]http://www.speech.kth.se/snack/

[4]http://www.r-project.org

Table 3: Difference of mean values between ASD and TD based on language and speech features from children's utterances. Each table cell notes which of the two classes has the greater mean on the corresponding feature (*: $p < 0.01$, **: $p < 0.005$).

WPS	**6 let.**	**laughter**	**adverb**	**pronoun**	**conjunctions**	**negations**	**quantifiers**	**numbers**	**social**
-	ASD*	-	-	-	-	-	-	-	TD**
affect	**cognitive**	**perceptual**	**biological**	**relativity**	**work**	**achievement**	**leisure**	**home**	**assent**
TD**	TD*	-	-	-	-	-	-	-	ASD**
nonfluent	**fillers**	**fsd**	**fcov**	**psd**	**pcov**	**speech rate**	**a3**	**h1h2**	**h1a3**
-	ASD*	TD**	TD*	-	-	-	-	-	ASD**

h1a3). In particular, we observe that the children with ASD tend to use monotonous intonation as reported in (Kanner, 1943). We do not confirm a significant differences in other features.

Next, we use principal component analysis and factor analysis to find features that have a large contribution based on large variance values. As a result of principal component analysis, features about fundamental frequency, power, and h1a3 have large variance in the first component, and the feature counting perceptual words also has large value in the second component. To analyze a different aspect of principal component analysis with rotated axes, we use factor analysis with the varimax rotation method. Figure 1 shows the result of factor analysis indicating that features regarding fundamental frequency and power have large variance. In addition, other features such as speech rate, a3, and h1a3 also have large variance. Here, we can see that for features such as statistics of fundamental frequency (fsd and fcov) and power (psd and pcov), the correlation coefficient between these features are over 80% ($p < 0.01$). For correlated features, we use only standard deviation in the following sections.

We also analyze important features to distinguish between children with ASD and TD by using a decision tree. Figure 2 shows the result of a decision tree with 10 leaves indicating that speech features fill almost all of the leaves (e.g. fsd is a most useful feature to distinguish between ASD and TD). In terms of the language features, we confirm that WPS and perceptual words are important for classification.

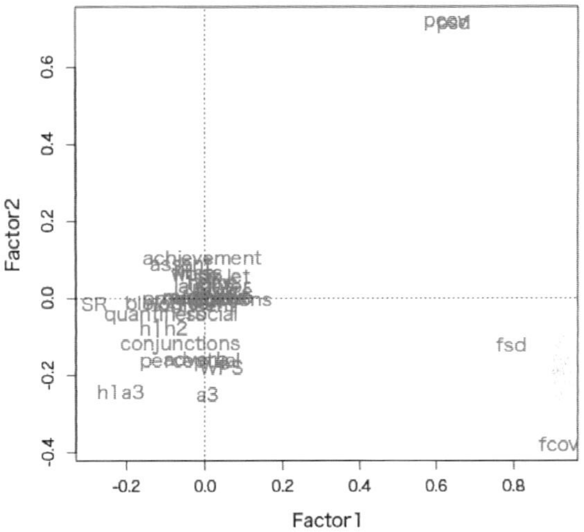

Figure 1: Factor analysis with varimax rotation method. First and second factors are indicated.

3.3 Classification

In this section, we examine the possibility of automatic identification of whether an utterance belongs to a speaker with ASD or TD. Based on the previous analysis, we prepare the following feature sets: 1) language features (Language), 2) speech features (Speech), 3) all features (All), 4) important features according to the t-test, principal component analysis, factor analysis, and decision tree (Selected), 5) important features according to the t-test that are not highly correlated (T-Uncor). The feature set of T-Uncor is as follows: 6 let., social, affect, cognitive, fillers, assent, fed, and h1a3. We also show the chance rate, which is a baseline of 50% because the number of utterances in each group is the same, and measure accuracy with 10-fold cross-validation and leave-one-speaker-out cross-validation using naive Bayes (NB) and support vector machines with a linear kernel (SVM). In the case of leave-one-speaker-out cross-validation, we use T-Uncor because the number of utterances without one speaker is too small to train using high dimensional feature sets.

Table 4 shows the result indicating that accuracies with almost all feature sets and classifiers are over 65%. The SVM with Selected achieves the best performance for the task of 10-fold cross-validation, and The SVM with T-Uncor achieves 66.7% for the task of leave-one-speaker-out. The accuracy for the task of leave-one-speaker-out on each speaker A1 to T2 is as follows: 78%, 60%, 53%, 51%, 82%, and 78%.

Table 4: Accuracy using Naive Bayes and SVM classifiers. The p-value of the t-test is measured compared to baseline (chance rate) (†: $p < 0.1$, *: $p < 0.01$)

Feature set	Accuracy [%]		
	Baseline	**NB**	**SVM**
Language		62.2†	70.3*
Speech		57.6	67.6*
All	50.0	65.0†	68.8*
Selected		67.4*	71.9*
T-Uncor		67.8†	68.1†
Per-Speaker	50.0	65.5†	66.7†

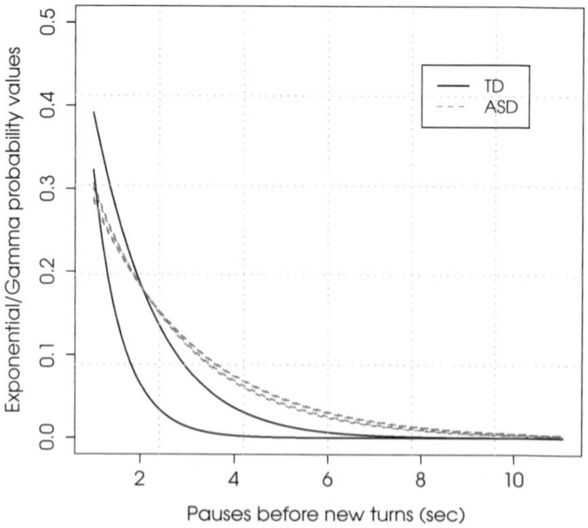

Figure 3: Gamma/Exponential pause distributions with parameters computed using Maximum Likelihood Estimation (MLE) for children with ASD and TD.

4 Narrative Level

In this section, we focus on the features of entire narratives, which allows us to examine other features of child-parent interaction for a better understanding of ASD and classification in children with ASD and TD. Each following subsection describes the procedure of feature extraction and analysis of characteristics at the narrative level. We consider pauses before new turns and unexpected words, which are mentioned in previous works, as well as words per minute.

4.1 Pauses Before New Turns

Heeman et al., (2010) reported that children with ASD tend to delay responses to their parent more than children with TD in natural conversation. In this paper, we examine whether a similar result is found in interactive narrative. We denote values of pauses before new turns as time between the end of the parent's utterance and the start of the child's utterance. We do not consider overlap of utterances. We test goodness of fit of pauses to a gamma and an exponential distribution based on (Theodora et al., 2013), because the later is a special case of gamma with a unity shape parameter, using the Kolmogorov-Smirnov test.

Figure 3 shows a fitting of pauses to gamma or exponential distributions, and we select a better fitted distribution. All subjects significantly fit ($p > 0.6$). As shown in Figure 3, we confirm that children with ASD tend to delay responses to their parent compared with children with TD. To reflect this information in our following experiments in automatic identification of ASD in narrative, we extract the expectation value of the exponential distribution

Heeman et al., (2010) also reported the relationship of the parent's previous utterance's type (question or non-question) and the child's pauses. We examine the relationship between the parent's previous question's type and pauses before new turns. For each of the children's utterances, we label the parent's utterance that directly precedes as either "open question," "closed question," or "non-question", and we calculate pause latency. Closed-questions are those which can be answered by a simple "yes" or "no," while open-questions are those which require more thought and more than a simple one-word answer. As shown in Table 5, children with ASD tend to delay responses to their parent to a greater extent than children with TD. We found no difference between open and closed questions, although a difference between questions and non-questions is observed. These results are consistent with those of previous work (Heeman et al., 2010) in terms of differences between questions and non-questions.

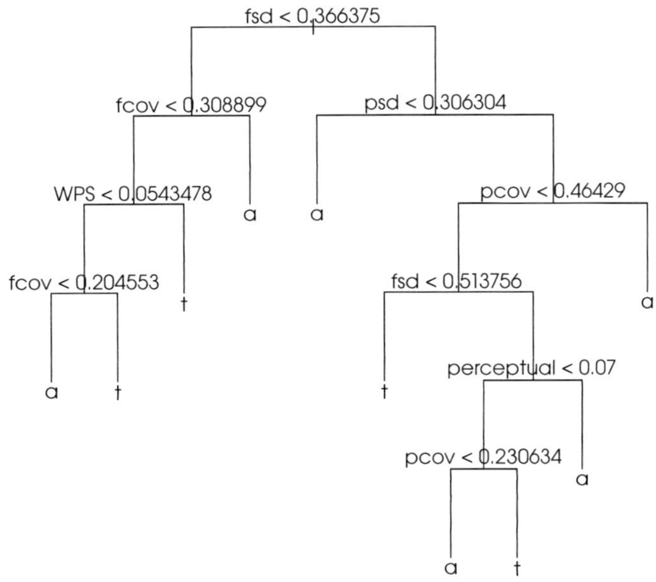

Figure 2: Decision tree with 10 leaves (a: ASD, t: TD).

Table 5: Relationship of pauses before new turns and parents' question types. The mean value and standard deviation are shown.

Question type	TD	ASD
Closed-question	0.47 (0.46)	1.61 (1.87)
Open-question	0.43 (0.34)	1.76 (1.51)
Non-question	0.95 (1.18)	2.60 (3.64)

Table 6: Mean value of words per minute.

Subj.	Averaged WPM
A1	18.25
A2	86.75
A3	23.75
A4	115.5
T1	99.25
T2	103.5

4.2 Words Per Minute

We analyze words per minute (WPM) in children with ASD and TD to clarify the relationship between ASD and frequency of speech. We use a total of 5 minutes of data in each narrative, and thus the total number of words are divided by 5 to calculate WPM. Table 6 shows the result. The data in this table indicates that some children with ASD have a significantly lower speaking rate than others with TD, but it is not necessarily the case that ASD will result in a low speaking rate such as the case of Asperger's syndrome (Asperger, 1944).

4.3 Unexpected Words

Characteristics of ASD include deficits in social communication, and these deficits affect inappropriate usage of words (Rouhizadeh et al., 2013). We evaluate these unexpected words using two measures, term frequency-inverse document frequency (TF-IDF) and log odds ratio. We use the following formulation to calculate TF-IDF for each child's narrative i and each word in that narrative j, where c_{ij} is the count of word j in narrative i. f_j is the number of narratives from the full data of child narratives containing that word j, and D is the total number of narratives (Rouhizadeh et al., 2013).

$$tf - idf_{ij} = (1 + \log c_{ij}) \log \frac{D}{f_j}$$

The log odds ratio, another measure used in information retrieval and extraction tasks, is the ratio between the odds of a particular word, j, appearing in a child's narrative, i. Letting the probability of a word appearing in a narrative be p_1 and the probability of that word appearing in all other narratives be p_2, we can express the odds ratio as follows:

$$\text{odds ratio} = \frac{\text{odds}(p_1)}{\text{odds}(p_2)} = \frac{p_1/(1-p_1)}{p_2/(1-p_2)}$$

A large TF-IDF and log odds score indicates that the word j is very specific to the narrative i, which in turn suggests that the word might be unexpected or inappropriate. In addition, because the overall amount of data included in the narratives is too small to robustly analyze these statistics for all words, we also check for the presence of each word in Japanese WordNet[5] and determine that if it exists in WordNet it is likely a common (expected) word. Table 7 shows the result of TF-IDF, log odds ratio, and their summation, and we confirm that there is no difference between children with ASD and TD. This result is different from that of previous work (Rouhizadeh et al., 2013). The children in that study were all telling the same story, and one possible explanation for this is due to the fact that in this work we do not use language-constricted data such as narrative retelling, and thus differences due to individuality are more prevalent.

Table 7: TF-IDF, log odds ratio, and their summation.

Subj.	TF-IDF	Log-odds	T+L
A1	0.50	1.01	1.52
A2	0.58	0.49	1.08
A3	0.66	1.23	1.89
A4	0.66	0.31	0.96
T1	0.74	0.49	1.23
T2	0.62	0.44	1.06

4.4 Classification

In this section, we examine the possibility of automatic classification of whether an interactive narrative belongs to children with ASD or TD. Because of the total number of subjects is small (n=4 for ASD, n=2 for TD), we perform classification with a K-NN classifier with K=1 nearest neighbour. As features, we compute the features mentioned in Section 3.1, and use the average over all utterances as the features for the entire narrative. Finally, we use pauses before new turns (expectation value of the exponential distribution), WPM, TF-IDF, log odds ratio, 6 let., social, affect, cognitive, assent, fillers, fsd, h1a3, and calculate accuracy with leave-one-speaker-out cross-validation.

As a result, we achieved an accuracy of 100% in classification between ASD and TD on the full-narrative level, which shows that these features are effective to some extent to distinguish children with ASD and TD. However, with only a total of 6 children, our sample size is somewhat small, and thus experiments with a larger data set will be necessary to draw more firm conclusions.

5 Data Comparison

As all our preceding experiments have been performed on data for Japanese child-parent pairs, it is also of interest to compare these results with data of children and parents from other cultures. In particular, we refer to the USC Rachel corpus (Mower et al., 2011) (the subjects are nine children with ASD) for comparison. Using the USC Rachel corpus, there is a report mentioning the relationship of parent's and child's linguistic information and pauses before new turns (Theodora et al., 2013). In this paper, we follow this work using Japanese data. The USC Rachel corpus includes a session of child-parent interaction, and the same transcription standard is used. We extract pauses before new turns, and short and long pauses are differentiated based on the 70th percentile of latency values for each child individually. We investigate the relationship between the parent and child's language information based on features used in Section 3.1, and short and long pauses.

Table 8 and 9 show significantly greater mean values performed using bootstrap significance testing on the means of the two pause types. By observing the values in the table, we can see that the trends are similar for both American and Japanese children. However, in terms of WPS, there is a difference. The American ASD children have greater means for WPS in the case of long pauses, while Japanese children have greater means for WPS in the case of short pauses. We analyze these differences in detail.

[5]http://www.omomimi.com/wnjpn/

Table 8: In the case of USC Rachel corpus, bootstrap on difference of means between short (S) and long (L) pauses based on linguistic features from child's and parent's utterances (†: $p < 0.1$, *: $p < 0.01$). Each table cell notes which of the two types of pauses has greater mean on the corresponding feature.

Subj.	Child				Parent		
	WPS	conj.	affect	nonflu.	adverb	cogn.	percept.
S1	L*	L*	S*	-	L*	L*	L*
S2	L*	L*	S†	L*	L*	L*	L*
S3	L*	L†	-	S†	L*	L*	L*
S4	-	-	-	L*	L*	L*	L*
S5	L†	-	-	-	L*	L*	L*
S6	L*	-	S*	-	L*	L*	-
S7	L†	-	S†	-	L†	-	-
S8	L*	-	-	-	L*	L*	L*
S9	-	-	-	S†	L*	L*	L*

Table 9: Bootstrap for pause differences in the Japanese corpus.

Subj.	Child				Parent		
	WPS	conj.	affect	nonflu.	adverb	cogn.	percept.
A1	S*	-	-	-	S*	L*	-
A2	S†	-	S*	-	L*	L*	L*
A3	S†	-	-	-	L*	L*	L*
A4	S*	-	-	-	-	-	-

In the Japanese corpus, we observe that WPS is larger in the case of short pauses. As we noticed that the child often utters only a single word for responses that follow a long pause, we analyzed the content of these single word utterances. As shown in Figure 4, for example, A1 tends to use a word related to assent when latency is long, and A4 tends to use a word related to filler, assent or others when latency is long. Though there are individual differences, we confirm that the Japanese children with ASD examined in this study tend to delay their responses before uttering one word. These characteristics may be related to the parent's question types and the child's cognitive process, and thus we need to examine these possibilities in detail.

6 Conclusion

In this work, we focused on differentiation of children with ASD and TD in terms of social communication, particularly focusing on language and speech features. Using narrative data, we examined several features on both the single utterance

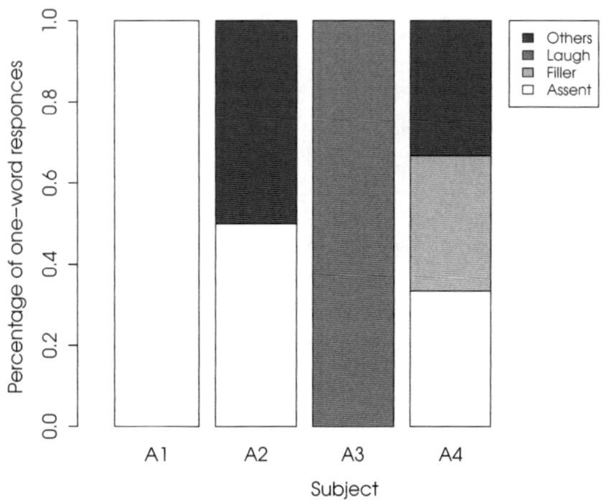

Figure 4: The language category of one-word responses in the case of a long pause.

level and the narrative level. We examined features mentioned in a number of previous works, as well as a few novel features. We confirmed about 70% accuracy in an evaluation over single utterances, and some narrative features also proved to have a correlation with ASD.

For future directions, we plan to perform larger scale experiments to examine the potential of these features for automated ASD screening. Given the results of this, we plan to move to applications including the development of dialogue systems for automatic ASD screening and social skills training.

Acknowledgments

We would like to thank the participants, children and their parents, in this study. We also thank Dr. Hidemi Iwasaka for his advice and support as clinician in pediatrics. A part of this study was conducted in Signal Analysis and Interpretation Laboratory (SAIL), University of Southern California. This study is supported by JSPS KAKEN 24240032.

References

American Psychiatric Association. 2013. *The Diagnostic and Statistical Manual of Mental Disorders: DSM 5*.

Asgari, Meysam, Alireza Bayestehtashk, and Izhak Shafran. 2013. Robust and Accurate Featuers for Detecting and Diagnosing Autism Spectrum Disorders. *Proceedings of Interspeech*, 191–194.

Asperger, H.. 1944. Die „Autistischen Psychopathen" im Kindesalter. *European Archives of Psychiatry and Clinical Neuroscience*, 117: 76–136.

Bone, D., Black, M. P., Lee, C. C., Williams, M. E., Levitt, P., Lee, S., and Narayanan, S.. 2012. Spontaneous-Speech Acoustic-Prosodic Features of Children with Autism and the Interacting Psychologist. *Proceedings of Interspeech.*

Chaspari, T., Gibson, D. B., Lee, C.-C., and Narayanan, S. S. 2013. Using physiology and language cues for modeling verbal response latencies of children with ASD. *Proceedings of ICASSP*, 3702–3706.

Davis, Megan, Kerstin Dautenhahn, CL Nehaniv, and SD Powell. 2004. Towards an Interactive System Facilitating Therapeutic Narrative Elicitation in Autism. *Proceedings of NILE.*

Dawson, Geraldine, Deborah Hill, Art Spencer, Larry Galpert, and Linda Watson.. 1990. Affective exchanges between young autistic children and their mothers. *Journal of Abnormal Child Psychology*, 18: 335–345.

de Marchena, A. and Inge-Marie E.. 2010. Conversational gestures in autism spectrum disorders: asynchrony but not decreased frequency. *Autism Research*, 3: 311–322.

Hanson M. H.. 1995. Glottal characteristics of female speakers. Harvard University, Ph.D. dissertation.

Heeman, P. A., Lunsford, R., Selfridge, E., Black, L., and Van Santen, J.. 2010. Autism and interactional aspects of dialogue. *Proceedings of SIGDIAL*, 249–252.

Kanner, L.. 1943. Autistic disturbances of affective contact. *Nervous Child*, 2: 217–250.

Kiss, G. and van Santen, J. P. H.. 2013. Estimating Speaker-Specific Intonation Patterns Using the Linear Alignment Model. *Proceedings of Interspeech* 354–358.

Kiss, G., van Santen, J. P. H., Prud'hommeaux, E. T., and Black, L. M.. 2012. Quantitative Analysis of Pitch in Speech of Children with Neurodevelopmental Disorders. *Proceedings of Interspeech.*

Lovaas, O Ivar, Robert Koegel, James Q Simmons, and Judith Stevens Long. 1973. Some generalisation and follow-up measures on autistic children in behaviour therapy. *Journal of Applied Behavior Analysis*, 6: 131–166.

Mairesse, Francois, Marilyn A Walker, Matthias R Mehl, and Roger K Moore. 2007. Using Linguistic cues for the automatic recognition of personality in conversation and text. *Journal of Artificial Intelligence Research*, 30: 457–500.

McCann, J. and Sue, P.. 2003. Prosody in autism spectrum disorders: a critical review. *International Journal of Language & Communication Disorders*, 38(4): 325–350.

Mower, E., Black, M. P., Flores, E., Williams, M., and Narayanan, S.. 2011. Rachel: Design of an emotionally targeted interactive agent for children with autism. *Proceedings of IEEE ICME*, 1–6.

Newton, A. T., Kramer, A. D. I., and McIntosh, D. N.. 2009. Autism online: a comparison of word usage in bloggers with and without autism spectrum disorders. *Proceedings of SIGCHI*, 463–466.

Paul, Rhea, Amy Augustyn, Ami Klin, and Fred R Volkmar. 2005. Perception and production of prosody by speakers with autism spectrum disorders. *Journal of Autism and Developmental Disorders*, 35: 205–220.

Pennebaker, James W, Martha E Francis, and Roger J Booth. 2005. Linguistic inquiry and word count: LIWC [Computer software] Austin, TX: liwc. net.

Rouhizadeh Masoud, Prud'hommeaux Emily, Roark Brian, and van Santen Jan. 2013. Distributional semantic models for the evaluation of disordered language. *Proceedings of NAACL-HLT*, 709–714.

Santen, Jan PH, Richard W Sproat, and Alison Presmanes Hill. 2013. Quantifying repetitive speech in autism spectrum disorders and language impairment. *Autism Research*, 6: 372–383.

Sharda, Megha, T Padma Subhadra, Sanchita Sahay, Chetan Nagaraja, Latika Singh, Ramesh Mishra, Amit Sen, Nidhi Singhal, Donna Erickson, and Nandini C Singh. 2010. Sounds of melody—Pitch patterns of speech in autism. *Neuroscience letters*, 478: 42–45.

Van Santen, Jan PH, Emily T Prud'hommeaux, Lois M Black, and Margaret Mitchell. 2010. Computational prosodic markers for autism. *Autism*, 14: 215–236.

Wallace, Charles J, Connie J Nelson, Robert Paul Liberman, Robert A Aitchison, David Lukoff, John P Elder, and Chris Ferris. 1980. A review and critique of social skills training with schizophrenic patients. *Schizophrenia Bulletin*, 6:42–63.

Mining Themes and Interests in the Asperger's and Autism Community

Yangfeng Ji, Hwajung Hong, Rosa Arriaga, Agata Rozga, Gregory Abowd, Jacob Eisenstein
School of Interactive Computing
Georgia Institute of Technology
{jiyfeng,hwajung,arriaga,agata,abowd,jacobe}@gatech.edu

Abstract

Discussion forums offer a new source of insight for the experiences and challenges faced by individuals affected by mental disorders. Language technology can help domain experts gather insight from these forums, by aggregating themes and user behaviors across thousands of conversations. We present a novel model for web forums, which captures both thematic content as well as user-specific interests. Applying this model to the Aspies Central forum (which covers issues related to Asperger's syndrome and autism spectrum disorder), we identify several topics of concern to individuals who report being on the autism spectrum. We perform the evaluation on the data collected from Aspies Central forum, including 1,939 threads, 29,947 posts and 972 users. Quantitative evaluations demonstrate that the topics extracted by this model are substantially more than those obtained by Latent Dirichlet Allocation and the Author-Topic Model. Qualitative analysis by subject-matter experts suggests intriguing directions for future investigation.

1 Introduction

Online forums can offer new insights on mental disorders, by leveraging the experiences of affected individuals — in their own words. Such insights can potentially help mental health professionals and caregivers. Below is an example dialogue from the Aspies Central forum,[1] where individuals who report being on the autism spectrum (and their families and friends) exchange advice and discuss their experiences:

- **User A**: *Do you feel paranoid at work? ... What are some situations in which you think you have been unfairly treated?*
- **User B**: *Actually I am going through something like that now, and it is very difficult to keep it under control...*
- **User A**: *Yes, yes that is it. Exactly ... I think it might be an Aspie trait to do that, I mean over think everything and take it too literally?*
- **User B**: *It probably is an Aspie trait. I've been told too that I am too hard on myself.*

Aspies Central, like other related forums, has thousands of such exchanges. However, aggregating insight from this wealth of information poses obvious challenges. Manual analysis is extremely time-consuming and labor-intensive, thus limiting the scope of data that can be considered. In addition, manual coding systems raise validity questions, because they can tacitly impose the pre-existing views of the experimenter on all subsequent analysis. There is therefore a need for computational tools that support large-scale *exploratory textual analysis* of such forums.

In this paper, we present a tool for automatically mining web forums to explore textual themes and user interests. Our system is based on Latent Dirichlet Allocation (LDA; Blei et al, 2003), but is customized for this setting in two key ways:

- By modeling sparsely-varying topics, we can easily recover key terms of interest, while retaining robustness to large vocabulary and small counts (Eisenstein et al., 2011).
- By modeling author preference by topic, we can quickly identify topics of interest for each user, and simultaneously recover topics that better distinguish the perspectives of each author.

The key technical challenge in this work lies in bringing together several disparate modalities into

[1] http://www.aspiescentral.com

Workshop on Computational Linguistics and Clinical Psychology: From Linguistic Signal to Clinical Reality, pages 97–106,
Baltimore, Maryland USA, June 27, 2014.

a single modeling framework: text, authorship, and thread structure. We present a joint Bayesian graphical model that unifies these facets, discovering both an underlying set of topical themes, and the relationship of these themes to authors. We derive a variational inference algorithm for this model, and apply the resulting software on a dataset gathered from Aspies Central.

The topics and insights produced by our system are evaluated both quantitatively and qualitatively. In a blind comparison with LDA and the author-topic model (Steyvers et al., 2004), both subject-matter experts and lay users find the topics generated by our system to be substantially more coherent and relevant. A subsequent qualitative analysis aligns these topics with existing theory about the autism spectrum, and suggests new potential insights and avenues for future investigation.

2 Aspies Central Forum

Aspies Central (AC) is an online forum for individuals on the autism spectrum, and has publicly accessible discussion boards. Members of the site do not necessarily have to have an official diagnosis of autism or a related condition. Neurotypical individuals (people not on the autism spectrum) are also allowed to participate in the forum. The forum includes more than 19 discussion boards with subjects ranging from general discussions about the autism spectrum to private discussions about personal concerns. As of March 2014, AC hosts 5,393 threads, 89,211 individual posts, and 3,278 members.

AC consists of fifteen public discussion boards and four private discussion boards that require membership. We collected data only from publicly-accessible discussion boards. In addition, we excluded discussion boards that were website-specific (announcement-and-introduce-yourself), those mainly used by family and friends of individuals on the spectrum (friends-and-family) or researchers (autism-news-and-research), and one for amusement (forum-games). Thus, we focused on ten discussion boards (aspergers-syndrome-Autism-and-HFA, PDD-NOS-social-anxiety-and-others, obsessions-and-interests, friendships-and-social-skills, education-and-employment, love-relationships-and-dating, autism-spectrum-help-and-support, off-topic-discussion, entertainment-discussion, computers-technology-discussion), in which AC users discuss their everyday expe-

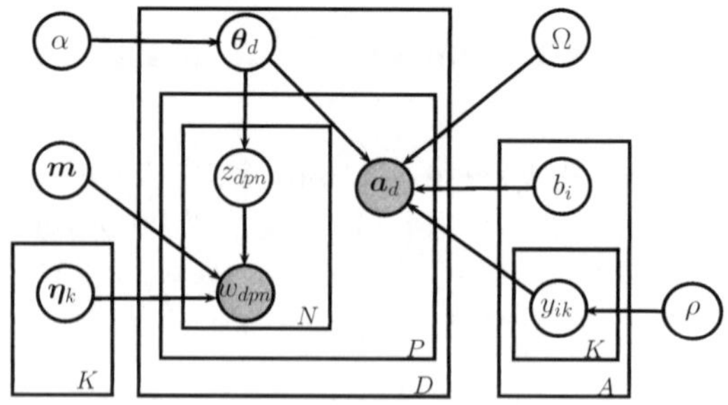

Figure 1: Plate diagram. Shaded notes represent observed variables, clear nodes represent latent variables, arrows indicate probabilistic dependencies, and plates indicate repetition.

riences, concerns, and challenges. Using the python library Beautiful Soup, we collected 1,939 threads (29,947 individual posts) from the discussion board archives over a time period from June 1, 2010 to July 27, 2013. For a given post, we extracted associated metadata such as the author identifier and posting timestamps.

3 Model Specification

Our goal is to develop a model that captures the preeminent themes and user behaviors from traces of user behaviors in online forums. The model should unite textual content with authorship and thread structure, by connecting these *observed variables* through a set of *latent variables* representing conceptual topics and user preferences. In this section, we present the statistical specification of just such a model, using the machinery of Bayesian graphical models. Specifically, the model descibes a stochastic process by which the observed variables are emitted from prior probability distributions shaped by the latent variables. By performing Bayesian statistical inference in this model, we can recover a probability distribution around the latent variables of interest.

We now describe the components of the model that generate each set of observed variables. The model is shown as a plate diagram in Figure 1, and the notation is summarized in Table 1.

3.1 Generating the text

The part of the model which produces the text itself is similar to standard latent Dirichlet allocation (LDA) (Blei et al., 2003). We assume a set of K latent topics, which are distributions over each word in a finite vocabulary. These topics are

Symbol	Description
D	number of threads
P_d	number of posts in thread d
N_p	number of word tokens in post p
α	parameter of topic distribution of threads
$\boldsymbol{\theta}_d$	the multinomial distribution of topics specific to the thread d
z_{dpn}	the topic associated with the nth token in post p of thread d
w_{dpn}	the nth token in post p of thread d
$\boldsymbol{a}_d$	authorship distribution for question post and answer posts in thread d respectively
y_{ik}	the topic-preference indicator of author i on topic k
b_i	the Gaussian distribution of author i's selection bias
$\boldsymbol{\eta}_k$	topic k in log linear space
$\boldsymbol{m}$	background topic
Ω	topic weights matrix
σ_λ^2	variance of feature weights
σ_b^2	variance of selection bias
ρ	prior probability of authors' preference on any topic

Table 1: Mathematical notations

shared among all D threads in the collection, but each thread has its own distribution over the topics.

We make use of the SAGE parametrization for generative models of text (Eisenstein et al., 2011). SAGE uses adaptive sparsity to induce topics that deviate from a background word distribution in only a few key words, without requiring a regularization parameter. The background distribution is written $\boldsymbol{m}$, and the deviation for topic k is written $\boldsymbol{\eta}_k$, so that $Pr(w = v|\boldsymbol{\eta}_k, \boldsymbol{m}) \propto \exp(m_v + \eta_{kv})$.

Each word token w_{dpn} (the nth word in post p of thread d) is generated from the probability distribution associated with a single topic, indexed by the latent variable $z_{dpn} \in \{1 \ldots K\}$. This latent variable is drawn from a prior $\boldsymbol{\theta}_d$, which is the probability distribution over topics associated with *all posts* in thread d.

3.2 Generating the author

We have metadata indicating the author of each post, and we assume that users are more likely to participate in threads that relate to their topic-specific preference. In addition, some people may be more or less likely to participate overall. We extend the LDA generative model to incorporate each of these intuitions.

For each author i, we define a latent preference vector $\boldsymbol{y}_i$, where $y_{ik} \in \{0, 1\}$ indicates whether the author i prefers to **answer** questions about topic k. We place a Bernoulli prior on each y_{ik}, so that $y_{ik} \sim \text{Bern}(\rho)$, where $\text{Bern}(y; \rho) = \rho^y(1-\rho)^{(1-y)}$. Induction of $\boldsymbol{y}$ is one of the key inference tasks for the model, since this captures topic-specific preference.

It is also a fact that some individuals will participate in a conversation regardless of whether they have anything useful to add. To model this general tendency, we add an "bias" variable $b_i \in \mathbb{R}$. When b_i is negative, this means that author i will be reluctant to participate even when she does have relevant interests.

Finally, various topics may require different levels of preference; some may capture only general knowledge that many individuals are able to provide, while others may be more obscure. We introduce a diagonal topic-weight matrix Ω, where $\Omega_{kk} = \omega_k \geq 0$ is the importance of preference for topic k. We can easily generalize the model by including non-zero off-diagonal elements, but leave this for future work.

The generative distribution for the observed author variable is a log-linear function of $\boldsymbol{y}$ and $\boldsymbol{b}$:

$$Pr(a_{di} = 1|\boldsymbol{\theta}_d, \boldsymbol{y}, \Omega, \boldsymbol{b}) = \frac{\exp(\boldsymbol{\theta}_d^\intercal \Omega \boldsymbol{y}_i + b_i)}{\sum_{j=1}^{A} \exp(\boldsymbol{\theta}_d^\intercal \Omega \boldsymbol{y}_j + b_j)} \tag{1}$$

This distribution is multinomial over authors; each author's probability of responding to a thread depends on the topics in the thread ($\boldsymbol{\theta}_d$), the author's preference on those topics ($\boldsymbol{y}_i$), the importance of preference for each topic (Ω), and the bias parameter b_i. We exponentiate and then normalize, yielding a multinomial distribution.

The authorship distribution in Equation (1) refers to a probability of user i authoring a single response post in thread d (we will handle question posts next). Let us construct a binary vector $\boldsymbol{a}_d^{(r)}$, where it is 1 if author i has authored any response posts in thread d, and zero otherwise. The probability distribution for this vector can be written

$$P(\boldsymbol{a}_d^{(r)}|\boldsymbol{\theta}_d, \boldsymbol{y}, \Omega, \boldsymbol{b}) \propto \prod_{i=1}^{A} \left(\frac{\exp(\boldsymbol{\theta}_d^\intercal \Omega \boldsymbol{y}_i + b_i)}{\sum_{j=1}^{A} \exp(\boldsymbol{\theta}_d^\intercal \Omega \boldsymbol{y}_j + b_j)} \right)^{a_{di}^{(r)}} \tag{2}$$

One of the goals of this model is to distinguish frequent responders (i.e., potential experts) from individuals who post questions in a given topic. Therefore, we make the probability of author i initiating thread d depend on the value $1 - y_{ki}$ for each topic k. We write the binary vector $\boldsymbol{a}_d^{(q)}$, where $a_{di}^{(q)} = 1$ if author i has written the question post, and zero otherwise. Note that there can only be one question post, so $\boldsymbol{a}_d^{(q)}$ is an indicator vector. Its probability is written as

$$p(\boldsymbol{a}_d^{(q)}|\boldsymbol{\theta}_d, \boldsymbol{y}, \Omega, \boldsymbol{b}) \propto \prod_{i=1}^{A} \left(\frac{\exp(\boldsymbol{\theta}_d^\intercal \Omega (\boldsymbol{1} - \boldsymbol{y}_i) + b_i)}{\sum_{j=1}^{A} \exp(\boldsymbol{\theta}_d^\intercal \Omega (\boldsymbol{1} - \boldsymbol{y}_j) + b_j)} \right)^{a_{di}^{(q)}} \tag{3}$$

We can put these pieces together for a complete distribution over authorship for thread d:

$$P(\boldsymbol{a}_d, |\boldsymbol{\theta}_d, \boldsymbol{y}, \Omega, \boldsymbol{b}) \propto \prod_{i=1}^{A} \left(\frac{\exp(\boldsymbol{\theta}_d^\intercal \Omega \boldsymbol{y}_i + b_i)}{\sum_{j=1}^{A} \exp(\boldsymbol{\theta}_d^\intercal \Omega \boldsymbol{y}_j + b_j)} \right)^{a_{di}^{(r)}} \cdot \prod_{i=1}^{A} \left(\frac{\exp(\boldsymbol{\theta}_d^\intercal \Omega (\mathbf{1} - \boldsymbol{y}_i) + b_i)}{\sum_{j=1}^{A} \exp(\boldsymbol{\theta}_d^\intercal \Omega (\mathbf{1} - \boldsymbol{y}_j) + b_j)} \right)^{a_{di}^{(q)}} \quad (4)$$

where $\boldsymbol{a}_d = \{\boldsymbol{a}_d^{(q)}, \boldsymbol{a}_d^{(r)}\}$. The probability $p(\boldsymbol{a}_d|\theta_d, \boldsymbol{y}, \Omega, \boldsymbol{b})$ combines the authorship distribution of authors from question post and answer posts in thread d. The identity of the original question poster does not appear in the answer vector, since further posts are taken to be refinements of the original question.

This model is similar in spirit to supervised latent Dirichlet allocation (sLDA) (Blei and McAuliffe, 2007). However, there are two key differences. First, sLDA uses point estimation to obtain a weight for each topic. In contrast, we perform Bayesian inference on the author-topic preference $\boldsymbol{y}$. Second, sLDA generates the metadata from the dot-product of the weights and $\bar{z}$, while we use $\boldsymbol{\theta}$ directly. The sLDA paper argues that there is a risk of overfitting, where some of the topics serve only to explain the metadata and never generate any of the text. This problem does not arise in our experiments.

3.3 Formal generative story

We are now ready to formally define the generative process of our model:

1. For each topic k
   (a) Set the word probabilities $\boldsymbol{\beta}_k = \frac{\exp(\boldsymbol{m}+\boldsymbol{\eta}_k)}{\sum_i \exp(m_i+\eta_{ki})}$
2. For each author i
   (a) Draw the selection bias $b_i \sim \mathcal{N}(0, \sigma_b^2)$
   (b) For each topic k
      i. Draw the author-topic preference level $y_{ik} \sim \text{Bern}(\rho)$
3. For each thread d
   (a) Draw topic proportions $\boldsymbol{\theta}_d \sim \text{Dir}(\alpha)$
   (b) Draw the author vector $\boldsymbol{a}_d$ from Equation (4)
   (c) For each post p
      i. For each word in this post
         A. Draw topic assignment $z_{dpn} \sim \text{Mult}(\boldsymbol{\theta}_d)$
         B. Draw word $w_{dpn} \sim \text{Mult}(\boldsymbol{\beta}_{z_{dpn}})$

4 Inference and estimation

The purpose of inference and estimation is to recover probability distributions and point estimates for the quantities of interest: the content of the topics, the assignment of topics to threads, author preferences for each topic, etc. While recent progress in probabilistic programming has improved capabilities for automating inference and estimation directly from the model specification,[2] here we develop a custom algorithm, based on variational mean field (Wainwright and Jordan, 2008). Specifically, we approximate the distribution over topic proportions, topic indicators, and author-topic preference $P(\boldsymbol{\theta}, \boldsymbol{z}, \boldsymbol{y}|\boldsymbol{w}, \boldsymbol{a}, \boldsymbol{x})$ with a mean field approximation

$$q(\boldsymbol{\theta}, \boldsymbol{z}, \boldsymbol{y}|\gamma, \phi, \psi) = \prod_{i=1}^{A}\prod_{k=1}^{K} q(y_{ik}|\psi_{ik}) \prod_{d=1}^{D}\prod_{p=1}^{P_d}\prod_{n=1}^{N_{p,d}} q(z_{dpn}|\phi_{dpn}) \prod_{d=1}^{D} q(\theta_d|\gamma_d) \quad (5)$$

where P_d is the number of posts in thread d, K is the number of topics, and N_p is the number of word tokens in post P_d. The variational parameters of $q(\cdot)$ are γ, ϕ, ψ. We will write $\langle\cdot\rangle$ to indicate an expectation under the distribution $q(\boldsymbol{\theta}, \boldsymbol{z}, \boldsymbol{y})$.

We employ point estimates for the variables $\boldsymbol{b}$ (author selection bias), $\boldsymbol{\lambda}$ (topic-time feature weights), $\boldsymbol{\eta}$ (topic-word log-probability deviations), and diagonal elements of Ω (topic weights). The estimation of $\boldsymbol{\eta}$ follows the procedure defined in SAGE (Eisenstein et al., 2011); we explain the estimation of the remaining parameters below.

Given the variational distribution in Equation (5), the inference on our topic model can be formulated as constrained optimization of this bound.

$$\begin{aligned} \min\ & \mathcal{L}(\gamma, \phi, \psi; \boldsymbol{b}, \boldsymbol{\lambda}, \Omega) \\ \text{s.t.}\ & \gamma_{dk} \geq 0 \quad \forall d, k \\ & \boldsymbol{\phi}_{dpn} \geq 0, \sum_k \phi_{dpnk} = 1 \quad \forall d, p, n \\ & 0 \leq \psi_{ik} \leq 1 \quad \forall i, k \\ & \omega_k \geq 0 \quad \forall k \end{aligned} \quad (6)$$

The constraints are due to the parametric form of the variational approximation: $q(\boldsymbol{\theta}_d|\gamma_d)$ is Dirichlet, and requires non-negative parameters;

[2]see http://probabilistic-programming.org/

$q(\boldsymbol{z}_{dpn}|\boldsymbol{\phi}_{dpn})$ is multinomial, and requires that $\boldsymbol{\phi}_{dpn}$ lie on the $K-1$ simplex; $q(y_{ik}|\psi_{ik})$ is Bernoulli and requires that ψ_{ik} be between 0 and 1. In addition, as a topic weight, ω_k should also be non-negative.

Algorithm 1 One pass of the variational inference algorithm for our model.

for $d = 1, \ldots, D$ **do**
  while not converged **do**
    for $p = 1, \ldots, P_d$ **do**
      for $n = 1, \ldots, N_{p,d}$ **do**
        Update ϕ_{dpnk} using Equation (7) for each $k = 1, \ldots, K$
      end for
    end for
    Update γ_{dk} by optimizing Equation (6) with Equation (10) for each $k = 1, \ldots, K$
  end while
end for
for $i = 1, \ldots, A$ **do**
  Update ψ_{ik} by optimizing Equation (6) with Equation (13) for each $k = 1, \ldots, K$
  Update $\hat{b}_i$ by optimizing Equation (6) with Equation (14)
end for
for $k = 1, \ldots, K$ **do**
  Update ω_k with Equation (15)
end for

4.1 Word-topic indicators

With the variational distribution in Equation (5), the inference on ϕ_{dpn} for a given token n in post p of thread d is same as in LDA. For the nth token in post p of thread d,

$$\phi_{dpnk} \propto \beta_{kw_{dpn}} \exp(\langle \log \theta_{dk} \rangle) \quad (7)$$

where $\boldsymbol{\beta}$ is defined in the generative story and $\langle \log \theta_{dk} \rangle$ is the expectation of $\log \theta_{dk}$ under the distribution $q(\theta_{dk}|\gamma_d)$,

$$\langle \log \theta_{dk} \rangle = \Psi(\gamma_{dk}) - \Psi(\sum_{k=1}^{K} \gamma_{dk}) \quad (8)$$

where $\Psi(\cdot)$ is the Digamma function, the first derivative of the log-gamma function.

For the other variational parameters γ and ψ, we can not obtain a closed form solution. As the constraints on these parameters are all convex with respect to each component, we employed a projected quasi-Newton algorithm proposed in (Schmidt et al., 2009) to optimize $\mathcal{L}$ in Equation (6). One pass of the variational inference procedure is summarized in Algorithm 1.Since every step in this algorithm will not decrease the variational bound, the overall algorithm is guaranteed to converge.

4.2 Document-topic distribution

The inference for document-topic proportions is different from LDA, due to the generation of the author vector $\boldsymbol{a}_d$, which depends on $\boldsymbol{\theta}_d$. For a given thread d, the part of the bound associated with the variational parameter $\boldsymbol{\gamma}_d$ is

$$\begin{aligned} \mathcal{L}_{\gamma_d} &= \langle \log p(\boldsymbol{\theta}_d|\alpha_d) \rangle + \langle \log p(\boldsymbol{a}_d|\boldsymbol{\theta}_d, \boldsymbol{y}, \Omega, \boldsymbol{b}) \rangle \\ &+ \sum_{p=1}^{P_d} \sum_{n=1}^{N_{p,d}} \langle \log p(z_{dpn}|\boldsymbol{\theta}_d) \rangle - \langle q(\boldsymbol{\theta}_d|\gamma_d) \rangle \end{aligned} \quad (9)$$

and the derivative of $\mathcal{L}_{\gamma_d}$ with respect to γ_{dk} is

$$\begin{aligned} \frac{d\mathcal{L}_{\gamma_d}}{d\gamma_{dk}} &= \Psi'(\gamma_{dk})(\alpha_{dk} + \sum_{p=1}^{P_d} \sum_{n=1}^{N_{p,d}} \phi_{dpnk} - \gamma_{dk}) \\ &- \Psi'(\sum_{k=1}^{K} \gamma_{dk}) \sum_{k=1}^{K} (\alpha_{dk} + \sum_{p=1}^{P_d} \sum_{n=1}^{N_{p,d}} \phi_{dpnk} - \gamma_{dk}) \\ &+ \frac{d}{d\gamma_{dk}} \langle \log p(\boldsymbol{a}_d|\boldsymbol{\theta}_d, \boldsymbol{y}, \Omega, \boldsymbol{b}) \rangle , \end{aligned} \quad (10)$$

where $\Psi'(\cdot)$ is the trigramma function. The first two lines of Equation (10) are identical to LDA's variational inference, which obtains a closed-form solution by setting $\gamma_{dk} = \alpha_{dk} + \sum_{p,n} \phi_{dpnk}$. The additional term for generating the authorship vector $\boldsymbol{a}_d$ eliminates this closed-form solution and forces us to turn to gradient-based optimization.

The expectation on the log probability of the authorship involves the expectation on the log partition function, which we approximate using Jensen's inequality. We then derive the gradient,

$$\begin{aligned} &\frac{\partial}{\partial \gamma_{dk}} \langle \log p(\boldsymbol{a}_d|\boldsymbol{\theta}_d, \boldsymbol{y}, \Omega, \boldsymbol{b}) \rangle \\ &\approx \omega_k \left(\sum_{i=1}^{A} a_{di}^{(r)} \psi_{ik} - A_d^{(r)} \sum_{i=1}^{A} \psi_{ik} \left\langle a_{di}^{(r)} | \boldsymbol{\theta}_d, \boldsymbol{y} \right\rangle \right) \\ &- \omega_k \left(\sum_{i=1}^{A} a_{di}^{(q)} \psi_{ik} - \sum_{i=1}^{A} \psi_{ik} \left\langle a_{di}^{(q)} | \boldsymbol{\theta}_d, \boldsymbol{y} \right\rangle \right) \end{aligned} \quad (11)$$

The convenience variable $A_d^{(r)}$ counts the number of distinct response authors in thread d; recall that there can be only one question author. The notation

$$\left\langle a_{di}^{(r)} | \boldsymbol{\theta}_d, \boldsymbol{y} \right\rangle = \frac{\exp(\langle \boldsymbol{\theta}^{\mathsf{T}} \rangle \Omega \langle \boldsymbol{y}_i \rangle + b_i)}{\sum_j \exp(\langle \boldsymbol{\theta}^{\mathsf{T}} \rangle \Omega \langle \boldsymbol{y}_j \rangle + b_j)},$$

represents the generative probability of $a_{di}^{(r)} = 1$ under the current variational distributions $q(\boldsymbol{\theta}_d)$ and $q(\boldsymbol{y}_i)$. The notation $\left\langle a_{di}^{(q)} | \boldsymbol{\theta}_d, \boldsymbol{y} \right\rangle$ is analogous, but represents the question post indicator $a_{di}^{(q)}$.

4.3 Author-topic preference

The variational distribution over author-topic preference is $q(y_{ik}|\psi_{ik})$; as this distribution is Bernoulli, $\langle y_{ik}\rangle = \psi_{ik}$, the parameter itself proxies for the topic-specific author preference — how much author i prefers to answer posts on topic k.

The part of the variational bound the relates to the author preferences is

$$\mathcal{L}_\psi = \sum_{d=1}^{D} \langle \log p(\boldsymbol{a}_d|\boldsymbol{\theta}_d, \boldsymbol{y}, \Omega, \boldsymbol{b})\rangle + \sum_{i=1}^{A}\sum_{k=1}^{K} \langle p(y_{ik}|\rho)\rangle - \sum_{i=1}^{A}\sum_{k=1}^{K} \langle q(y_{ik}|\psi_{ik})\rangle \quad (12)$$

For author i on topic k, the derivative of $\langle \log p(\boldsymbol{a}_d|\boldsymbol{\theta}_d, \boldsymbol{y}, \Omega, \boldsymbol{b})\rangle$ for document d with respect to ψ_{ik} is

$$\frac{d}{d\psi_{ik}} \langle \log P(\boldsymbol{a}_d|\boldsymbol{\theta}_d, \boldsymbol{y}, \Omega, \boldsymbol{b})\rangle \approx \langle\theta_{dk}\rangle\,\omega_k \left(a_{di}^{(r)} - \left\langle a_{di}^{(r)}|\boldsymbol{\theta}_d, \boldsymbol{y}\right\rangle - a_{di}^{(q)} + \left\langle a_{di}^{(q)}|\boldsymbol{\theta}_d, \boldsymbol{y}\right\rangle\right), \quad (13)$$

where $\langle\theta_{dk}\rangle = \frac{\gamma_{dk}}{\sum_{k'}\gamma_{dk'}}$. Thus, participating as a respondent increases ψ_{ik} to the extent that topic k is involved in the thread; participating as the questioner decreases ψ_{ik} by a corresponding amount.

4.4 Point estimates

We make point estimates of the following parameters: author selection bias b_i and topic-specific preference weights ω_k. All updates are based on maximum a posteriori estimation or maximum likelihood estimation.

Selection bias For the selection bias b_i of author i given a thread d, the objective function in Equation (6) with the prior of $b_i \sim \mathcal{N}(0, \sigma_b^2)$ is minimized by a quasi-Newton algorithm with the following derivative

$$\frac{\partial}{\partial b_i} \langle \log P(\boldsymbol{a}_d|\boldsymbol{\theta}_d, \boldsymbol{y}, \Omega, \boldsymbol{b})\rangle \approx a_{d,i}^{(r)} - \left\langle a_{di}^{(r)}|\boldsymbol{\theta}_d, \boldsymbol{y}\right\rangle + a_{d,i}^{(q)} - \left\langle a_{di}^{(q)}|\boldsymbol{\theta}_d, \boldsymbol{y}\right\rangle \quad (14)$$

The zero-mean Gaussian prior shrinks b_i towards zero by subtracting b_i/σ_b^2 from this gradient. Note that the gradient in Equation (14) is non-negative whenever author i participates in thread d. This means any post from this author, whether question posts or answer posts, will have a positive contribution of the author's selection bias. This means that any activity in the forum will elevate the selection bias b_i, but will not necessarily increase the imputed preference level.

Topic weights The topic-specific preference weight ω_k is updated by considering the derivative of variational bound with respect to ω_k

$$\frac{\partial \mathcal{L}}{\partial \omega_k} = \sum_{d=1}^{D} \frac{\partial}{\partial \omega_k} \langle p(\boldsymbol{a}_d|\boldsymbol{\theta}_d, \boldsymbol{y}, \Omega, \boldsymbol{b})\rangle \quad (15)$$

where for a given document d,

$$\frac{\partial}{\partial \omega_k} \langle \log p(\boldsymbol{a}_d|\boldsymbol{\theta}_d, \boldsymbol{y}, \Omega, \boldsymbol{b})\rangle \approx \langle\theta_{dk}\rangle\,\omega_k \cdot \sum_{i=1}^{A} \psi_{ik}\left(a_i^{(r)} - a_i^{(q)} + \left\langle a_{di}^{(q)}|\boldsymbol{\theta}_d, \boldsymbol{y}\right\rangle - A_d^{(r)}\left\langle a_{di}^{(r)}|\boldsymbol{\theta}_d, \boldsymbol{y}\right\rangle\right)$$

Thus, ω_k will converge at a value where the observed posting counts matches the expectations under $\langle \log p(\boldsymbol{a}_d|\boldsymbol{\theta}_d, \boldsymbol{y}, \Omega, \boldsymbol{b})\rangle$.

5 Quantitative Evaluation

To validate the topics identified by the model, we performed a manual evaluation, combining the opinions of both novices as well as subject matter experts in Autism and Asberger's Syndrome. The purpose of the evaluation is to determine whether the topics induced by the proposed model are more coherent than topics from generic alternatives such as LDA and the author-topic model, which are not specifically designed for forums.

5.1 Experiment Setup

Preprocessing Preprocessing was minimal. We tokenized texts using white space and removed punctuations at the beginning/end of each token. We removed words that appear less than five times, resulting in a vocabulary of the 4903 most frequently-used words.

Baseline Models We considered two baseline models in the evaulation. The first baseline model is latent Dirichlet allocation (LDA), which considers only the text and ignores the metadata (Blei et al., 2003). The second baseline is the Author-Topic (AT) model, which extends LDA by associating authors with topics (Rosen-Zvi et al., 2004; Steyvers et al., 2004). Both baselines are implemented in the Matlab Topic Modeling Toolbox (Steyvers and Griffiths, 2005).

Parameter Settings For all three models, we set $K = 50$. Our model includes the three tunable parameters ρ, the Bernoulli prior on topic-specific expertise; σ_b^2, the variance prior on use selection bias; and α, the prior on document-topic distribution. In the following experiments, we chose $\rho = 0.2$, $\sigma_b^2 = 1.0$, $\alpha = 1.0$. LDA and AT share two parameters, α, the symmetric Dirichlet prior for document-topic distribution; β, the symmetric Dirichlet prior for the topic-word distribution. In both models, we set $\alpha = 3.0$ and $\beta = 0.01$. All parameters were selected in advance of the experiments; further tuning of these paramters is left for future work.

5.2 Topic Coherence Evaluation

To be useful, a topic model should produce topics that human readers judge to be *coherent*. While some automated metrics have been shown to cohere with human coherence judgments (Newman et al., 2010), it is possible that naive raters might have different judgments from subject matter experts. For this reason, we focused on human evaluation, including both expert and novice opinions. One rater, R1, is an author of the paper (HH) and a Ph.D. student focusing on designing technology to understand and support individuals with autism spectrum disorder. The remaining three raters are not authors of the paper and are not domain experts.

In the evaluation protocol, raters were presented with batteries of fifteen topics, from which they were asked to select the three most coherent. In each of the ten batteries, there were five topics from each model, permuted at random. Thus, after completing the task, all 150 topics — 50 topics from each model — were rated. The user interface of topic coherence evaluation is given in Figure 2, including the specific prompt.

We note that this evaluation differs from the "intrusion task" proposed by Chang et al. (2009), in which raters are asked to guess which word was randomly inserted into a topic. While the intrusion task protocol avoids relying on subjective judgments of the meaning of "coherence," it prevents expert raters from expressing a preference for topics that might be especially useful for analysis of autism spectrum disorder. Prior work has also shown that the variance of these tasks is high, making it difficult to distinguish between models.

Table 2 shows, for each rater, the percentage of topics were chosen from each model as the most coherent within each battery. On average, 80% of the topics were chosen from our proposed model. If all three models are equally good at discovering coherent topics, the average percentage across three models should be roughly equal. Note that the opinion of the expert rater R1 is generally similar to the other three raters.

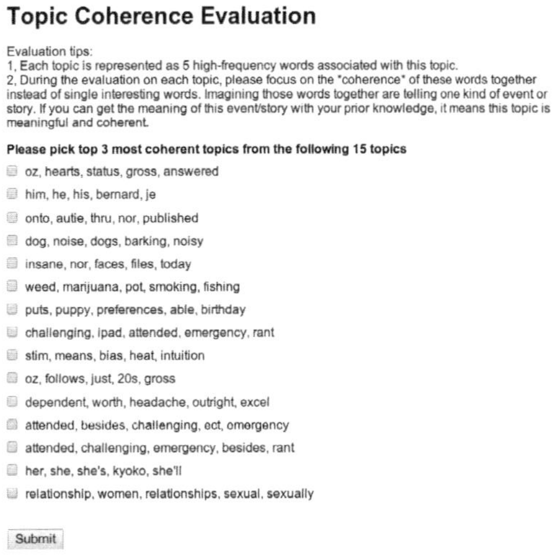

Figure 2: The user interface of topic coherence evaluation.

	Rater				
Model	R1	R2	R3	R4	Average
Our model	70%	93%	80%	77%	80%
AT	17%	7%	13%	10%	12%
LDA	13%	0%	7%	13%	8%

Table 2: Percentage of the most coherent topics that are selected from three different topic models: our model, the Author-Topic Model (AT), and latent Dirichlet allocation (LDA).

6 Analysis of Aspies Central Topics

In this section, we further use our model to explore more information about the Aspies Central forum. We want to examine whether the autism-related topics identified the model can support researchers to gain qualitative understanding of the needs and concerns of autism forum users. We are also interested in understanding the users' behavioral patterns on autism-related topics. The analysis task has three components: first we will describe the interesting topics from the autism domain perpective. Then we will find out the proportion of each topic, including autism related topics. Finally, in order to understand the user activity patterns on these autism related topics we will derive the topic-specific preference ranking of the users from our model.

Index	Proportion	Top keywords	Index	Proportion	Top keywords
1	1.7%	dont im organization couldnt construction	2	2.6%	**yah supervisor behavior taboo phone**
3	2.2%	game watched games fallout played	4	3.5%	**volunteering esteem community art self**
5	1.1%	**nobody smell boss fool smelling**	6	3.2%	firefox razor blades pc console
7	3.4%	doesn't it's mandarin i've that's	8	2.1%	**diagnosed facessenses visualize visual**
9	1.7%	obsessions bookscollecting library authors	10	2.6%	ptsd central cure neurotypical we
11	1.2%	stims mom nails lip shoes	12	1.8%	**classroom campus tag numbers exams**
13	1.6%	battery hawke charlie ive swing	14	1.9%	divorce william women marryrates
15	0.1%	chocolate pdd milk romance nose	16	5.8%	kinda holland neccesarily employment bucks
17	0.6%	eat burgers jokes memory foods	18	2.4%	dryer martial dream wake schedule
19	3.7%	**depression beleive christianity buddhism becouse**	20	1.4%	grudges pairs glasses museum frames
21	0.4%	alma star gods alien sun	22	2.6%	**facebook profiles befriend friendships friends**
23	0.4%	trilogy sci-fi cartoon iphone grandma	24	2.7%	flapping stuffed toes curse animal
25	1.5%	**empathy smells compassion emotions emotional**	26	1.7%	males evolution females originally constructive
27	0.5%	list dedicate lists humor song	28	4.6%	nts aspies autie qc intuitive
29	2.7%	captain i'm film anime that's	30	3.6%	homeless pic wild math laugh
31	3.3%	**shave exhausting during terrified products**	32	5.6%	you're you your yourself hiring
33	4.6%	dictionary asks there're offend fog	34	1.5%	grade ed school 7th diploma
35	1.0%	cave blonde hair bald disney	36	1.9%	**diagnosis autism syndrome symptoms aspergers**
37	1.3%	song joanna newsom rap favorites	38	1.8%	poetry asleep children ghosts lots
39	2.1%	heat iron adhd chaos pills	40	3.6%	bike zone rides zoning worrying
41	1.2%	uk maths team teams op	42	0.8%	book books read reading kindle
43	1.0%	husband narcissist husband's he hyper	44	1.1%	**songs guitar drums music synth**
45	1.3%	**autism disorder spectrum disorders pervasive**	46	0.7%	dog noise dogs barking noisy
47	0.6%	**relationship women relationships sexual sexually**	48	0.9%	**weed marijuana pot smoking fishing**
49	0.9%	him he his bernard je	50	2.0%	her she she's kyoko she'll

Table 3: 50 topics identified by our model. The "proportion" columns show the topic proportions in the dataset. Furthermore, 14 topics are highlighted as interesting topics for autism research.

Table 3 shows all 50 topics from our model. For each topic, we show the top five words related to this topic. We further identified fourteen topics (highlighted with **blue** color), which are particularly relevant to understand autism.

Among the identified topics, there are three popular topics discussed in the Aspies Central forum: topic 4, topic 19 and topic 31. From the top word list, we identified that topic 4 is composed of keywords related to psychological (e.g., self-esteem, art) and social (e.g., volunteering, community) well-being of the Aspies Central users. Topic 19 includes discussion on mental health issues (e.g., depression) and religious activities (e.g., believe, christianity, buddhism) as coping strategies. Topic 31 addresses a specific personal hygiene issue — helping people with autism learn to shave. This might be difficult for individuals with sensory issues: for example, they may be terrified by the sound and vibration generated by the shaver. For example, topic 22 is about making friends and maintaining friendship; topic 12 is about educational issues ranging from seeking educational resources to improving academic skills and adjusting to college life.

In addition to identifying meaningful topics, another capability of our model is to discover users' topic preferences and expertise. Recall that, for user i and topic k, our model estimates a author-topic preference variable ψ_{ik}. Each ψ_{ik} ranges from 0 to 1, indicating the probability of user i to answer a question on topic k. As we set the prior probability of author-topic preference to be 0.2, we show topic-author pairs for which $\psi_{ik} > 0.2$ in Table 4.

Topic	User index
5	USER_1, USER_2, USER_3, USER_4, USER_5
8	USER_1, USER_2, USER_6, USER_5, USER_7
12	USER_1, USER_2, USER_4, USER_8, USER_3
19	USER_1, USER_2, USER_3, USER_4, USER_7
22	USER_1, USER_2, USER_3, USER_9, USER_7
31	USER_1, USER_3, USER_2, USER_6, USER_10
36	USER_1, USER_2, USER_4, USER_3, USER_11
45	USER_1, USER_3, USER_4, USER_12, USER_13
47	USER_2, USER_14, USER_15, USER_16 , USER_6
48	USER_5, USER_4, USER_6, USER_9, USER_2

Table 4: The ranking of user preference on some interesting topics (we replace user IDs with user indices to avoid any privacy-related issue). USER_1 is the moderator of this forum. In total, our model identifies 16 user with high topic-specific preference from 10 interesting topics. For the other 4 interesting topics, there is no user with significantly high preference.

The dominance of USER_1 in these topics is explained by the fact that this user is the moderator of the forum. Besides, we also find some other users participating in most of the interesting topics, such as USER_2 and USER_3. On the other hand, users like USER_14 and USER_15 only show up in few topics. This observation is supported by their activities on discussion boards. Searching on the Aspies Certral forum, we found most answer posts of user USER_15 are from the board "love-relationships-and-dating".

7 Related Work

Social media has become an important source of health information (Choudhury et al., 2014). For example, Twitter has been used both for mining both public health information (Paul and Dredze, 2011) and for estimating individual health status (Sokolova et al., 2013; Teodoro and Naaman, 2013). Domain-specific online communities, such Aspies Central, have their own advantages, targeting specific issues and featuring more close-knit and long-term relationships among members (Newton et al., 2009).

Previous studies on mining health information show that technical models and tools from computational linguistics are helpful for both understanding contents and providing informative features. Sokolova and Bobicev (2011) use sentiment analysis to analyze opinions expressed in health-related Web messages; Hong et al. (2012) focus on lexical differences to automatically distinguish schizophrenic patients from healthy individuals.

Topic models have previously been used to mine health information: Resnik et al. (2013) use LDA to improve the prediction for neuroticism and depression on college students, while Paul and Dredze (2013) customize their *factorial* LDA to model the joint effect of drug, aspect, and route of administration. Most relevantly for the current paper, Nguyen et al. (2013) use LDA to discover autism-related topics, using a dataset of 10,000 posts from ten different autism commnities. However, their focus was on automated classification of communities as autism-related or not, rather than on analysis and on providing support for qualitative autism researchers. The applicability of the model developed in our paper towards classification tasks is a potential direction for future research.

In general, topic models capture latent themes in document collections, characterizing each document in the collection as a mixture of topics (Blei et al., 2003). A natural extension of topic models is to infer the relationships between topics and metadata such as authorship or time. A relatively simple approach is to represent authors as an aggregation of the topics in all documents they have written (Wagner et al., 2012). More sophisticated topic models, such as Author-Topic (AT) model (Rosen-Zvi et al., 2004; Steyvers et al., 2004) assume that each document is generated by a mixture of its authors' topic distributions. Our model can be viewed as one further extension of topic models by incorporating more metadata information (authorship, thread structure) in online forums.

8 Conclusion

This paper describes how topic models can offer insights on the issues and challenges faced by individuals on the autism spectrum. In particular, we demonstrate that by unifying textual content with authorship and thread structure metadata, we can obtain more coherent topics and better understand user activity patterns. This coherence is validated by manual annotations from both experts and non-experts. Thus, we believe that our model provides a promising mechanism to capture behavioral and psychological attributes relating to the special populations affected by their cognitive disabilities, some of which may signal needs and concerns about their mental health and social well-being.

We hope that this paper encourages future applications of topic modeling to help psychologists understand the autism spectrum and other psychological disorders — and we hope to obtain further validation of our model through its utility in such qualitative research. Other directions for future work include replication of our results across multiple forums, and applications to other conditions such as depression and attention deficit hyperactivity disorder (ADHD).

Acknowledgments

This research was supported by a Google Faculty Award to the last author. We thank the three reviewers for their detailed and helpful suggestions to improve the paper.

References

David M. Blei and Jon D. McAuliffe. 2007. Supervised Topic Models. In *NIPS*.

David M. Blei, Andrew Y. Ng, and Michael I. Jordan. 2003. Latent dirichlet allocation. *the Journal of machine Learning research*, 3:993–1022.

Jonathan Chang, Jordan L. Boyd-Graber, Sean Gerrish, Chong Wang, and David M. Blei. 2009. Reading Tea Leaves: How Humans Interpret Topic Models. In Yoshua Bengio, Dale Schuurmans, John D. Lafferty, Christopher K. I. Williams, and Aron Culotta, editors, *NIPS*, pages 288–296. Curran Associates, Inc.

Munmun De Choudhury, Meredith Ringel Morris, and Ryen W. White. 2014. Seeking and Sharing Health Information Online: Comparing Search Engines and Social Media. In *Procedings of CHI*.

Jacob Eisenstein, Amr Ahmed, and Eric P. Xing. 2011. Sparse Additive Generative Models of Text. In *ICML*.

Kai Hong, Christian G. Kohler, Mary E. March, Amber A. Parker, and Ani Nenkova. 2012. Lexical Differences in Autobiographical Narratives from Schizophrenic Patients and Healthy Controls. In *Proceedings of the 2012 Joint Conference on Empirical Methods in Natural Language Processing and Computational Natural Language Learning*, pages 37–47. Association for Computational Linguistics, July.

David Newman, Jey Han Lau, Karl Grieser, and Timothy Baldwin. 2010. Automatic evaluation of topic coherence. In *Human Language Technologies: The 2010 Annual Conference of the North American Chapter of the Association for Computational Linguistics*, pages 100–108. Association for Computational Linguistics.

A. Taylor Newton, Adam D.I. Kramer, and Daniel N. McIntosh. 2009. Autism online: a comparison of word usage in bloggers with and without autism spectrum disorders. In *Proceedings of the SIGCHI Conference on Human Factors in Computing Systems*, pages 463–466. ACM.

Thin Nguyen, Dinh Phung, and Svetha Venkatesh. 2013. Analysis of psycholinguistic processes and topics in online autism communities. In *Multimedia and Expo (ICME), 2013 IEEE International Conference on*, pages 1–6. IEEE.

Michael J. Paul and Mark Dredze. 2011. You Are What You Tweet: Analyzing Twitter for Public Health. In *ICWSM*.

Michael J. Paul and Mark Dredze. 2013. Drug Extraction from the Web: Summarizing Drug Experiences with Multi-Dimensional Topic Models. In *Proceedings of the 2013 Conference of the North American Chapter of the Association for Computational Linguistics: Human Language Technologies*, pages 168–178, Atlanta, Georgia, June. Association for Computational Linguistics.

Philip Resnik, Anderson Garron, and Rebecca Resnik. 2013. Using Topic Modeling to Improve Prediction of Neuroticism and Depression in College Students. In *Proceedings of the 2013 Conference on Empirical Methods in Natural Language Processing*.

Michal Rosen-Zvi, Thomas Griffiths, Mark Steyvers, and Padhraic Smyth. 2004. The Author-Topic Model for Authors and Documents. In *UAI*.

Mark Schmidt, Ewout van den Berg, Michael P. Friedlander, and Kevin Muphy. 2009. Optimizing Costly Functions with Simple Constraints: A Limited-Memory Projected Quasi-Netton Algorithm. In *AISTATS*.

Marina Sokolova and Victoria Bobicev. 2011. Sentiments and Opinions in Health-related Web messages. In *Proceedings of the International Conference Recent Advances in Natural Language Processing 2011*, pages 132–139, Hissar, Bulgaria, September. RANLP 2011 Organising Committee.

Marina Sokolova, Stan Matwin, Yasser Jafer, and David Schramm. 2013. How Joe and Jane Tweet about Their Health: Mining for Personal Health Information on Twitter. In *Proceedings of the International Conference Recent Advances in Natural Language Processing RANLP 2013*, pages 626–632, Hissar, Bulgaria, September. INCOMA Ltd. Shoumen, BULGARIA.

Mark Steyvers and Thomas Griffiths. 2005. Matlab Topic Modeling Toolbox 1.4.

Mark Steyvers, Padhraic Smyth, and Thomas Griffiths. 2004. Probabilistic Author-Topic Models for Information Discovery. In *KDD*.

Rannie Teodoro and Mor Naaman. 2013. Fitter with Twitter: Understanding Personal Health and Fitness Activity in Social Media. In *Proceedings of the 7th International Conference on Weblogs and Social Media*.

Claudia Wagner, Vera Liao, Peter Pirolli, Les Nelson, and Markus Strohmaier. 2012. It's not in their tweets: Modeling topical expertise of Twitter users. In *ASE/IEEE International Conference on Social Computing*.

Martin J. Wainwright and Michael I. Jordan. 2008. Graphical models, exponential families, and variational inference. *Foundations and Trends in Machine Learning*, 1(1-2):1–305.

Toward Macro-Insights for Suicide Prevention: Analyzing Fine-Grained Distress at Scale

Christopher M. Homan[1] **Ravdeep Johar**[1] **Tong Liu**[1]
Megan Lytle[2] **Vincent Silenzio**[2] **Cecilia O. Alm**[3]
[1] Golisano College of Computing and Information Sciences, Rochester Institute of Technology
[2] Department of Psychiatry, University of Rochester Medical Center
[3] College of Liberal Arts, Rochester Institute of Technology
{cmh[§] | rsj7209[$] | tl8313[$] | Megan_Lytle[†] | Vincent_Silenzio[†] | coagla[$]}
[§]@cs.rit.edu [$]@rit.edu [†]@urmc.rochester.edu

Abstract

Suicide is a leading cause of death in the United States. One of the major challenges to suicide prevention is that those who may be most at risk cannot be relied upon to report their conditions to clinicians. This paper takes an initial step toward the automatic detection of suicidal risk factors through social media activity, with no reliance on self-reporting. We consider the performance of annotators with various degrees of expertise in suicide prevention at annotating microblog data for the purpose of training text-based models for detecting suicide risk behaviors. Consistent with crowdsourcing literature, we found that novice-novice annotator pairs underperform expert annotators and outperform automatic lexical analysis tools, such as Linguistic Inquiry and Word Count.

1 Introduction

Suicide is among the leading causes of death for individuals 10–44 years of age in the United States (Heron and Tejada-Vera, 2009). Indeed, while mortality rates for most illnesses decreased between 2008 and 2009, the rate of suicide increased by 2.4% (Heron and Tejada-Vera, 2009). The lifetime prevalence for suicidal ideation is 5.6–14.3% in the general population, and as high as 19.8–24.0% among youth (Nock et al., 2008).

The first step toward suicide *prevention* is to identify, ideally in consultation with clinical experts, the risk factors associated with suicide. Due to social stigma among other sociocultural factors (Crosby et al., 2011), individuals at risk for committing suicide may not always reach out to professionals or, if they do, provide them with accurate information. They may not even realize their own level of suicide risk before it is too late. Self-reporting, then, is not an entirely reliable means of detecting and assessing suicide risk, and research on suicide prevention can benefit from also exploring other channels for assessing risk.

For instance, individuals may be more inclined to seek support from informal resources, such as social media, instead of seeking treatment (Crosby et al., 2011; Bruffaerts et al., 2011; Ryan et al., 2010). Evidence suggests that youth and emerging adults usually prefer to seek help from their friends and families; however, higher levels of suicidal ideation are associated with lower levels of help-seeking from both formal or informal resources (Deane et al., 2001).

These patterns in help-seeking behavior suggest that social media might be an important channel for discovering those at risk for—and even preventing—suicide. Internet- and telecommunications-driven activity is revolutionizing the social sciences by providing data, much of it publicly available, on human activity in situ, at volumes and a level of time and space granularity never before approached. Can such data improve clinical preventative study and measures by providing access to at-risk individuals who would otherwise go undetected, and by leading to better science about suicide risk behaviors?

The stress-diathesis model for suicidal behavior (Mann et al., 1999) suggests that they might. It says that (1) objective states, such as depression or life events, as well as subjective states and traits, such as substance abuse or family history of depression, suicide, or substance abuse, are among the risk factors that contribute to suicidal ideation and (2) the presence of these factors could eventually lead to either externalizing (e.g., interper-

Workshop on Computational Linguistics and Clinical Psychology: From Linguistic Signal to Clinical Reality, pages 107–117,
Baltimore, Maryland USA, June 27, 2014.

sonal violence) or internalizing aggression (e.g., attempting suicide).

Since the stress-diathesis model was developed using risk factors for suicidal behavior, and because it makes a connection between internalized and externalized acts, it is a suitable framework for analyzing publicly available linguistic data from social media outlets such as Twitter. Data from social media can be seen as a kind of natural experiment on depression and suicidal ideation that is unburdened by such sample biases as the willingness of individuals to take part in research and/or seek out formal sources of support. Moreover, this approach may provide information about individuals who are unlikely to engage in formal help-seeking behaviors, or may inform effective methods of natural helping. Thus, this macro-level approach to monitoring suicidal behaviors may have future implications not only for identifying individuals who have a higher prevalence for suicidal behaviors but it could eventually lead to additional methods for enhancing protective factors against suicide.

In this paper, we take steps toward the automatic detection of suicide risk among individuals via social media. Suicide ideation is a complex behavior and its connection to suicide itself remains poorly understood. We focus on a particular aspect of suicidality, namely *distress*. While not equivalent to suicide ideation, according to Nock et al. (2010) distress is an important risk factor in suicide, and one that is observable from microblog text, though admittedly observing suicide risk behavior is a subjective and noisy venture.

Lehrman et al. (2012) conducted an early study on the computational modeling of distress based on short forum texts, yet left many areas wide open for continued study. For example, analysis at scale is one such open issue. More specifically, Pestian and colleagues (Matykiewicz et al., 2009; Pestian et al., 2008) used computational methods to understand suicide notes. However, when it comes to preventive contexts, such data are less insightful. For preventive health, access to real-time health-related data that dynamically evolve can allow us to address macro-level analysis. Social media provide an additional opportunity to model the phenomena of interest at scale.

We use methods that take advantage of lexical analysis to retrieve microblog posts (tweets) from Twitter and compare the performance of human annotators—one being an expert, and others not—to rate the level of distress of each tweet.

Clinical expert annotation, rather than general-purpose tools for content and sentiment analysis such as LIWC (Linguistic Inquiry and Word Count) by Pennebaker et al. (2001), provides a basis for text-based statistical modeling. We show that expertise-based keyword retrieval, departing from knowledge about contributing risk factors, results in better interannotator agreement in both novice-novice and novice-expert annotation when the keywords reflect the task at hand.

2 Related Work

Data on suicide traditionally comes from health-care organizations, large-scale studies, or self reporting (Crosby et al., 2011; Horowitz and Ballard, 2009). These sources are limited by sociocultural barriers (Crosby et al., 2011), such as stigma and shame. Moreover, data on suicide is never particularly reliable because suicide is a fundamentally subjective, complex phenomenon with a low base rate. For these reasons, many researchers tend to focus on the relationship between risk factors and suicidal behavior, without relying heavily on theoretical models (Nock et al., 2008).

Approximately one-third of all individuals who reported suicidal ideation in their lifetime made a plan to commit suicide. Nearly three-quarters of those who reported making a suicide plan actually attempted. The odds of attempting suicide increased exponentially when individuals endorsed three or more risk factors, e.g., having a mood or substance abuse disorder (Kessler et al., 1999).

Demographics, previous suicide attempts, mental health concerns (i.e., depression, substance abuse, suicidal ideation, self-harm, or impulsivity), family history of suicide, interpersonal conflicts (i.e., family violence or bullying), and means for suicidal behavior (e.g., firearms), are commonly cited risk factors for suicidal behavior (Nock et al., 2008; Crosby et al., 2011; Gaynes et al., 2004; Harriss and Hawton, 2005; Shaffer et al., 2004; Brown et al., 2000).

Regarding the use of annotation for predictive modeling, evidence suggests that when it comes to judgments that involve clinical phenomena, experts and novices behave differently (Li et al., 2012; Womack et al., 2012). Such distinctions intuitively make sense, as the learning of medical domain knowledge requires advanced education in conjunction with substantial practical field experience.

In a task such as medical image inspection, the subtle cues that point an observer to evidence that allow them to identify a clinical condition, while accessible to experts with training and perceptual expertise to guide their exploration, are likely to be missed by novices who lack that background and clinical understanding. Such expertise can then be integrated into human-centered health-IT systems (Guo et al., 2014), in order to introduce novel ways to retrieve medical images and take advantage of an understanding of which information is useful. It is reasonable to assume that this knowledge gap also applies to other knowledge-intensive clinical domains such as mental health. In this study, we explore this question and study if novice vs. expert annotation makes a difference for identifying distress in social media texts, as well as what the impact of expert vs. novice annotation is for subsequent computational modeling with the annotated data.

Affect in language is a phenomenon that has been studied in the speech and text analysis domains, and in many others (Calvo and D'Mello, 2010). Clearly, emotion is a key element in the human experience, but it is notoriously difficult to pin down and scholars in the affective sciences lack a single agreed-upon definition for emotion. Accordingly, different theoretical constructs have been proposed to describe affect and affect-related behaviors (Picard, 1997). In addition, research on affect in language has shown that such phenomena tend to be subjective, lack real ground truth (often resulting in moderate kappa scores), and have particularly fuzzy semantics in the gray zone where neutrality and emotion meet (Alm, 2008). These kinds of problem characteristics bring with them their own set of demanding challenges from a computational perspective (Alm, 2011). Yet, the nature of such problems make them incredibly important to study, despite the challenges involved.

Sentiment analysis has been widely studied in a number of computational settings, including on various social networking sites. A rather substantial body of work already exists on the use of Twitter to study emotion (Bollen et al., 2011b; Dodds et al., 2011; Wang et al., 2012; Pfitzner et al., 2012; Kim et al., 2012; Bollen et al., 2011a; Pfitzner et al., 2012; Bollen et al., 2011c; Mohammad, 2012; Golder and Macy, 2011; De Choudhury et al., 2012a; De Choudhury et al., 2012b; De Choudhury et al., 2013; De Choudhury and Counts, 2013; Hannak et al., 2012; Thelwall et al., 2011; Pak and Paroubek, 2010). For instance, Golder and and Macy study aggregate global trends in "mood," and show, among other things, that people wake up in a relatively good mood that decays as the day progresses (Golder and Macy, 2011). Bollen et al. (2011c) show that tweets from users who took a standard diagnostic instrument for mood are often tied to current events, such as elections and holidays.

Relatively little of this work has focused on suicide or related psychological conditions. Masuda et al. (2013) study suicide on mixi (a Japanese social networking service). Cheng et al. (2012) consider the ethical and political implications of online data collection for suicide prevention. Jashinsky et al. (2013) show correlations between frequency in tweets related to suicide and actual suicide in the 50 United States of America. Sadilek et al. (2014) study depression on Twitter. De Choudhury and collaborators studied depression—in general and post-partum—in Twitter (De Choudhury et al., 2012a; De Choudhury et al., 2012b; De Choudhury et al., 2013; De Choudhury and Counts, 2013) and Facebook (De Choudhury et al., 2014). Homan et al. (2014) investigate depression in TrevorSpace. A number of social theories of suicide have been proposed (Wray et al., 2011), but most of this work was with respect to offline social systems.

3 Methods

Our methods involve four main phases: (1) We filtered a corpus, obtained from Sadilek et al. (2012), of approximately 2.5 million tweets from 6,237 unique users in the New York City area that were sent during a 1-month period between May and June, 2010, into a set of 2,000 tweets that are relatively likely to be centered around suicide risk factors. (2) We annotated each of these 2,000 tweets with their level of distress, and also analyzed the annotations in detail. (3) We then trained support vector machines and topic models with the annotated data, except for a held-out subset of 200 tweets. (4) Finally, we assessed the effectiveness of these methods on the held-out data.

Source tweets	Number of tweets	2,535,706
	Unique geo-active users	6,237
	"Follows" relationships	102,739
	"Friends" relationships	31,874
Filtered tweets	Number of tweets	2,000
	Unique users	1,467
	Unique unigrams	1,714,167
	Unique bigrams	9,246,715
	Unique trigrams	1,306,1142
Categories distribution	LIWC sad	1,370
	Depressive feeling	283
	Suicide ideation	123
	Depression symptoms	72
	Self harm	67
	Family violence/discord	47
	Bullying	10
	Gun ownership	10
	Drug abuse	6
	Impulsivity	6
	Prior suicide attempts	2
	Suicide around individual	2
	Psychological disorders	2

Table 1: Summary statistics and thematic category distributions of the collected dataset. The data were collected from NYC. Geo-active users are those who geo-tag (i.e., automatically post the GPS location of) their tweets relatively frequently (more than 100 times per month).

depressive feeling	tired of living, leave this world, wanna die, hate my job, feeling guilty, deserve to die, desire to end own life, feeling ignored, tired of everything, feeling blue, have blues
depression symptoms	sleeping pill, have insomnia, sleep forever, sleep disorder
drug abuse	clonazepam, drug overdose, imipramine
prior suicide attempts	tried suicide
suicide ideation	commit suicide, committing suicide, feeling suicidal, want to suicide, shoot myself, a gun to head, hang myself, intention to die
self harm	hurt myself, cut myself
psychological disorders	sleep apnea
family violence discord	lost my friend, argument with wife, argument with husband, shouted at each other

Table 2: Filtering terms added to those from Jashinsky et al. (2013).

3.1 Filtering tweets

In order to facilitate the discovery of distress-related tweets, we first (a) converted all text to lower case; (b) stripped out punctuation and special characters; and (c) mapped informal terms (such as abbreviations and netspeak) to more standard ones, based on the noslang dictionary.[1]

We then used two different methods to filter tweets that are relatively likely to center on suicide risk factors. We used LIWC to capture 1,370 tweets by sampling randomly from among the 2,000 tweets with the highest LIWC sad score. LIWC has been widely used to estimate emotion in online social networks, and specifically to mood on Twitter. This slight amount of randomness in filtering tweets this way was intended to avoid selecting obvious false positives, such as the use of "sad" in nicknames.

Next, we adopted a collection of inclusive search terms/phrases from Jashinsky et al. (2013), which was designed specifically for capturing tweets related to suicide risk factors, and applied them to our source corpus. We added to these more terms, from (Crosby et al., 2011) (see Table 2). These terms yielded 630 tweets.

[1]http://www.noslang.com/dictionary

3.2 Novice and Expert Tweet Annotation

We then divided the resulting set of 2,000 filtered tweets (1,370 from the LIWC sad dimension and 630 from suicide-specific search terms), into two randomized sets of 1,000 tweets each. Both sets had the same proportion of LIWC-filtered and suicide-specific-filtered tweets. A novice annotated the first set and a counseling psychologist with experience in suicide related research annotated the second set. A second novice annotated a subset of 250 tweets of the first set, to reveal interannotator agreement between novices, as one might expect a novice without training to be less systematic. (The annotators were among the authors.) Each tweet in each set was rated on a four-point scale (H, ND, LD, HD) according to the level of distress evident (Table 3).

Each tweet to be annotated was provided with context in the form of the three tweets before and after the tweet to be annotated that the tweeter made, along with the timestamp of those tweets and the thematic categories to which the tweet belonged, based on the filtering process (Figure 1).

3.3 Modeling

We then mapped each tweet to a feature space composed of the unigrams, bigrams, and trigrams in the corpus. For example, a simple tweet "I am

```
978: Date: XXXX
   -3: dat man on maury is overreacting!!
       he juss doin dat cuz he on
       tv [-0:24:39]
   -2: @XXXX cedes!!! [-0:21:25]
   -1: yesssss! da weatherman was wronq
       no rainy ass prom days!! yesss
        prom is 2day guys!! class
        of 2010! [-0:02:56]
>>> @XXXX awwww thanks trae-trae
    1: rt @XXXX: abt 2 hop in a kab
       to skool i wouldn't dare spend
       over 2 dollars to get somewhere
       i dnt wanna be n da first
       place! [+0:00:57]
    2: @XXXX yeaa [+0:03:59]
    3: @XXXX wassup? [+0:05:28]
Msg_id: XXXX   [Distress: ND, LIWC Sad: No]
```

Figure 1: Example input for annotator. The tweet to be annotated is indicated by >>>. Annotators were given context in the form of the three tweets immediately preceding—and the three tweets immediately following—the tweet to be annotated that the tweeter made, along with the relative time at which each tweet was made. Each numerical label denotes one of these context tweets. (Tweeter information has been blanked out.)

Code	Distress Level
H	happy
ND	no distress
LD	low distress
HD	high distress

Table 3: Distress-related categories used to annotate the tweets.

so happy" was represented as the following *feature vector*: {I, am, so, happy, I am, am so, so happy, I am so, am so happy}. Each feature is associated with its tf-idf score (Manning et al., 2008).

We performed topic modeling on our dataset. A *topic* is a set of lexical items that are likely to occur in the same tweet. Topic models are capable of associating words with similar meanings and distinguishing among the different meanings of a single word. We used latent Dirichlet allocation (LDA) (Blei et al., 2003) to create these topics. Before doing so, we removed stop words and words that occur only once in the dataset. We then applied LDA algorithm on the data to discover three topics using 100 iterations.

We used support vector machines (SVMs) (Joachims, 1998), a machine learning method that is used to train a classification model that can assign class labels to previously unseen tweets, to assess the power of our annotations. SVMs treat each tweet as a point in an extremely high dimensional space (one dimension per uni-, bi-, and trigram in the corpus). SVMs are a form of *linear separator* that can also distinguish between nonlinearly separable classes of data by warping the feature space (though in our case we perform no such warping, or *kernelization*). They have proven to be an extremely effective tool in classifying text in numerous settings, including Twitter.

4 Results

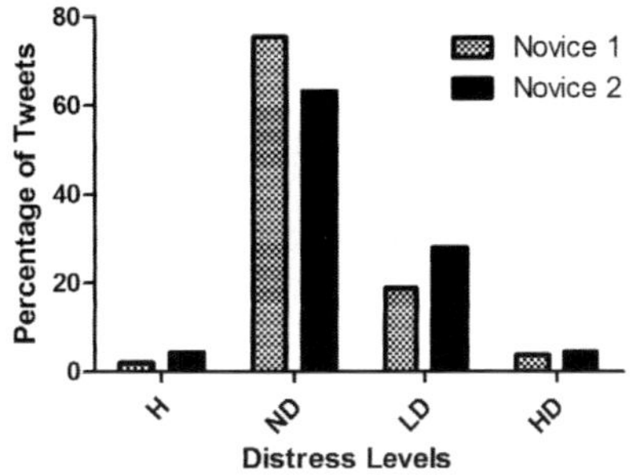

Figure 2: Distribution of distress level annotations on the tweets annotated by Novices 1 and 2 (N=250, identical set).

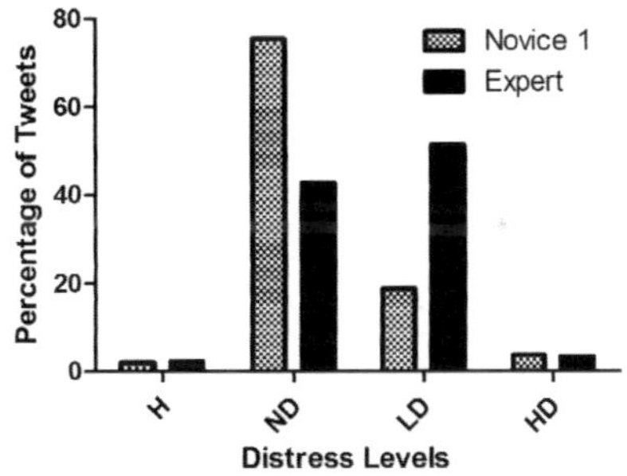

Figure 3: Distribution of distress level annotations from Novice 1 and Expert. Note the these two datasets are disjoint (N = 1000 tweets, respectively).

Figure 2 shows the distribution of annotation labels for the subset of tweets that Novices 1 and 2 both annotated, and Figure 3 compares the overall annotation distributions between Novice 1 and the Expert. Interestingly, the novices are relatively conservative, compared to the expert, in assigning distressed labels, whereas the expert exhibits a higher sensitivity toward low distress than either of the novices. This suggests that it is important in this domain not to rely too much on novice judgments, as novices are not trained to pick up on subtle cues—in contrast to the clinically trained eye.

Note that there are very few happy tweets, which confirms that our filtering was effective in removing tweets of the opposite polarity.

Filtering method	Kappa
LIWC sad	0.4
Thematic suicide risk factors	0.6
Both	0.5

Table 4: Cohen kappa interannotator agreement between Novice 1 and 2.

	H	ND	LD	HD
H	0	2	0	0
ND	1	85	2	1
LD	0	22	9	0
HD	0	1	0	2

Table 5: Confusion matrix between Novices 1 and 2 on annotations of the LIWC-sad-based filtered tweets.

	H	ND	LD	HD
H	4	6	0	0
ND	0	55	12	1
LD	0	12	22	5
HD	0	1	3	4

Table 6: Confusion matrix between Novices 1 and 2 on annotations of tweets filtered by Jashinsky et al. (2013)'s thematic suicide risk factors inclusion terms.

Table 4 shows the Cohen kappa score between Novices 1 and 2, when high and low distress vs. no distress and happy, are grouped in a single category and Tables 5—7 show the confusion matrices between Novices 1 and 2. In all cases the kappa score is moderate. However, it clearly improves when annotation is restricted to just those tweets filtered using the suicide-thematic inclusion terms of Jashinsky et al. (2013). This again seems to point to the usefulness of including clinical experts into the training process.

Due to their sensitive nature, we decided not to provide examples of high distress tweets. Here are two examples of tweets labeled as low distress by two annotators.

- `insomnia night#56325897521365!! sheesh can't deal w/ this shit! i have class in the morning got dammit....`

	H	ND	LD	HD
H	4	8	0	0
ND	1	140	14	2
LD	0	34	31	5
HD	0	2	3	6

Table 7: Confusion matrix between Novices 1 and 2 on annotations of all common tweets between the two annotators.

- `@XXXX i'm still sad thoo. i feel neglected! and i miss XXXX`

And here are two examples of tweets labeled as no distress by two annotators.

- `i did mad push-ups tryna get that cut up look, then look at myself after a shower ... #plandidntwork; thats #whyiaintgotomiami`
- `my son is gonna have blues eyes and nappy hair! yes yes yes`

The above examples are rather clear cut, however in many cases the tweets were more ambiguous, even when annotators had the preceding and succeeding three tweets from the user of the tweet to be annotated to rely on for context. While context and time offset information was useful for annotators, distress annotation is clearly a challenging task, as the confusion matrices in Tables 5–6 reveal. The lower agreement levels, and particularly the fuzzy border between 'no distress' and 'low distress' are completely in line with prior research, discussed above, on affective language phenomena.

Another filtering and annotation challenge involves tweets with mixed emotion, such as:

- `as much as i hate my job some of the people i work with are amazing.`

Beyond the targeted annotation categories of distress level, there were emerging themes of aggression, privilege and oppression, and daily struggles, among others. For instance, jobs were a popular source of distress:

- `i friggin hate these bastards my job grimey ass bastards knew i wanted the day off and tell me some next shit`
- `hate my job wit a passion! hate everyl there.. they better do sumthin about it, or im out!`

Personal bias may have impacted annotation decisions. For instance, numerous tweets contained irony and dark humor, which may result in annotators underestimating or overlooking actual distress. In addition, by pulling data from Twitter, any non-Twitter context behind the tweets is lost. For example, a few individuals retweeted in a sarcastic manner about what individuals should say to someone who is considering suicide:

- `you wish!!! rt @XXXX: i think suicide is funny. especially once my mom does it`
- `rt @XXXX: what do i say to a person thats asking me for advice becuz they thinking bout committing suicide when i see there point? lmao`

Without knowing the circumstances of the original message (beyond the provided context window) it is difficult to classify such tweets.

Finally, a number of tweets seemed to show compassion or empathy for others experiencing stress. This suggests to us the profound role that social support places in well-being and depression, that one's friends and associates can also provide clues into one's emotional state, and that social media can reveal such behavior.

- `rt @XXXX: damn now what do i do? i feel empty as f$% damit!! breathe ocho, *tears* from liberty city to (cont) http://XXXX`
- `@XXXX that's just sad i feel for you`

High Distress	Random
feel like, wanna cry, get hurt, miss 2, ima miss, win lose, tired everything, broke bitches, gun range, one person	good morning, last night, happy birthday, look like, bout 2, can't wait, video , know (cont), chris brown, jus got
commit suicide, miss you!, miss baby, feel empty, committing suicide, tired living, sleep forever, lost phone, left alone, :(miss	feel like, let know, make sure, bout go, time get, don't get, wats good, . ., don't want, jus saw
hate job, feel sad, tummy hurts, lost friend, feel helpless, leave alone, don't wanna, worst feeling, leave world, don't let	don't know, let's go, looks like, what's good, go sleep, even tho, hell yea, new single, r u?, don't wanna

Table 8: Topic analysis on bigrams of tweets labeled as high distress vs. randomly selected tweets from the larger, unlabeled dataset. The high distress tweets clearly convey strong negative affect.

Table 8 shows the results of a 3-category topic model on bigrams. The first column is taken just from tweets labeled high distress by any one of the three annotators (72 tweets total). The second column comes from a randomly-chosen sample of 2000 tweets from the 2.3 million tweet corpus. These results show that the lexical contents of the annotated tweets are recognizeably different from the random sample. By our judgement, the topical groupings in the rows of the high distress column are all clearly marked by strong negative affect, and additionally they could arguably be labeled—from top to bottom—as: "failure and defeat," "loss," and "loneliness." The rows of the second column are less clear cut, and appear to reflect a much broader scope of topics. One interesting aspect of the second, random column is that recording artist Chris Brown had released a new album during the collection period, which seems to explain why his name appeared.

Training	Testing	Precision	Recall	F-Measure
N1	N1	0.53	0.63	0.58
N1	E	0.58	0.27	0.37
E	E	0.59	0.71	0.64
E	N1	0.34	0.85	0.48
N1 + E	N1 + E	0.33	0.41	0.37

Table 9: Performance of SVM-based classification when the training and testing sets are alternately Novice 1 (N1) or the Expert (E). Because we focus on distress classification, we report precision, recall and F-measure for the distress class, which combines LD and HD into a single class with respect to binary (distress vs. non-distress) classification. In each case, a held-out set of 100 randomly selected tweets compose the test set and the remaining 900 tweets from that annotator compose the training set. The last row shows when the two training sets (respectively, test sets) are combined into a single set of 1800 (respectively, 200) tweets.

For classification, because we are most interested in being able to separate distressed from non-distressed tweets, we combine low distress and high distress into a single distress class, and no distress and happy into a non-distress class. Table 9 shows the performance of the SVM-based classifier when trained and tested on the Expert and Novice 1 training sets. Four themes emerge: (1) the SVM classifier is much more accurate (in terms of F-measure) when the testing and training data come from the same annotator (test and training data are disjoint), and the best performance comes from the expert-annotated data. (2) When testing and training data are from different annotators, the F-measure performance of the SVM is lower when the training set is from the novice rather than the expert. (3) When testing and training data are from different annotators, the SVM has lower recall and higher precision when the training set is from the novice rather than the expert. This is in part because the Expert was more sensitive to distress than Novice 1. It is premature to draw conclusions from this observation, but perhaps this shows that training with expert-labeled annotations is preferable to using novice-labeled data, espectially when our goal is to discover distressful tweets for the purpose of identifying at-risk individuals and err on the side of caution (high recall). (4) Integrating more but mixed data does not improve performance.

5 Discussion

As previously mentioned, many of the risk factors for suicidal behavior may be linked to other expressions of distress, such as aggression and interpersonal violence (Mann et al., 1999). The goal of this study is to determine the feasibility of classifying distress to enable further study of expressed suicidal behaviors. Consistent with the stress diathesis model for suicidal behavior, aggression was an emerging theme that arose from the data. Here are some examples:

- @XXXX i don't feel sad 4 him. he gets pissed n says wat he wants then sends out fony apologies
- @XXXX cuz he's n a relationship with that horseface bitch & he lied 2 me & i feel so used & worthless now

Some individuals tweeted about feeling empty, hopeless, angry, frustrated, and alone. Behaviors indicating bullying and schadenfreude were also observed. While these are all risk factors for internalizing aggression (i.e., suicidal behavior), they are also associated with externalized aggression. In addition to overt expressions of anger and violence, many of the humorous, ironic tweets also had an aggressive undertone.

5.1 Limitations

As ground truth, we rely on tweets hand-annotated by expert and novice for classification. However, the mental state of another individual, observed from a few lines of text often written in an informal register is necessarily hard to discern and, even under less noisy conditions, extremely subjective; even the observers' personal understandings of such concepts as "distress" may differ drastically. This makes annotation quite a challenge, and does not reveal in an objective fashion a tweeter's true mental state. As we have mentioned earlier, self-reporting has its own limitations, yet it is often regarded as the gold standard for ground truth about emotional state. Part of the problem in assessing the effectiveness of self-reporting is the relative rareness by which suicide occurs, and by the inherent subjectivity of the act, which makes any data on suicide fuzzy. We hope to explore in future work the relationship between clinical observation in both on- and off-line settings and self-reporting, including the integration of natural language data of patients from clinical settings. We also hope to explore distress annotation from different perspectives and levels of context.

Higher levels of suicidal ideation have an inverse relationship with all types of help-seeking and a positive correlation with the decision to not seek support (Deane et al., 2001). Thus, we would expect suicidal individuals to generally be less active on social media than those who are not. Nevertheless, a number of studies have shown a positive correlation between online social network use and negative mood. Perhaps this means in part that individuals who are depressed are slower to disengage on- rather than off-line.

6 Conclusion

We studied the performance of different approaches to training systems to detect evidence of suicide risk behavior in microblog data. We showed that both the methods used to automatically collect training sets, as well as the expertise level of the annotator affect greatly the performance of automatic systems for detecting suicide risk factors. In general, our study and its results—from filtering via data annotation to classification—confirmed the critical importance of bringing clinical expertise into the computational modeling loop.

Acknowledgments

This work was supported by a grant of the Kodak Endowed Chair Fund from the Golisano College of Computing and Information Sciences at RIT and NSF award SES-1111016.

References

Cecilia Ovesdotter Alm. 2008. *Affect in Text and Speech*. Ph.D. thesis, University of Illinois at Urbana Champaign.

Cecilia Ovesdotter Alm. 2011. Subjective natural language problems: Motivations, applications, characterizations, and implications. In *Proceedings of 49th Annual Meeting of the Assoc. for Computational Linguistics: Human Language Technologies, Portland, OR*, pages 107–112.

David M. Blei, Andrew Y. Ng, and Michael I. Jordan. 2003. Latent Dirichlet allocation. *Journal Machince Learning Research*, 3:993–1022, March.

Johan Bollen, Bruno Gonçalves, Guangchen Ruan, and Huina Mao. 2011a. Happiness is assortative in online social networks. *Artificial Life*, 17(3):237–251.

Johan Bollen, Huina Mao, and Xiaojun Zeng. 2011b. Twitter mood predicts the stock market. *Journal of Computational Science*, 2(1):1–8.

Johan Bollen, Alberto Pepe, and Huina Mao. 2011c. Modeling public mood and emotion: Twitter sentiment and socio-economic phenomena. In *Proceedings of the Fifth International AAAI Conference on Weblogs and Social Media*, pages 450–453.

Gregory K Brown, Aaron T Beck, Robert A Steer, and Jessica R Grisham. 2000. Risk factors for suicide in psychiatric outpatients: A 20-year prospective study. *Journal of Consulting and Clinical Psychology*, 68(3):371.

Ronny Bruffaerts, Koen Demyttenaere, Irving Hwang, Wai-Tat Chiu, Nancy Sampson, Ronald C Kessler, Jordi Alonso, Guilherme Borges, Giovanni de Girolamo, Ron de Graaf, et al. 2011. Treatment of suicidal people around the world. *The British Journal of Psychiatry*, 199(1):64–70.

Rafael A. Calvo and Sidney D'Mello. 2010. Affect detection: An interdisciplinary review of models, methods, and their applications. *IEEE Transactions on Affective Computing*, 1(1):18–37.

Qijin Cheng, Shu-Sen Chang, and Paul SF Yip. 2012. Opportunities and challenges of online data collection for suicide prevention. *The Lancet*, 379(9830):e53–e54.

Alex E Crosby, LaVonne Ortega, and Cindi Melanson. 2011. *Self-directed violence surveillance: Uniform definitions and recommended data elements*. Centers for Disease Control and Prevention, National Center for Injury Prevention and Control, Division of Violence Prevention.

Munmun De Choudhury and Scott Counts. 2013. Understanding affect in the workplace via social media. In *16th ACM Conference on Computer Supported Cooperative Work and Social Media (CSCW 2013)*, pages 303–316. ACM.

Munmun De Choudhury, Scott Counts, and Michael Gamon. 2012a. Not all moods are created equal! Exploring human emotional states in social media. In *6th International AAAI Conference on Weblogs and Social Media*.

Munmun De Choudhury, Michael Gamon, and Scott Counts. 2012b. Happy, nervous or surprised? Classification of human affective states in social media. In *6th International AAAI Conference on Weblogs and Social Media*.

Munmun De Choudhury, Scott Counts, and Eric Horvitz. 2013. Major life changes and behavioral markers in social media: case of childbirth. In *Proceedings of the 2013 conference on Computer supported cooperative work*, pages 1431–1442. ACM.

Munmun De Choudhury, Scott Counts, Eric J Horvitz, and Aaron Hoff. 2014. Characterizing and predicting postpartum depression from shared facebook data. In *Proceedings of the 17th ACM conference on Computer Supported Cooperative Work & Social Computing*, pages 626–638. ACM.

Frank P Deane, Coralie J Wilson, and Joseph Ciarrochi. 2001. Suicidal ideation and help-negation: Not just hopelessness or prior help. *Journal of Clinical Psychology*, 57:901–914.

Peter Sheridan Dodds, Kameron Decker Harris, Isabel M Kloumann, Catherine A Bliss, and Christopher M Danforth. 2011. Temporal patterns of happiness and information in a global social network: Hedonometrics and twitter. *PloS one*, 6(12):e26752.

Bradley N Gaynes, Suzanne L West, Carol A Ford, Paul Frame, Jonathan Klein, and Kathleen N Lohr. 2004. Screening for suicide risk in adults: A summary of the evidence for the US Preventive Services Task Force. *Annals of Internal Medicine*, 140(10):822–835.

S.A. Golder and M.W. Macy. 2011. Diurnal and seasonal mood vary with work, sleep, and daylength across diverse cultures. *Science*, 333(6051):1878–1881.

Xuan Guo, Rui Li, Cecilia Ovesdotter Alm, Qi Yu, Jeff Pelz, Pengcheng Shi, and Anne Haake. 2014. Infusing perceptual expertise and domain knowledge into a human-centered image retrieval system: A prototype application. In *Proceedings of the Symposium on Eye Tracking Research and Applications*, pages 275–278. ACM.

Aniko Hannak, Eric Anderson, Lisa Feldman Barrett, Sune Lehmann, Alan Mislove, and Mirek Riedewald. 2012. Tweetin in the rain: Exploring societal-scale effects of weather on mood. In *Proceedings of the 6th International AAAI Conference on Weblogs and Social Media (ICWSM12)*.

Louise Harriss and Keith Hawton. 2005. Suicidal intent in deliberate self-harm and the risk of suicide: The predictive power of the suicide intent scale. *Journal of Affective Disorders*, 86(2):225–233.

Melonie Heron and Betzaida Tejada-Vera. 2009. Deaths: Leading causes for 2005. *National Vital Statistics Reports: From the Centers for Disease Control and Prevention, National Center for Health Statistics, National Vital Statistics System*, 58(8):1–97.

Christopher M Homan, Naiji Lu, Xin Tu, Megan C Lytle, and Vincent Silenzio. 2014. Social structure and depression in TrevorSpace. In *Proceedings of the 17th ACM Conference on Computer Supported Cooperative Work & Social Computing*, pages 615–625. ACM.

Lisa M Horowitz and Elizabeth D Ballard. 2009. Suicide screening in schools, primary care and emergency departments. *Current Opinion in Pediatrics*, 21(5):620–627.

Jared Jashinsky, Scott H Burton, Carl L Hanson, Josh West, Christophe Giraud-Carrier, Michael D Barnes, and Trenton Argyle. 2013. Tracking suicide risk factors through Twitter in the US. *Crisis*, pages 1–9.

T. Joachims. 1998. Text categorization with support vector machines: Learning with many relevant features. In *European Conference on Machine Learning (ECML)*, pages 137–142, Berlin. Springer.

Ronald C Kessler, Guilherme Borges, and Ellen E Walters. 1999. Prevalence of and risk factors for lifetime suicide attempts in the national comorbidity survey. *Archives of General Psychiatry*, 56(7):617–626.

Suin Kim, J Bak, and Alice Oh. 2012. Do you feel what I feel? Social aspects of emotions in Twitter conversations. In *Proceedings of the AAAI International Conference on Weblogs and Social Media.*

Michael Lehrman, Cecilia Ovesdotter Alm, and Ruben Proano. 2012. Detecting distressed vs. non-distressed affect state in short forum texts. In *Proceedings of the Workshop on Language in Social Media (LSM 2012) at the Conference of the North American Chapter of the Association for Computational Linguistics-Human Language Technologies, Montreal, Canada*, pages 9–18.

Rui Li, Jeff Pelz, Pengcheng Shi, and Anne Haake. 2012. Learning image-derived eye movement patterns to characterize perceptual expertise. In *CogSci*, pages 1900–1905.

J John Mann, Christine Waternaux, Gretchen L Haas, and Kevin M Malone. 1999. Toward a clinical model of suicidal behavior in psychiatric patients. *American Journal of Psychiatry*, 156(2):181–189.

Christopher D. Manning, Prabhakar Raghavan, and Hinrich Schütze. 2008. *Introduction to Information Retrieval*. Cambridge University Press, New York, NY, USA.

Naoki Masuda, Issei Kurahashi, and Hiroko Onari. 2013. Suicide ideation of individuals in online social networks. *PloS one*, 8(4):e62262.

Pawel Matykiewicz, Wlodzislav Duch, and John P. Pestian. 2009. Clustering semantic spaces of suicide notes and newsgroup articles. In *Proceedings of the Workshop on BioNLP, Boulder, Colorado*, pages 179–184.

Saif M Mohammad. 2012. # Emotional tweets. In *Proceedings of the First Joint Conference on Lexical and Computational Semantics-Volume 1: Proceedings of the main conference and the shared task, and Volume 2: Proceedings of the Sixth International Workshop on Semantic Evaluation*, pages 246–255. Association for Computational Linguistics.

Matthew K Nock, Guilherme Borges, Evelyn J Bromet, Christine B Cha, Ronald C Kessler, and Sing Lee. 2008. Suicide and suicidal behavior. *Epidemiologic Reviews*, 30(1):133–154.

Matthew K Nock, Jennifer M Park, Christine T Finn, Tara L Deliberto, Halina J Dour, and Mahzarin R Banaji. 2010. Measuring the suicidal mind implicit cognition predicts suicidal behavior. *Psychological Science*, 21(4):511–517.

Alexander Pak and Patrick Paroubek. 2010. Twitter as a corpus for sentiment analysis and opinion mining. In *Proceedings of Conference on Language Resources and Evaluation.*

James W Pennebaker, Martha E Francis, and Roger J Booth. 2001. Linguistic inquiry and word count: Liwc 2001. *Mahway: Lawrence Erlbaum Associates*, 71:2001.

John P. Pestian, Pawel Matykiewicz, and Jacqueline Grupp-Phelan. 2008. Using natural language processing to classify suicide notes. In *BioNLP 2008: Current Trends in Biomedical Natural Language Processing, Columbus, Ohio*, pages 96–97.

René Pfitzner, Antonios Garas, and Frank Schweitzer. 2012. Emotional divergence influences information spreading in twitter. *Proceedings of the 6th International AAAI Conference on Weblogs and Social Media (ICWSM12)*, pages 2–5.

Rosalind W. Picard. 1997. *Affective Computing*. MIT Press, Cambridge, MA, USA.

Megan L Ryan, Ian M Shochet, and Helen M Stallman. 2010. Universal online interventions might engage psychologically distressed university students who are unlikely to seek formal help. *Advances in Mental Health*, 9(1):73–83.

Adam Sadilek, Henry A Kautz, and Vincent Silenzio. 2012. Predicting disease transmission from geo-tagged micro-blog data. In *Association for the Advancement of Articial Intelligence*.

Adam Sadilek, Christopher Homan, Walter S. Lasecki, Vincent Silenzio, and Henry Kautz. 2014. Modeling fine-grained dynamics of mood at scale. In *WSDM 2014 Workshop on Diffusion Networks and Cascade Analytics*.

David Shaffer, Michelle Scott, Holly Wilcox, Carey Maslow, Roger Hicks, Christopher P Lucas, Robin Garfinkel, and Steven Greenwald. 2004. The Columbia SuicideScreen: Validity and reliability of a screen for youth suicide and depression. *Journal of the American Academy of Child & Adolescent Psychiatry*, 43(1):71–79.

Mike Thelwall, Kevan Buckley, and Georgios Paltoglou. 2011. Sentiment in Twitter events. *Journal of the American Society for Information Science and Technology*, 62(2):406–418.

Wenbo Wang, Lu Chen, Krishnaprasad Thirunarayan, and Amit P Sheth. 2012. Harnessing Twitter 'Big Data' for automatic emotion identification. In *Privacy, Security, Risk and Trust (PASSAT), 2012 International Conference on and 2012 International Confernece on Social Computing (SocialCom)*, pages 587–592. IEEE.

Kathryn Womack, Wilson McCoy, Cecilia Ovesdotter Alm, Cara Calvelli, Jeff B. Pelz, Pengcheng Shi, and Anne Haake. 2012. Disfluencies as extra-propositional indicators of cognitive processing. In *Proceedings of the Workshop on Extra-Propositional Aspects of Meaning in Computational Linguistics*, pages 1–9. Association for Computational Linguistics.

Matt Wray, Cynthia Colen, and Bernice Pescosolido. 2011. The sociology of suicide. *Annual Review of Sociology*, 37:505–528.

Towards Assessing Changes in Degree of Depression through Facebook

H. Andrew Schwartz[†] **Johannes Eichstaedt**[†] **Margaret L. Kern**[†] **Gregory Park**[†]
Maarten Sap[†] **David Stillwell**[‡] **Michal Kosinski**[‡] and **Lyle Ungar**[†]
[†]Psychology and Computer & Information Science, University of Pennsylvania
[‡]Psychometrics Centre, University of Cambridge
hansens@seas.upenn.edu

Abstract

Depression is typically diagnosed as being present or absent. However, depression severity is believed to be continuously distributed rather than dichotomous. Severity may vary for a given patient daily and seasonally as a function of many variables ranging from life events to environmental factors. Repeated population-scale assessment of depression through questionnaires is expensive. In this paper we use survey responses and status updates from 28,749 Facebook users to develop a regression model that predicts users' degree of depression based on their Facebook status updates. Our user-level predictive accuracy is modest, significantly outperforming a baseline of average user sentiment. We use our model to estimate user changes in depression across seasons, and find, consistent with literature, users' degree of depression most often increases from summer to winter. We then show the potential to study factors driving individuals' level of depression by looking at its most highly correlated language features.

1 Introduction

Depression, a common mental disorder, greatly contributes to the economic, social, and physical burden of people worldwide. Along with other mental disorders it has been related to early termination of education, unstable marriages, teenage pregnancy, financial problems, role impairment, heart disease, and other negative outcomes (Kessler and Bromet, 2013; Lichtman et al., 2014)

Currently, depression is primarily assessed through surveys. Diagnoses require a medical or psychological evaluation, and are typically classified into discrete categories (absent, mild, moderate, severe). Clinicians rely on retrospective reports by patients to monitor symptoms and treatment. Unobtrusive assessments based on language use in Facebook and social media usage could amend both the self-help resources available to patients as well as repertoire of clinicians with richer information. Such a tool could allow for more frequent and fine grained (i.e., continuously scored) assessment and could provide contextualized information (e.g. specific words and online activities that are contributing to the user's depression score).

Here, we predict and characterize one's *degree of depression* (*DDep*) based on their language use in Facebook. Datasets connecting surveyed depression with language in Facebook are rare at best. To operationalize *DDep*, we use the depression facet scores of the "Big 5" item pool (Goldberg, 1999) from the MyPersonality dataset. This provides a continuous value outcome, for which we fit a regression model based on ngrams, LDA topics, and lexica usage. By predicting continuous values, rather than classes, one can track changes in *DDep* of varying size across time; we find significantly more users' *DDep* increases from summer to winter than vice-versa.

Our primary contribution is the exploration of predicting continuous-valued depression scores from individuals' social media messages. To the best of our knowledge this has not previously been studied, with other social media and depression work focused on discrete classes: present or absent. We compare our predictive model of *DDep* to one derived from a state-of-the-art sentiment lexicon and look at changes across seasons. Finally, we characterize *DDep* by looking at its top ngram and topic correlates.

Workshop on Computational Linguistics and Clinical Psychology: From Linguistic Signal to Clinical Reality, pages 118–125,
Baltimore, Maryland USA, June 27, 2014.

2 Background

2.1 Depression

Depression is generally characterized by persistent low mood, poor concentration, fatigue, and little interest in normally enjoyable activities. Depression can range from mild to severe, and can occur as an acute episode (major depressive episode), extend chronically over time (major depressive disorder, persistent depressive disorder), reoccur after a period of remission (recurrent depression), or occur at specific periods (seasonal affective disorder, postpartum depression, premenstrual dysphoric disorder). Prevalence rates vary; the World Health Organization estimates that over 350 million people worldwide have a depressive disorder, with many more reporting at least some symptoms (Organization, 2012). In the U.S., in the World Health Mental Survey, over half of the respondents (62%) endorsed at least one diagnostic stem questions for depression, with 19.2% meeting criteria for at least one major depressive episode (Kessler et al., 2010).

Although depression has long been defined as a single disease with a set of diagnostic criteria, it often occurs comorbidly with other psychological and physical disorders. Anxiety, anger, and other psychological disorders often co-occur with depression, and some have suggested that anxiety and depression are different manifestations of the same underlying pathology (Mineka et al., 1998). An expert panel convened by the American Heart Association recently recommended that depression be considered a formal risk factor for heart disease (Lichtman et al., 2014). Depression has been related to a range of physical conditions, including asthma, cancer, cardiovascular disease, diabetes, and chronic pain (Kessler and Bromet, 2013), although the causal direction is confounded; it may be that other factors cause both depression and physical illness (Friedman and Kern, 2014).

As noted previously, assessing degree of depression as a continuous value allows us to look at changes in depression across time. There has been longstanding interest and discussion of seasonal patterns of depression, with observations of seasonal depressive patterns apparent in ancient times, and the first systematic description occurring in 1984 (Westrin and Lam, 2007). Commonly called Seasonal Affective Disorder (SAD), the DSM-V now refers to this pattern as recurrent major depressive disorder with a seasonal pattern. A clinical diagnosis of seasonal depression requires that two major depressive episodes have occurred in the past two years, with the onset and remission showing a regular temporal pattern (predominantly with onset occurring in the fall/winter and full remission in spring/summer).

Patients with depression often have common symptoms of low energy, reduced or intensified psychomotor movements, low concentration, indecisiveness, and thoughts of death, as well as related symptoms such as fatigue, insomnia, and weight gain. A challenge in diagnosis is that it relies on a patient's historical report, and other possible causes such as physical illness must be ruled out. Further, with stigmas against mental illness and feats about seeking treatment, many cases go unrecognized, causing considerable burden on the individual and society as a whole. Prevalence rates vary, but rigorous reviews suggest a prevalence of .4% in the U.S., although estimates have been reported as high as 10% (Blazer et al., 1998; Magnusson and Partonen, 2005).

There are a number of different hypotheses about the pathophysiology of S A D, including circadian, neurotransmitter, and genetic causes (Lam and Levitan, 2000). Reviews suggest that light therapy is an effective and well-tolerated treatment, with effects equal to or larger than antidepressants (Golden et al., 2005; Lam and Levitan, 2000; Thompson, 2001; Westrin and Lam, 2007). Attempts to explain why light therapy is so effective have included shifting photoperiods (light-dark cycles, with less light in the winter), changes in melotonin secretion, and circadian phase shifts (Lam and Levitan, 2000).

One related explanation for the photoperiod effect is latitude, with the prevalence of seasonal depression increasing with growing distance from the equator. Although there has been some support for this hypothesis in the U.S. (Rosen et al., 1990), findings in other countries have been mixed (Mersch et al., 1999). Although latitude may play some role, other factors such as climate, genetic vulnerability, and the sociocultural context may have a stronger impact.

Altogether, inconsistent results suggest that there is considerable variation in the magnitude, causes and manifestations of seasonal depression, much of which is not fully understood, in part due to diagnostic issues (Lam and Levitan, 2000). A

Dislike myself.
Am often down in the dumps.
Have frequent mood swings.
Feel desperate.
Feel comfortable with myself. (-)
Seldom feel blue. (-)
Am very pleased with myself. (-)

Table 1: The seven items of the depression facet from the 100-item International Personality Item Pool (IPIP) proxy to the NEO-PI-R (Goldberg, 1999). (-) indicates a reverse coded item.

weekly or even daily depression assessment tool would allow us to more fully understand the seasonal and other temporal changes in depression.

We use the "depression facet" scores derived from a subset of the "big-5" personality items. Specifically, depression is one of several facets (e.g. anger, depression, anxiety, self-consciousness, impulsiveness, vulnerability) of the neuroticism personality factor. Neuroticism refers to individual differences in the tendency to experience negative, distressing emotions, and behavioral and cognitive styles that result from this (McCrae and John, 1992). It includes traits such as tension, depression, frustration, guilt, and self-consciousness, and is associated with low self-esteem, irrational thoughts and behaviors, ineffective coping styles, and somatic complaints.

Various scales have been developed to measure neuroticism, such as the Eysenck Personality Questionnaire (Eysenck and Eysenck, 1975) and the NEO-PI-R (Costa and McCrae, 1992). Some items on these scales overlap with self-reported items that screen for depression (e.g., personality item: "I am often down in the dumps"; depression screening item: "how often have you been feeling down, depressed, or hopeless?"; see Table 1.), such that the personality items effectively provide a proxy measure of depressive tendencies.

2.2 Related Work

Depression has been linked with many online behaviors. In fact, even Internet usage itself seems to vary as a function of being depressed(Katikalapudi et al., 2012). Other behaviors include social networking (Moreno et al., 2011) and differences in location sharing on Facebook (Park et al., 2013).

Most related to our work, are those using linguistic features to assess various measures of depression. For example, De Choudhury et al. (2013) used online posting behavior, network characteristics, and linguistic features when trying to predict depression rather than find its correlates. They used crowdsourcing to screen Twitter users with the CES-D test (Beekman et al., 1997), while others analyzed one year of Facebook status updates for DSM diagnostic critera of a Major Depressive Episode (Moreno et al., 2011). In addition, Park et al. (2013) predicted results of the Beck Depression Inventory (Beck et al., 1961).

While previous works have made major headway toward automatic depression assessment tools from social media, to the best of our knowledge, none have tried to predict depression as a continuum rather than a discrete, present or absent, attribute. For instance, Neuman et al. (2012) classified blog posts based on whether they contained signs of depression, and De Choudhury et al. (2013) classified which newfound mothers would suffer from postpartum depression.

3 Predicting Degree of Depression

3.1 Method

Dataset. We used a dataset of 28,749 nonclinical users who opted into a Facebook application ("MyPersonality"; Kosinski and Stillwell, 2012) between June 2009 and March 2011, completed a 100-item personality questionnaire (an International Personality Item Pool (IPIP) proxy to the NEO-PI-R (Goldberg, 1999), and shared access to their status updates containing at least 500 words. Users wrote on average of 4,236 words (69,917,624 total word instances), and a subset of 16,507 users provided gender and age, in which 57.0% were female and the mean age was 24.8.

The dataset was divided into *training* and *testing* samples. In particular, the testing sample consisted of a random set of 1000 users who wrote at least 1000 words and completed the personality measure, while the training set contained the 27,749 remaining users.

Degree of depression. We estimated user-level degree of depression (*DDep*) as the average response to seven *depression* facet items, which are nested within the larger Neuroticism item pool. For each item, users indicated how accurately short phrases described themselves (e.g., "often feel blue", "dislike myself"; responses ranged from 1 = very inaccurate to 5 = very accu-

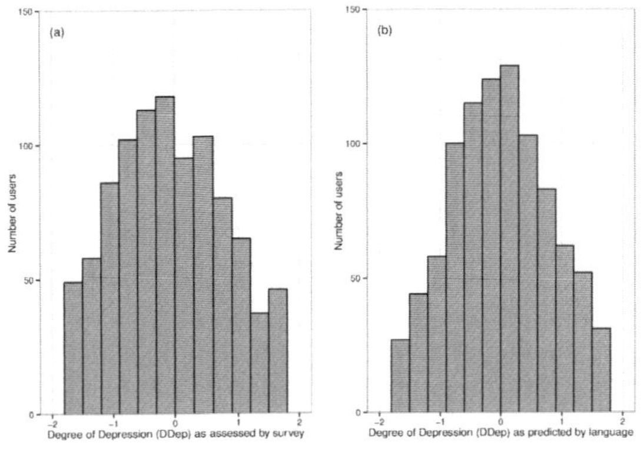

Figure 1: Histograms of (a) survey-assessed and (b) predicted user-level degree of depression $DDep$.

rate). Figure 1a shows the distribution of survey-assessed DDep (standardized). The items can be seen in Table 1.

Figure 2 shows the daily averages of survey-assessed $DDep$, collapsed across years. A LOESS smoother over the daily averages illustrates a seasonal trend, with depression rising over the winter months and dropping during the summer.

Regression modeling. In order to get a continuous value output from our model, we explored regression techniques over our training data. Since this first work exploring regression was concerned primarily with language content, our features for predicting depression were based entirely on language use (other social media activity and friend networks may be considered in future work). These features can be broken into four categories:

ngrams: Ngrams of order to 1 to 3, found via HappierFunTokenizer, and restricted to those used by at least 5% of users (resulting in 10,450 ngrams). The features were encoded as relative frequency of mentioning each ngram (ng):

$$rel\_freq(user, ng) = \frac{freq(user, ng)}{\sum_{ng' \in ngs} freq(user, ng')}$$

topics: 2000 LDA derived Facebook topics.[1] Usage was calculated as the probability of the topic given the user:

$$usage(top|user) = \sum_{ng \in topic} p(top|ng) * rel\_freq(user, ng)$$

[1] downloaded from wwbp.org/data.html

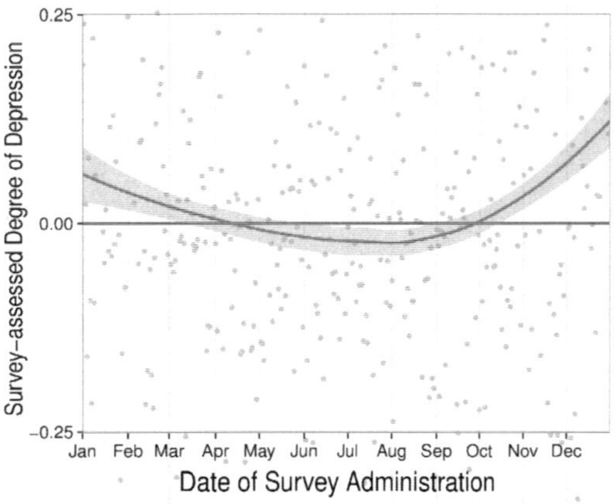

Figure 2: Seasonal trends in degree of depression as assessed by surveys. Red line is a LOESS smoothed trend (+/- 1 SE) over the average of scores from users who completed the survey on that day.

lexica: 64 LIWC categories (Pennebaker et al., 2007) as well as the sentiment lexicon from NRC Canada (Mohammad et al., 2013).[2] Usage of a lexicon (lex) was calculated similar to the LDA topics, where w is the weight of the word in the lexicon in the case of sentiment and always 1 in the case of LIWC which has no weights:

$$usage(lex, user) = \sum_{ng \in lex} w(ng, lex) * rel\_freq(user, ng)$$

number of words: Encoded simply as the integer value for that user.

We used penalized linear regression to fit our features to *DDep*. We experimented with a few penalization types over the training set and settled on $L2$ ("ridge regression"), using Principal Components Analysis to first reduce the ngram and topic features to 10 % of their original size. In order to ensure users tested provided an adequate amount of features, we only tested over those with at least 1,000 words. However, we found that including more users in our training set at the expense of words per user increased model accuracy. Thus, we only required our training data users to mention 500 words, essentially allowing more noise in order to increase the number of training examples.

We also experimented with training models on two sets of messages: *all messages* and the subset of messages written in the same three-month season as the survey administration (*season only*

[2] downloaded from www.saifmohammad.com

Model	Season test (r)	All test (r)
$Baseline_{sentiment}$	.124	.149
$Season$	.321	.340
All	.351	**.386**

Table 2: Accuracy of various models against test sets containing only messages from the *season* and year in which the user took the survey as well as a test using all of user's messages. Models: $Baseline_{sentiment}$ a model based on a state-of-the-art sentiment lexicon (Mohammad et al., 2013); $Season$: model trained on messages sent only during the same season and year in which each user took the survey; All model trained on all messages of each user.

messages). Because the degree of depression may vary over time, we reasoned that messages written closer to survey administration might better reflect the degree of depression assessed by the survey. When generating predictions on users in the test set, we applied both the all messages model and the season only messages model to features from all messages and then to just the features from the same season as the survey administration.

3.2 Evaluation and Results

We evaluated accuracy using the Pearson correlation coefficient r between our predictions and survey-assessed $DDep$. As a baseline, we built a regression model simply using the NRC sentiment (Mohammad et al., 2013) feature.

Accuracies are shown in Table 2. Accuracy was highest ($r = .386$) when we trained a model over all messages from users in the training set and then applied this model to all messages by users in the test set. Though our model allows for seasonal change in depression, we suspect the test across all messages was more accurate than that of only using the season in which the users depression was assessed due to the larger amount messages and language features provided to the model.

Both models (season-only messages, and all messages) gave significant ($p < 0.05$) improvement over the baseline ($r = .149$) and though these accuracies may look small, it's worth noting that a correlation above $r = 0.3$ is often regarded as a strong link between a behavior and a psychological outcome (Meyer et al., 2001). Still, we fit many behavior variables (i.e., language use features) to an outcome and so we might hope

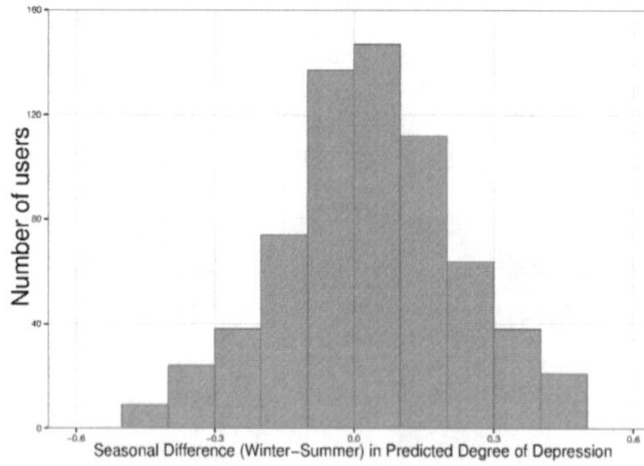

Figure 3: Histogram of differences between winter and summer predictions of user-level $DDep$. Average user-level predicted $DDep$ values were significantly higher in the winter months ($t = 4.63$, $p < .001$).

for higher variance explained. We suspect having more users to train on and taking more features into account could improve results. For example, people who nearly stopped writing for a season would be thrown out of our analyses since it is completely based on language content, even though they are more likely to be depressed (social isolation is a common symptom in depression). Similarly, we do not use demographics in our models, even though women are more likely to become depressed than men.

To assess individual seasonal changes in degree of depression, we predicted summer and winter $DDep$ values for each user with at least 1000 words across both summer-only and winter-only messages, respectively. We then compared the differences across the seasonal predictions; Figure 3 shows the distribution of user-level seasonal differences across 676 users with sufficient language for both seasonal predictions. In line with the trends seen in survey data, average user-level $DDep$ values, as predicted by language, were significantly higher in the winter months ($t = 4.63$, $p < .001$).

4 Differential Language Analysis

Figure 4 shows the 100 ngrams most highly correlated with depression score across the 21,913 Facebook users in our dataset writing at least 1,000 words. Unlike typical word clouds, the clouds represent language that differentiates users scoring high on depression. The size of a word represents its correlation with depression (larger

= stronger), the color its relative frequency (grey = rarely used, blue = moderately used, red = frequently used).

The f-word emerges as both the most correlated feature (as indicated by the size of the word) and is highly frequent (indicated by the red color). Together with words such as 'pissed' and 'bloody', these curse words suggest hostility or aggression. Similarly, words such has 'hate' and 'lonely' suggest negative social relationships.

Perhaps surprisingly, the words 'depression' and 'depressed' emerge as highly correlated features. These face valid features occur infrequently (as indicated by their grey color), yet are strongly associated with depressive tendencies, demonstrating the high statistical power of our approach applied to this large dataset in identifying significant but rarely used language features. The both frequent and highly correlated word 'why' hints at signs of hopelessness and meaninglessness, a core feature of depressive disorders.

As illustrated in Figure 5, extending the words and phrase results, automatically derived topics demonstrate substantial overlap with the major clinical symptoms of major depressive disorder (American Psychiatric Association et al., 2013). Hopelessness and meaninglessness are seemingly expressed by 'hopeless' and 'helpless'. Perhaps the most noticable symptom of depression, depressed mood, is expressed in topics mentioning 'feel', 'crap', 'sad', and 'miserable'.

Depression often affects psychomotor function, either in terms of fatigue and low energy or inversely as insomnia and hyperactivity. Such symptoms are reflected in words such as 'tired', and 'sleep'. Depression is often expressed somatically through bodily symptoms, captured through 'hurt', 'my head' and 'pain'.

One of the most predictive questions on depressive screening questionnaires asks about suicidal thought, which appears with topics related to thoughts of death, with words such as 'kill', 'die', and 'dying'.

Topics also reflected hostility, aggression, and negative relationships with other people. Loneliness has emerged as one of the strongest predictors of physical morbidity and mortality (Hawkley and Cacioppo, 2010), and both 'lonely' and 'alone' appear as some of the most correlated single words. Given such striking descriptive results, future work might try to detect depression associated conditions as well such as insomnia, loneliness, and aggression.

Figure 5: Top ten topics most positively correlated with depression (from $r = .14$ at top to $r = .11$ at bottom). All are significant at a Bonferroni-corrected threshold of $p < 0.001$. Word size corresponds to prevalence within the topics.

5 Conclusion

Depression can be viewed as a continuous construct that changes over time, rather than simply as being a disease that one has or does not have. We showed that regression models based on Facebook language can be used to predict an individual's degree of depression, as measured by a depression facet survey. In line with survey seasonal trends and the broader literature, we found that language-based predictions of depression were higher in the winter than the summer, suggesting that our

Figure 4: The 100 ngrams most correlated with *DDep* (ranging from $r = .05$ to $r = .10$). All are significant at a Bonferroni-corrected threshold of $p < 0.001$. Ngram size corresponds to correlation strength (larger words are more distinguishing). Color corresponds to relative frequency (red if frequent, blue moderate, grey infrequent).

continuous predictions are capturing small, yet meaningful within-person changes. With further development of regression models, many users write enough on Facebook that we could estimate changes in their level of depression on a monthly or even weekly basis. Such estimates, correlated with word use over time offers potential both for research at the group-level ("What are the social and environmental determinants of depression?", "How well are talk or medication-based interventions working?") as well as, eventually, for medical and therapeutic application at the individual level ("How well am I doing and what depression-relevant thoughts or behaviors have I disclosed in the past week?").

References

APA American Psychiatric Association, American Psychiatric Association, et al. 2013. Diagnostic and statistical manual of mental disorders.

Aaron T Beck, Calvin H Ward, Mock Mendelson, Jeremiah Mock, and JK Erbaugh. 1961. An inventory for measuring depression. *Archives of general psychiatry*, 4(6):561.

Aartjan TF Beekman, DJH Deeg, J Van Limbeek, AW Braam, MZ De Vries, W Van Tilburg, et al. 1997. Criterion validity of the Center for Epidemiologic Studies Depression scale (CES-D): results from a community-based sample of older subjects in The Netherlands. *Psychological medicine*, 27(1):231–236.

Dan G Blazer, Ronald C Kessler, and Marvin S Swartz. 1998. Epidemiology of recurrent major and minor depression with a seasonal pattern. The National Comorbidity Survey. *The British Journal of Psychiatry*, 172(2):164–167.

Paul T Costa and Robert R McCrae. 1992. Professional manual: revised NEO personality inventory (NEO-PI-R) and NEO five-factor inventory (NEO-FFI). *Odessa, FL: Psychological Assessment Resources*.

Munmun De Choudhury, Scott Counts, and Eric Horvitz. 2013a. Predicting postpartum changes in emotion and behavior via social media. In *Proceedings of the 2013 ACM annual conference on Human factors in computing systems*, pages 3267–3276. ACM.

Munmun De Choudhury, Michael Gamon, Scott Counts, and Eric Horvitz. 2013b. Predicting depression via social media. In *AAAI Conference on Weblogs and Social Media*.

Hans Jurgen Eysenck and Sybil Bianca Giuletta Eysenck. 1975. *Manual of the Eysenck Personality Questionnaire (junior and adult)*. Hodder and Stoughton.

Howard S Friedman and Margaret L Kern. 2014. Personality, Well-Being, and Health*. *Psychology*, 65(1):719.

Lewis R Goldberg. 1999. A broad-bandwidth, public domain, personality inventory measuring the lower-level facets of several five-factor models. *Personality psychology in Europe*, 7:7–28.

Robert N Golden, Bradley N Gaynes, R David Ekstrom, Robert M Hamer, Frederick M Jacobsen, Trisha Suppes, Katherine L Wisner, and Charles B Nemeroff. 2005. The efficacy of light therapy in the treatment of mood disorders: a review and meta-analysis of the evidence. *American Journal of Psychiatry*, 162(4):656–662.

Louise C Hawkley and John T Cacioppo. 2010. Loneliness matters: a theoretical and empirical review of consequences and mechanisms. *Annals of Behavioral Medicine*, 40(2):218–227.

R Katikalapudi, Sriram Chellappan, Frances Montgomery, Donald Wunsch, and Karl Lutzen. 2012. Associating Internet usage with depressive behavior among college students. *Technology and Society Magazine, IEEE*, 31(4):73–80.

Ronald C. Kessler and Evelyn J. Bromet. 2013. The Epidemiology of Depression Across Cultures. *Annual Review of Public Health*, 34(1):119–138, Mar.

Ronald C Kessler, Howard G Birnbaum, Victoria Shahly, Evelyn Bromet, Irving Hwang, Katie A McLaughlin, Nancy Sampson, Laura Helena Andrade, Giovanni de Girolamo, Koen Demyttenaere, et al. 2010. Age differences in the prevalence and co-morbidity of DSM-IV major depressive episodes: results from the WHO World Mental Health Survey Initiative. *Depression and anxiety*, 27(4):351–364.

M. Kosinski and D.J. Stillwell. 2012. myPersonality Project. *http://www.mypersonality.org/wiki/*.

Raymond W Lam and Robert D Levitan. 2000. Pathophysiology of seasonal affective disorder: a review. *Journal of Psychiatry and Neuroscience*, 25(5):469.

Judith H Lichtman, Erika S Froelicher, James A Blumenthal, Robert M Carney, Lynn V Doering, Nancy Frasure-Smith, Kenneth E Freedland, Allan S Jaffe, Erica C Leifheit-Limson, David S Sheps, et al. 2014. Depression as a Risk Factor for Poor Prognosis Among Patients With Acute Coronary Syndrome: Systematic Review and Recommendations A Scientific Statement From the American Heart Association. *Circulation*.

Andres Magnusson and Timo Partonen. 2005. Focus Points. *CNS Spectr*, 10(8):625–634.

Robert R McCrae and Oliver P John. 1992. An introduction to the five-factor model and its applications. *Journal of personality*, 60(2):175–215.

Peter Paul A Mersch, Hermine M Middendorp, Antoinette L Bouhuys, Domien GM Beersma, and Rutger H van den Hoofdakker. 1999. Seasonal affective disorder and latitude: a review of the literature. *Journal of affective disorders*, 53(1):35–48.

Gregory J Meyer, Stephen E Finn, Lorraine D Eyde, Gary G Kay, Kevin L Moreland, Robert R Dies, Elena J Eisman, Tom W Kubiszyn, and Geoffrey M Reed. 2001. Psychological testing and psychological assessment: A review of evidence and issues. *American psychologist*, 56(2):128–165.

S Mineka, D Watson, and LA Clark. 1998. Comorbidity of anxiety and unipolar mood disorders. *Annual review of psychology*, 49:377.

Saif M. Mohammad, Svetlana Kiritchenko, and Xiaodan Zhu. 2013. NRC-Canada: Building the State-of-the-Art in Sentiment Analysis of Tweets. In *Proceedings of the seventh international workshop on Semantic Evaluation Exercises (SemEval-2013)*, Atlanta, Georgia, USA, June.

Megan A Moreno, Lauren A Jelenchick, Katie G Egan, Elizabeth Cox, Henry Young, Kerry E Gannon, and Tara Becker. 2011. Feeling bad on Facebook: Depression disclosures by college students on a social networking site. *Depression and anxiety*, 28(6):447–455.

Yair Neuman, Yohai Cohen, Dan Assaf, and Gabbi Kedma. 2012. Proactive screening for depression through metaphorical and automatic text analysis. *Artificial intelligence in medicine*, 56(1):19–25.

World Health Organization. 2012. *Depression fact sheet.* http://www.who.int/mediacentre/factsheets/fs369/en/.

Sungkyu Park, Sang Won Lee, Jinah Kwak, Meeyoung Cha, and Bumseok Jeong. 2013. Activities on Facebook Reveal the Depressive State of Users. *Journal of medical Internet research*, 15(10).

James W. Pennebaker, C.K. Chung, M. Ireland, A. Gonzales, and R.J. Booth. 2007. The development and psychometric properties of LIWC2007. *Austin, TX, LIWC. Net.*

Leora N Rosen, Steven D Targum, Michael Terman, Michael J Bryant, Howard Hoffman, Siegfried F Kasper, Joelle R Hamovit, John P Docherty, Betty Welch, and Norman E Rosenthal. 1990. Prevalence of seasonal affective disorder at four latitudes. *Psychiatry research*, 31(2):131–144.

C Thompson. 2001. Evidence-based treatment. *Seasonal affective disorder: practice and research*, pages 151–158.

Asa Westrin and Raymond W Lam. 2007. Seasonal affective disorder: a clinical update. *Annals of Clinical Psychiatry*, 19(4):239–246.

Author Index